"A pleasure to read. We can see Jamison let go of her carefully wrought personal narrative and open herself to the unknown...In her world, astonishment is always just around the corner."

—Sheila McClear, *Washington Post*

"Sharply analytic and deeply personal...*Make It Scream, Make It Burn* is a heady hybrid of journalism, memoir, and criticism...This is a writer who is incapable of being uninteresting."

—Heller McAlpin, National Public Radio

"Like the glass in a kaleidoscope, Jamison's fine-tuned attention seems capable of refracting whatever subject it touches. When I finally looked up from the page it was with a renewed sense of wonder."

—Cornelia Channing, *The Paris Review*

"A dazzling collection about the outer reaches of human connection... Acute in her analysis and nourishing in her observations, Jamison is at the height of her powers here as she investigates what we owe one another."

—Adrienne Westenfeld, *Esquire*

"Leslie Jamison's astonishingly formidable, restless intellect has gifted us two monumental works of nonfiction...Here, she turns her exacting eye on subjects such as the loneliest whale in the world and a Croatian museum filled with the effluvia of failed relationships."

—Michelle Hart, *O, The Oprah Magazine*

"Jamison can pin an idea with the speed and fluidity of a pro athlete. She thinks ethically but feels aesthetically. Her writing, although lyrical, proceeds with a precise, searching sobriety—each sentence a controlled swoon."

—Katy Waldman, *The New Yorker*

"Provocative... Compassionate, curious, and humble... Rather than pretending to have the 'honesty' of a mythical, objective observer, Jamison acknowledges that she has skin in the game, and her wise, urgent writing is stronger for it." —Chris Hewitt, *Minneapolis Star Tribune*

"In this essay collection, Leslie Jamison confronts the challenges of love, loss, motherhood, and more. She brings readers the world's loneliest whale and the Museum of Broken Relationships, and finds reasons to be joyful even in the hard work of being human." —Kelly Wynne, *Newsweek*

"Stunning... Essential... *Make It Scream, Make It Burn* expands on the efforts of *The Empathy Exams*... Here we see the territory Jamison's writing inhabits: self-questioning while at the same time empathetic, dubious and credible at once... What Jamison is after is a kind of radical honesty: the ongoing inquiry of a mind at work." —David L. Ulin, *Four Columns*

"A masterwork... Leslie Jamison has long been known as a force in American writing for both her intellect and empathy... Jamison draws connections to her own life—a challenging dance that can only be pulled off by the most masterful of writers." —Louis Cheslaw, *Condé Nast Traveler*

"Insightful and searching, exciting and staggering. Jamison interweaves memoir, journalism, and cultural criticism into essays that explore topics like motherhood, romance, and relationships." —*Good Housekeeping*

"A roaming, wide-ranging collection, grounded through Jamison's lucid, unflinching prose, leading to a singularly empathetic, moving reading experience." —*Nylon*

"As riveting as ever, Jamison's writing elicited within me many of the same responses I felt while reading her previous essay collection, *The Empathy Exams*: enlightenment, amusement, and, of course, empathy itself."

—Zakiya Harris, *The Rumpus*

"Jamison is one of my favorite working essayists...In *Make It Scream, Make It Burn*, she dances between the personal, the critical, and the observational, showing her deftness when it comes to each form."

—Jeva Lange, *The Week*

"Richly diverse...The pieces in *Make It Scream, Make It Burn* are all written with care and intricacy, drawing readers in and making us care...Jamison's observational skills, genuine empathy, and lack of sentimentality create an intelligent blending of journalism, scholarship, and memoir."

—Pam Kingsbury, *Library Journal*

"Leslie Jamison is a master of blending memoir, criticism, and journalism...Her characteristic fusion of the intellectual and emotional is in full force here, cementing comparisons of her work to that of Joan Didion and Susan Sontag."

—Christy Lynch, *Bookpage*

"To fortify and enlarge the world through eloquence—apt descriptions of Jamison's new collection...Another wonderful book from this gifted writer."

—Nick Ripatrazone, *The Millions*

"Lyrical...There is something distinctly empowering in Jamison's employment of the self—in her collapsing of the theoretical and the experienced."

—Katherine Lucky, *Commonweal Magazine*

"Illuminating and ruminative...Jamison is positively brilliant when penetrating a subject and unraveling its layers of meaning...Fans of the author's unique brand of perceptiveness will be delighted."

—*Publishers Weekly*

ALSO BY LESLIE JAMISON

NONFICTION

The Recovering: Intoxication and Its Aftermath
The Empathy Exams: Essays

FICTION

The Gin Closet

MAKE IT
SCREAM,
MAKE IT
BURN

ESSAYS

LESLIE JAMISON

BACK BAY BOOKS
Little, Brown and Company
New York Boston London

Back Bay Books / Little, Brown and Company
Hachette Book Group
1290 Avenue of the Americas, New York, NY 10104
littlebrown.com

Originally published in hardcover by Little, Brown and Company, September 2019
First Back Bay trade paperback edition, October 2020

Back Bay Books is an imprint of Little, Brown and Company, a division of Hachette Book Group, Inc. The Back Bay Books name and logo are trademarks of Hachette Book Group, Inc.

The publisher is not responsible for websites (or their content) that are not owned by the publisher.

The Hachette Speakers Bureau provides a wide range of authors for speaking events. To find out more, go to hachettespeakersbureau.com or call (866) 376-6591.

The essays in this book previously appeared, sometimes in significantly different form, in the following publications: "Up in Jaffna" (as "The Two Faces of Paradise") in *Afar;* "52 Blue" in *The Atavist;* "The Quickening" and "Sim Life" in *The Atlantic;* "Layover Story" (as "Baggage Claims") and "We Tell Ourselves Stories in Order to Live Again" (as "Giving up the Ghost") in *Harper's;* "No Tongue Can Tell" in the *Los Angeles Review of Books;* "The Long Trick" (as "Saudades") in the *Mississippi Review;* "Rehearsals" in *The Nervous Breakdown;* "Daughter of a Ghost" (as "In the Shadow of a Fairy Tale") in the *New York Times Magazine;* "Make It Scream, Make It Burn" in the *Oxford American;* and "Maximum Exposure" (as "Going Back") and "Museum of Broken Hearts" (as "The Breakup Museum") in the *Virginia Quarterly Review.*

ISBN 978-0-316-25963-7 (hc) / 978-0-316-25965-1 (pb)
LCCN 2019931414

10 9 8 7 6 5 4 3 2 1

LSC-C

Printed in the United States of America

For my father,
Dean Tecumseh Jamison

When do our senses know any thing so utterly as
when we lack it?

    —Marilynne Robinson, *Housekeeping*

CONTENTS

— I —

LONGING

52 Blue

December 7, 1992. Whidbey Island, Puget Sound. The world wars were over. The other wars were over: Korea, Vietnam. The Cold War was finally over, too. The Whidbey Island Naval Air Station remained. So did the Pacific, its waters vast and fathomless beyond an airfield named for an airman whose body was never found: William Ault, who died in the Battle of the Coral Sea. This is how it goes. The ocean swallows human bodies whole and makes them immortal. William Ault became a runway that sends other men into the sky.

At the Naval Air Station, the infinite Pacific appeared as finite data gathered by a network of hydrophones spread along the ocean floor. Initially used to monitor Soviet subs during the Cold War, these hydrophones had since been turned toward the sea itself, transforming its formless noises into something measurable: pages of printed graphs rolling out of a spectrograph machine.

On that particular December day in 1992, petty officer second class Velma Ronquille heard a strange sound. She stretched it out on a different spectrogram so she could see it better. She couldn't quite believe that it was coming in at 52 hertz. She beckoned one of the audio technicians. He needed to come back, she said. He needed to take another look. The technician came back. He took another look. His name was Joe George. Velma told him, "I think this is a whale."

Joe thought, *Holy cow*. It hardly seemed possible. The sound pattern looked like the call of a blue whale, but blue whales usually came in somewhere between 15 and 20 hertz—an almost imperceptible rumble, on the periphery of what the human ear can detect. Fifty-two hertz was off the charts. But here it was, right in front of them, the audio signature of a creature moving through Pacific waters with a singularly high-pitched song.

Whales make calls for a number of reasons: to navigate, to find food, to communicate with one another. For certain whales, including humpbacks and blues, songs also play a role in sexual selection. Blue males sing louder than females, and the volume of their singing—at more than 180 decibels—makes them the loudest animals in the world. They click and grunt and trill and hum and moan. They sound like foghorns. Their calls can travel thousands of miles through the ocean.

Because this whale's frequency was unprecedented, the folks at Whidbey kept tracking him for years, every migration season, as he made his way south from Alaska to Mexico. They figured it was a he, as only males sing during mating season. His path wasn't unusual, only his song—along with the fact that they never detected any other whales around him. He always seemed to be alone. This whale was calling out high, and apparently to no one—or at least, no one seemed to be answering. The acoustic technicians called him 52 Blue. A scientific report would eventually acknowledge that no other whale calls with similar characteristics had ever been reported. "It is perhaps difficult to accept," the report conceded, that "there could have been only one of this kind in this large oceanic expanse."

*   *   *

The drive from Seattle to Whidbey Island took me through the plainspoken pageantry of Washington State industry: massive stacks of cut lumber, rivers clogged with tree trunks like fish trapped in pens, towers of candy-colored shipping containers near Skagit port, and a collection of dirty white silos near Deception Pass Bridge, its steel span looming majestically over Puget Sound—hard-sparkling water glinting with shards of sunlight nearly two hundred feet below. On the far side of the bridge, the island felt pastoral and otherworldly, almost defensive. LITTER AND IT WILL HURT, one sign read. Another said, SPACE HEATERS NEED SPACE. Whidbey Island often calls itself the longest island in America, but this isn't strictly true. "Whidbey is long," the *Seattle Times* observed in 2000, "but let's not stretch it." It's long enough to hold a kite festival, a mussel festival, an annual bike race (the Tour de Whidbey), four inland lakes, and a yearly murder-mystery game that turns the entire town of Langley, population 1,035, into a crime scene.

Joe George, the technician who first identified 52 Blue, still lives in a modest hillside home perched on the northern end of Whidbey, about six miles from the air station. When I visited, he answered the door smiling—a burly man with silver hair, no-nonsense but friendly. Though he hadn't worked at the air station for twenty years, he was still able to get us past security with his Navy ID. He told me he uses it whenever he comes back to the base to drop off his recycling. Outside the officers' club, men in flight suits were drinking cocktails on a wooden deck. The coastline was ragged and beautiful beyond—waves crashing onto dark sand, salt wind moving through the evergreens.

Joe explained that when he worked at the air station, his team—the team responsible for processing audio data from the hydrophones—was fairly disconnected from the rest of the base. It was a question of security, he said. When we reached his old building, I saw what he meant. It was surrounded by double fences topped with razor wire. He told me that some of the other servicemen on base used to think his building was some kind of prison. They never knew what it was for. When I asked him what he had thought those strange sounds had been, back in 1992, before he realized they were whale calls, he said, "I can't tell you that. It's classified."

Back at his house, Joe pulled out a sheaf of papers from his days spent tracking 52 Blue. They were computer maps documenting nearly a decade of migratory patterns, the whale's journey each season marked by a different color—yellow, orange, purple—in the crude lines of mid-'90s computer graphics. Joe showed me charts of 52's song and explained the lines and metrics so I could compare its signature with more typical whale noise: the lower frequencies of regular blues, the much higher frequencies of humpbacks. Blue-whale songs hold various kinds of sounds—long purrs and moans, constant or modulated—and 52 Blue's vocalizations showed these same distinctive patterns, only on a wildly different frequency, one just above the lowest note on a tuba. The brief recorded clip of 52 he played me, sped up for human hearing, sounded ghostly: a reedy, pulsing, searching sound, the aural equivalent of a beam of light murkily visible through thick fog on a moonlit night.

Joe clearly enjoyed explaining his charts and maps. It seemed to have something to do with his love for organization and order. As he proudly showed me the fruits of his various and somewhat surprising hobbies—his impressive collection of carnivorous plants and the bees he raised to feed them, or the pristine musket he'd built from a kit for one of his eighteenth-century fur-trapper rendezvous reenactments—a clear penchant for care and conscientiousness emerged. He had a deep desire to be accurate and meticulous about everything he did. As he showed me the cobra lilies, his favorite plants, he explained how their translucent hoods trick trapped flies into exhausting themselves by flying toward the light—evidently impressed by the economy and ingenuity of their design—and then carefully fixed a frost cloth over their curled green backs to protect them from the cold.

I sensed that Joe enjoyed the chance to pull out his old whale charts. They took him back to the days when the story of 52 was still unfolding, and he was right in the middle of it. Joe told me he'd arrived at Whidbey after several years of what was technically classified as "arduous duty" on a base in Iceland, though he explained that those years weren't particularly arduous at all; his kids built snowmen by the Blue Lagoon. Joe was a good candidate for Whidbey. He was already trained as an acoustic technician, already prepared for the work that happened in his squat little bunker behind the razor-wire fences.

The hydrophone tracking program—also known as the Sound Surveillance System, or SOSUS—was a bit of a "bastard child," Joe told me. After the Cold War ended, without Soviet submarines to listen to, the Navy needed more convincing about how the expensive hydrophone array could earn its keep. The work that emerged surprised even the ones who started doing it. Darel Martin, an acoustic technician who worked with Joe at Whidbey, described it like this: "We went from being experts on sharks of steel to tracking living, breathing animals." He said: "It's just endless what you can hear out of the ocean." Now the mystery of one particular whale survives as a man sitting at his kitchen table, pulling out weathered folders to point out the ordinary-looking graph of an extraordinary song.

July 2007, Harlem, New York. Leonora knew she was going to die. Not just someday, but soon. She'd been suffering from fibroids and bleeding for years, sometimes so heavily that she was afraid to leave her apartment. She grew obsessed with blood: thinking about blood, dreaming about blood, writing poems about blood. She stopped working as a case supervisor for the city, a job she'd held for more than a decade. At that point, Leonora was forty-eight years old. She had always been a self-sufficient person; she'd been working since she was fourteen. She'd never been married, though she'd had offers. She liked to know that she could support herself. But this was a new level of isolation. One family member told her, "You are in a very dark place," and said she no longer wanted to see her.

By summer things had gotten worse. Leonora felt truly ill: relentless nausea, severe constipation, aches across her whole body. Her wrists were swollen, her stomach bloated, her vision blurred with jagged spirals of color. She could hardly breathe when she was lying down, so she barely slept. When she did sleep, her dreams were strange. One night she saw a horse-drawn hearse moving across the cobblestone streets of another century's Harlem. She picked up the horse's reins, looked it straight in the eye, and knew it had come for her. She felt so convinced she was going to die that she unlocked her apartment door so her neighbors wouldn't have trouble removing her body. She called her doctor to tell her as much—*I'm pretty sure I'm going to die*—and her doctor got pissed, said she needed to call the paramedics, that she was going to live.

As the paramedics were wheeling Leonora away from her apartment on a gurney, she asked them to turn around and take her back so she could lock the door. This was how she knew she'd regained faith in her own life. If she wasn't going to die, she didn't want to leave her door unlocked.

That request, asking the paramedics to turn around, is the last thing Leonora can remember before two months of darkness. That night in July was the beginning of a medical odyssey—five days of surgery, seven weeks in a coma, six months in the hospital—that would eventually deliver her, in her own time and her own way, to the story of 52 Blue.

* * *

During the years when Joe and Darel were tracking 52 Blue, they worked under the supervision of Bill Watkins, an acoustic expert from Woods Hole who came across the country to Whidbey Island every few months to hear about what they'd found. Everyone who told me about Watkins spoke of him in almost mythic terms. The number of languages he spoke kept changing every time I heard it: six, twelve, thirteen. One of his former research assistants claimed it was twenty. He'd been born to Christian missionaries stationed in French Guinea. According to Darel, Watkins had hunted elephants with his father when he was a kid. "He could actually hear twenty hertz, which is extremely low for any human," Darel told me. "You and I can't hear that...but he could actually hear the elephants in the distance. And he would tell his dad which way to go."

Over the course of his career, Watkins developed much of the technology and methodology that made it possible to record and analyze whale songs: whale tags, underwater playback experiments, location methods. He developed the first tape recorder capable of capturing whale vocalizations.

For Joe and Darel, 52 Blue's unusual frequency was interesting mainly because it made him easy to track. You could always distinguish his call, so you always knew where he was traveling. Other whales were harder to tell apart, their patterns of motion harder to discern. The possibility of particularity—*this* whale, among all whales—allowed for an ongoing relationship to 52 as an individual creature, while other whales blurred into a more anonymous collective body.

52's particularity, as well as his apparent isolation, lent him a certain sheen of personality. "We always laughed when we were tracking him," Darel told me. "We said, 'Maybe he's heading to Baja for the lady blues.'" Darel's jokes echoed with the familiarity of affectionate condescension, the way frat brothers might talk about the runt of a pledge class who never had much luck with girls: *52 struck out, looked again, tried again. 52 never let up with that song.* It was something more than a job. Darel bought his wife a whale necklace during the years he spent tracking 52, and she still wears it.

Joe had his own fixations. "One time he disappeared for over a *month*," he said of 52, his inflection registering a mystery that clearly still engaged him. And at the end of the month, when they finally picked him up again, he was farther out in the Pacific than he'd ever been. Why was there that gap? Joe wondered. What had happened during that time?

Watkins was the driving force behind the whale tracking, but he couldn't keep it running forever. After 9/11, Joe explained, all the money disappeared for good.

As it turned out, however, the saga of 52 was just beginning. After the Woods Hole researchers published their findings about 52 Blue for the first time — in 2004, three years after the funding dried up — they started getting inundated with notes about the whale. Bill Watkins had died a month after the paper was accepted, so it was his former research assistant, a woman named Mary Ann Daher, who found herself receiving this flood of letters. They weren't typical pieces of professional correspondence. They came, as *New York Times* reporter Andrew Revkin wrote at the time, "from whale lovers lamenting the notion of a lonely heart of the cetacean world" or from people who identified with the whale for other reasons: because he seemed restless or independent, because he sang his own song.

After Revkin's story ran that December, headlined "Song of the Sea, a Cappella and Unanswered," more letters flooded Woods Hole. (One marine-mammal researcher quoted in the story, Kate Stafford, may have inadvertently fanned the flames: "He's saying, 'Hey, I'm out here.' Well, nobody is phoning home.") These letters came from the heartbroken and the deaf; from the lovelorn and the single; the once bitten, twice shy and the twice bitten, forever shy — people who identified with the whale or hurt for him, ached for whatever set of feelings they projected onto him.

A legend was born: the loneliest whale in the world.

In the years since, 52 Blue—or 52 Hertz, as he is known to many of his devotees—has inspired numerous sob-story headlines: not just "The Loneliest Whale in the World" but "The Whale Whose Unique Call Has Stopped Him Finding Love"; "A Lonely Whale's Unrequited Love Song"; "There Is One Whale That Zero Other Whales Can Hear and It's Very Alone: It's the Saddest Thing Ever, and Science Should Try to Talk to It." There have been imaginative accounts of a solitary bachelor headed down to the Mexican Riviera to troll haplessly for the biggest mammal babes alive, "his musical mating calls ringing for hours through the darkness of the deepest seas…broadcasting a wide repertory of heartfelt tunes."

A singer in New Mexico, unhappy at his day job in tech, wrote an entire album dedicated to 52; another singer in Michigan wrote a kids' song about the whale's plight; an artist in upstate New York made a sculpture out of old plastic bottles and called it *52 Hertz*. A music producer in Los Angeles started buying cassette tapes at garage sales and recording over them with 52's song, the song that was quickly becoming a kind of sentimental seismograph suggesting multiple story lines: alienation and determination; autonomy and longing; not only a failure to communicate but also a dogged persistence in the face of this failure. People have set up Twitter accounts to speak for him, including @52_Hz_Whale, who gets right to the point:

Helloooooooo?! Yoooohoooooo! Is anyone out there? #SadLife

I'm so lonely. :'(#lonely #ForeverAlone

*   *   *

Leonora woke up in St. Luke's–Roosevelt Hospital in September 2007, in the aftermath of a seven-week coma but still near the beginning of the medical odyssey that would deliver her to 52 Blue. Across the course of five days of surgery, the doctors had removed nearly three feet of her intestines in order to cut out all the necrotic tissue that had rotted around a severe intestinal blockage. Then they'd put her in the coma to help her recover more efficiently. But so much recovery remained ahead of her. She couldn't walk. She had trouble remembering words, and she could barely speak anyway—her trachea was so scarred from all the tubes that had been thrust down it during her coma. She couldn't count past ten. She couldn't even quite count to ten. But she pretended. She didn't let on. She didn't want other people to see her struggling.

Leonora had grown up around struggle, raised mostly by her grandmother, a determined and resourceful woman, four feet eleven and blind from diabetes, who'd come to the States from Chennai by way of Trinidad. She'd always told Leonora that her people back in India thought America was full of golden sidewalks. But Leonora remembers the part of Harlem where she grew up, a neighborhood near Bradhurst Avenue, as something of an urban war zone during her high-school years in the mid-'70s, with its own police task force and sky-high murder rates. When Leonora got interested in photography one summer, people started calling her Death Photographer because so many of her subjects ended up as victims of violence.

Leonora was determined to leave, eventually saving enough bartending money to fund a trip to Paris, where she spent a blurry year walking up and down the Boulevard Saint-Michel with a corkscrew in her hand; taking a trip to Capri, where she and a friend met a pair of amorous lifeguards, broke into an abandoned villa, and ate bread and jam off the dusty kitchen table. Back in New York, Leonora met a man she almost married, but when they went to the courthouse, she got such terrible cramps that she had to go to the bathroom and realized it was her body telling her: *Don't do this*. She listened. She stayed in the bathroom until the offices closed; a police officer had to get her out.

She got a job as a case manager for the city, working with clients on food stamps or welfare, but grew increasingly isolated in her personal life. By the time she was hospitalized in July 2007, she'd retreated from the world so much that her time in the hospital felt less like an abrupt rupture and more like the continuation of her descent.

For Leonora, the hardest part of the recovery process was losing her self-sufficiency, realizing that she could no longer be independent or take care of herself. As she regained her voice, she started to grow more comfortable asking for what she needed. When she eventually realized the source of a stench she'd grown aware of—that it was her own hair, matted with blood—she demanded that one of the doctors cut it, and it turned out looking pretty good. They joked that the doctor might have a second career as a hairdresser.

During the six months she spent at the hospital and various rehab facilities, Leonora felt abandoned. She didn't have many visitors. It seemed like everyone in her life was fleeing her damage, pushing her away because they didn't want to be around her sickness. She assumed her illness made them uncomfortable because it reminded them of their own mortality. When people did visit, she perceived a dark energy coming from them; it nauseated her. When her father came to see her, he told her over and over that she looked like her mother—a woman he hadn't spoken about in many years. She felt that her illness raised long-buried emotions of anger and loss in him.

Leonora was cut off from others, and from the world itself. She couldn't even watch television because it gave her headaches. It was late one night, alone and trolling the internet, that she came upon the story of 52 Blue. By then the story of the whale had been floating around the internet for several years. But it resonated for Leonora with a particular urgency. "He was speaking a language that no one else could speak," she told me. "And here I was without a language. I had no more language to describe what had happened to me...I was like him. I had nothing. No one to communicate with. No one was hearing me. No one was hearing him. And I thought: *I hear you. I wish you could hear me.*"

Like the whale's, she felt that her own language was adrift. She was struggling to come back to any sense of self, much less find the words for what she was thinking or feeling. The world seemed to be pulling away, and the whale offered an echo of this difficulty. She remembers thinking, *I wish I could speak whale.* She found a strange kind of hope in the possibility that 52 Blue knew he wasn't alone. "I was like: Here he is. He's talking. He's saying something. He's singing. And nobody's really understanding, but there are people listening. I bet he knows people are listening. He must feel it."

The hunt for an elusive whale is the most famous story in the history of American literature. *Hast thou seen the White Whale?* But as much as *Moby-Dick* is about the quest for an animal, or for revenge, it's also about the quest for metaphor—the attempt to understand what can't be understood. Ishmael calls the whiteness of the whale "a dumb blankness, full of meaning." Full of many meanings, actually: divinity and its absence, primal power and its refusal, the possibility of revenge and the possibility of annihilation. "Of all these things the Albino whale was the symbol," Ishmael explains. "Wonder ye then at the fiery hunt?"

When I first began looking into the story of 52 Blue, I reached out to Mary Ann Daher at Woods Hole, hoping she could help me understand how the story of this whale had jumped the bounds of science and become something more like a rallying cry. Her role in the story was curious. She'd become the unwitting confessor for a growing flock of devotees simply because her name was on a paper recounting work for which she'd been a research assistant years before. "I get all sorts of emails," she told one reporter at the time, "some of them very touching—genuinely; it just breaks your heart to read some of them—asking why I can't go out there and help this animal." Eventually the media attention started to grate on her. "It's been pretty painful," she told another reporter in 2013. "You name the country and I've had a phone call, wanting to get information. And I haven't worked on this since 2006 or so...and...oh God, [Watkins would] be dismayed, to put it mildly."

I was eager to speak with Daher anyway. I pictured the two of us at Woods Hole, meeting by the sea, locking eyes, nursing cups of coffee in the salt air. How did it feel to get those letters? I'd ask her. And she'd tell me about the tug on her heart each time, her in-box turned into confessional booth. Perhaps she'd recite one from memory, the one that had moved her the most: *He is hope and loss at once.* I'd hear some break in her voice, and I'd copy her words. I'd copy the break. I'd make note of her scientific neutrality showing the strain at its seams, nearly torn open by a lonely stranger's helpless wonder.

It could have gone like that. Perhaps there is another world in which it did. This world, however, holds only her refusal to return my emails. The Woods Hole media-relations representative made it very clear: Daher was done talking about the whale; done refusing to make assumptions about the whale; done correcting other people's assumptions about the whale. She'd already said everything she had to say.

The last journalist Daher agreed to talk to was a writer named Kieran Mulvaney. The transcript of their conversation gives a sense of her wariness and aggravation. "We don't know what the heck it is," she said, when asked about the cause of 52's odd song. "Is he alone? I don't know. People like to imagine this creature just out there swimming by his lonesome, just singing away and nobody's listening. But I can't say that...Is he successful reproductively? I haven't the vaguest idea.

Nobody can answer those questions. Is he lonely? I hate to attach human emotions like that. Do whales get lonely? I don't know. I don't even want to touch that topic."

Daher never agreed to speak to me. She never agreed to pass along the letters she'd received from all the people who had been moved by this animal. So I went looking for them on my own.

At first, they were just voices out of the digital ether: a Polish tabloid photographer, an Irish farmers' cooperative employee, an American Muslim woman who associated 52 Blue with the Prophet Yunus. They congregated at a Facebook page dedicated to the whale, where most of the messages converged on two themes: feeling bad for 52 and wanting to find 52. Denise posted one message—"find 52 hertz"—over and over and over again one morning: at 8:09, 8:11, 8:14, 8:14 (a second time), and 8:16. A woman named Jen wrote, "Just want to give it a hug."

Shorna, a twenty-two-year-old in Kent, England, told me that learning about 52 gave her a way to understand the isolation she felt after her brother was killed when she was thirteen—the abiding conviction that her grief was nothing anyone else could ever understand. Her family didn't want to talk about it. Therapists were telling her what she should feel. The whale never told her what to feel. It just gave a shape to what she already felt, which was that she was "on a different wave length to other people." Juliana was a nineteen-year-old English major at the University of Toronto who told me she understood the whale as "the epitome of every person who's ever felt too weird to love." For her, he represented anyone "wandering alone," or anyone, herself included, "trying to find someone who accepts us for our weaknesses and faults."

Zbigniew, a twenty-six-year-old photo editor at the biggest daily tabloid in Poland, decided to get the outline of 52 Blue tattooed across his back after the end of a six-year relationship:

> i was deeply in love. but as it came out she was treating me like a second category person in relationship... i was devastadcm mainy becose i have given her everything i could, and i thought she would do the same for me. [Because] of her i lost connection with important friends. View of the wasted time made me sad...Story of 52 hz whale made me happy. For me he is symbol of being alone in a positive way...He is like a steatement, that despite being alone he lives on.

For Zee, as he calls himself, 52 came to represent the lonely days after the breakup, watching sad movies alone at home with his two cats, Puma and Fuga. "For long time i was 'singing' in other frequency then everybody around," he wrote to me. But for him the whale also represented resilience: "this is what my life looks like for last 2 years. im swiming slowly through my part of ocean, trying to find poeple like me, Patient, going past life being sure that im not crippled but special in positive way."

The tattoo was a way for Zee to honor what the whale had meant to him, and to communicate that meaning—to sing at a frequency that might be understood. It stretches across his upper back, the "only place on my body huge enough to make it look awesome." Behind a detailed rendering of Moby-Dick, another one of Zee's fixations, there is a second whale, a ghost whale: just a negative space of bare skin defined by an outline of ink. Rather than illustrating 52 Blue, Zee's tattoo evoked the fact that he hadn't ever been seen.

Sakina, a twenty-eight-year-old medical actor living in Michigan, associates 52 with a different kind of loss—a more spiritual struggle. I first saw her in a YouTube video, wearing a hijab, describing how the story of 52 immediately made her think of the prophet Yunus, who was swallowed by a whale. "It makes sense that the loneliest whale feels lonely," she says. "Because he had a prophet with him, inside of him, and now he doesn't." I met Sakina in a coffee shop in downtown Ann Arbor, where she told me that learning about 52 Blue had evoked certain lonely periods of her childhood. (She grew up Muslim in New Mexico.) But she hadn't imagined the whale hungry for love so much as for a sense of purpose, craving a prophet to swallow or a prophecy to fulfill. She wondered: "Is he aching for the divinity again?"

David, an Irish father of two, identified with 52 Blue more deeply after he lost his job at Waterford Crystal, where he had been working for more than two decades. He wrote a song lamenting that he'd "followed sorrow like Whale 52 Hertz," and then moved to Galway with his wife to forge a new life. "I am told by everyone that Galway will be good for me," he wrote to me at the time. At the age of forty-seven, he was starting with a singing group and going back to school. "I have taken the discovery of the Whale as a signal from the depths that I am close to discovery...All I really know is that the 52 Hertz Whale is out there singing and that makes me feel less alone."

Six months later, David wrote to tell me that his wife had left him after twenty-five years of marriage. They could barely speak to each other. Life in Galway wasn't what he'd expected. His singing group had been a bust. But he still found solace in the whale. "I know that she's still out there," he wrote, imagining her as a female, perhaps as a soul mate. "I see others searching. Maybe I won't be alone for much longer."

T he natural world has always offered itself as a screen for human projection. The Romantics called this the pathetic fallacy. Ralph Waldo Emerson called it "intercourse with heaven and Earth." We project our fears and longings onto everything we're not—every beast, every mountain—and in this way we make them somehow kin. It's an act of humbling and longing and claiming all at once. Often, we're not even aware that we're doing it. Decades after amateur astronomer Percival Lowell claimed to have seen canals on Mars and shadowy "spokes" on Venus, interpreting both as signs of alien life, an optometrist figured out that the settings on Lowell's telescope— its magnification and narrow aperture—meant that it was essentially projecting the interior of his eye onto the planets he was observing. The spokes of Venus were the shadows of his blood vessels, swollen from hypertension. He wasn't seeing other life; he was seeing the imprint of his own gaze.

When Emerson claimed that "every appearance in nature corresponds to some state of the mind," he understood this correspondence as a kind of completion. "All the facts in natural history taken by themselves have no value but are barren, like a single sex," he argued, suggesting that human projection effectively fertilized the egg. It not only brought meaning to the "barren" body of natural history, Emerson suggested, but offered sustenance to man himself, becoming "part of his daily food."

Though Emerson celebrated this process, he also interrogated its implications. "We are thus assisted by natural objects in the expression of particular meanings, but how great a language to convey such pepper-corn informations!" he wrote. "We are like travelers using the cinders of a volcano to roast their eggs." He wondered whether it robbed the natural world of its integrity to deploy it as metaphor: "Have mountains, and waves, and skies, no significance but what we consciously give them, when we employ them as emblems of our thoughts?" Roasting an egg on volcano cinders might be an apt way of describing what it means to use a giant whale to embody dorm-room homesickness or post-breakup ennui. *Is he lonely? I hate to attach human emotions like that.*

There used to be a name for the kind of people who like to tell tall tales about animals: nature fakers. Teddy Roosevelt himself issued a scathing public condemnation of what he called "yellow journalism of the woods." These syrupy accounts of the natural world projected human logic onto animal behaviors, spinning tales of wild fowl setting their own broken legs in mud-made casts, or crows convening schoolrooms for their young. "I know as President I ought not do this," he wrote, but criticized them anyway. "He is not a student of nature at all who sees not keenly but falsely, who writes interestingly and untruthfully, and whose imagination is used not to interpret facts but to invent them." Roosevelt was especially concerned about "fact-blindness": the possibility that telling fake stories about nature might blind us to the true ones. This is the danger of making the whale lonely or prophethungry, asking the duck to set a mud cast for his own broken leg—the possibility that feeling too much awe about the nature we've invented will make us unable to appreciate the nature in which we live.

Roosevelt's argument finds a strange modern echo in a Twitter account called @52Hurts, whose bio imagines the whale protesting his own symbolic status: "I am no symbol, no metaphor. I am not the metaphysics you feel stirring in you, no stand-in for your obsessions. I am a whale." Many of his tweets are nonsense—"Ivdhggv ahijhd ajhlkjhds"—but something about them seems honest. They are the tweets of a whale that doesn't know why he's on Twitter, whose jumbled language protests the projection of language onto him at all. His gibberish is more interested in what *isn't* legible than in forcing the unknown into false legibility. It's more interested in acknowledging the gaps than in voicing the projections we hurl across them.

When I first reached out to Leonora, she responded immediately to welcome me into the "vast vibrational pool" of 52 devotees. We met in Harlem's Riverbank State Park on a March afternoon caught between winter and spring. The wind was chilly off the Hudson.

Leonora moved carefully and chose her words with the same deliberate attention. Riverbank was clearly a special place for her. She was eager to explain that the park had been built on top of a sewage-treatment facility. She seemed proud of how it had turned ugly necessity into possibility. Riverbank had also been an important part of her rehabilitation process. It was the place she'd practiced walking after coming out of her coma. She'd been embarrassed at the thought of her home-care aide watching her stumble at every step, so she went to the park instead. The park didn't judge. It just let her practice.

As we walked past a row of withered garden plots, Leonora told me she hadn't gotten a cold all winter because of her vitamins. She'd been taking a "barrage" of them ever since she died. That's how she described her illness and coma: as a process of dying and coming back to life. "My ticket back came with conditions," she said. She had to learn to take care of herself—hence the vitamins, the art classes, and the desire to start growing her own vegetables this spring. She was hoping to get one of the small gardens that the park association was going to auction off before summer. The plots were down by the running track, full of the residue of winter: shriveled stalks, leaves withered to a crisp, bent lattices that had once held tomatoes and would hold them again. Leonora said she wanted to plant peppers and parsley, a small crop perched above a sewage plant. It would be a way of saying, *We do what we can with what we have.* She'd come back from her coma in pieces. She was still putting those pieces back together into a life.

A red-bellied robin hopped across one of the garden plots, right in front of us, and Leonora couldn't believe we were seeing it. It was too early in spring. She told me we needed to wish on it. This was part of her three-day rule: when she asks the universe a question, she always gets an answer in three days, in a dream or a visitation—maybe an animal or something as simple as the smell of lavender. She is open to messages from everything, all the time, in languages that aren't even recognizable as languages at all.

We walked inside and settled at the snack bar, by the ice rink, where an elementary-school hockey team was practicing. The Squirts. Leonora told me this was the last place in New York where you could still get coffee for a dollar. This was her home turf. The guys behind the counter knew her order before she ordered it. The guy riding by in a motorized wheelchair said hello. The guy lurking by the register wanted her to sign a petition for a candidate for parks superintendent.

At our table, Leonora pulled out a large notebook to show me some of her pen and pencil sketches of 52 Blue. "He obsesses me," she explained. "I was trying to get a sense of what he looks like." But she told me her early drawings were "muddled." So she looked at photographs of other whales. "But I still wasn't finding *him*. He's so elusive." She kept sketching him anyway. She was working on a painting of 52 for the final exhibition of an art class she was taking at the park's recreation center.

The first time Leonora ever listened to 52's song, she told me, she played it back at least fifty times. She once dreamed about swimming with him: he was in a pod of whales, no longer alone, and she was moving with them at what felt like a hundred miles per hour—her head huge, her body sleek and hairless. Her coma recovery was full of dreams about water, always rivers and oceans rather than lakes or ponds. The water needed to be in motion, rather than stagnant or still. After her dream about 52, she woke up astonished. "I was moved by it," she said. "All I could do was just lie there and think, *What was that? What was that?*"

Leonora's sense of connection to 52 had always been about two things at once: communication and autonomy. He represented her difficulties in recovery—her failed attempts to speak—but also the independence that these difficulties had taken away. While others saw the whale as heartbroken, because he couldn't find a companion, Leonora saw him as a creature that didn't need one. He was a representation of her own capacity to live alone. It was a capacity she cherished, and it was precisely what her illness had imperiled.

It bothered Leonora that people conflated 52's aloneness with loneliness. It bothered her that people conflated *her* aloneness with loneliness. Apropos of very little, she told me, "I haven't been in a relationship since the last century. I haven't been on a date." She said it worried other people in her life, friends and family members who tried to set her up. "It's like a woman is not a whole person until she has a man." But it didn't worry her. "I've never felt lonely. There is not this lonely factor. I am *alone*. But I am not lonely, okay? I go over to a friend's, I buy cases of wine, I have people over, I cook."

It was hard not to hear a hint of *doth protest too much* in her insistence. But I was also hearing an argument for the importance of humility: Don't assume the contours of another person's heart. Don't assume its desires. Don't assume that being alone means being lonely. Leonora told me that she hopes 52 is never found. "I pray they don't. I like to believe that I'll see him in my dreams."

I just don't know what it is, the fascination with this whale," Joe George told me, while we sat at his dining room table. "To me it's just science." Which made the tray of cookies that sat between us even more charming—all of them shaped like whales, with frosted tails, various pastel shades of green and pink and periwinkle, and "52" written in matching shades of icing. Joe's daughter had made them for us. He was pleased to offer them to me but also seemed a bit sheepish. They were complicit in the whimsy of a phenomenon he couldn't quite wrap his mind around.

He told me it felt odd to have funding for the whale tracking cut so suddenly and unequivocally—to feel like no one cared about what they were doing—and then to see his whale resurface so many years later in such a strange, refracted form. Suddenly *everyone* cared, but for reasons that didn't really make sense to Joe, a man more worried about doing his job right than mining it for metaphor.

At a certain point, Joe told me, the whale called 52 Hertz stopped coming in at 52 hertz. The last time they tracked him, his call was more like 49.6 hertz. It could have been a kind of delayed puberty, or else a function of size, his growing form pulling his vocalizations down into lower frequencies.

It's another lesson in humility—the possibility that an elusive animal might stop flashing its old calling card, that the physical creature might render all our mythical projections moot. It's as if we have tuned our hearts to a signal that no longer exists. Which means there is no way to find what we've been looking for, only—perhaps—a way to find what that creature has become.

After a spring spent getting to know Leonora, I went back to Riverbank State Park for her class's final art show. It was an early summer day of celebration. The beginning keyboard class played "When the Saints Go Marching In" under giant beige industrial fans. A group of elderly women did a synchronized dance to bubblegum-pop, waving matching fans and wearing white capri pants with bright sapphire and coral-pink shirts. One of the park staff leaned close to whisper in my ear, "These are our seniors. They like to get down."

Leonora, wearing lavender pants and a pink scrunchie, was taking photos and rolling around a shopping cart full of her artwork. She showed me her painting of 52 Blue hanging on a hallway wall: a whale painted in flat acrylics, flying over a rainbow, over an ocean. The decoupaged figure of a woman was riding him—or flying with him, it wasn't entirely clear—and Leonora said it was a photograph of her taken years ago, though she'd obscured the face so it wouldn't be just *her*. It could be anyone. The woman's head was ducking close to the whale, as if she were listening to something he was saying. "Someone asked me, 'Is the whale kissing you?'" Leonora told me. "And I said, 'Maybe he is.'"

When a young woman wearing the green shirt of park staff walked by, Leonora explained to her, without apology or introduction: "This is 52 Hertz. Just how I imagined him." As if everyone would know the whale, or should—as if the project of imagining his distant body should be familiar to us all.

Over the course of our conversations during the previous few months, I'd come to understand Leonora's attachment to the whale as something her whole life had been building toward. If she thought of her medical crisis as a culmination—the intestinal blockage as an accretion of traumas from all across her life, experiences she endured but never let herself cry or talk about, until they cluttered her insides and finally made her ill—then it seemed the whale offered another kind of gathering: a vessel in which the accumulation of a lifetime of longings might reside. She had a deep desire to understand her life as something structured by patterns, woven through with signs and signals and voices. She was hungry for a logic that might arrange all the isolated points of her experience into a legible constellation. During one of our talks, she told me she thought of me whenever she saw a robin, because we'd seen one together. I told her that two weeks after we saw that robin, I'd met the man I wanted to marry. It wasn't three days, but still. It was something.

During another one of our visits at the rec-center snack bar, Leonora told me she believed the whale might be the last of his kind—as she would be the last of hers, in a way, because she doesn't have any kids. She hated how people considered her childlessness an insufficiency.

Her artwork was the closest thing she had to progeny, and that was okay with her. It didn't seem like an accident that she used the words "resurrection," "rebirth," and "second birth" to describe her coma and its aftermath, or that we kept coming back to the subject of babies, to having them or not having them. It didn't seem like coincidence that birth was such a big part of how she thought about all this. She'd bled for years. And at the end of all that blood, when she came back from death, it was like she gave birth to herself.

As I left Riverbank State Park that last day, Leonora handed me a small painting: a robin with a red breast, tiny claws, and a single beady eye. She said the red on his breast symbolized activation. I thought of the man I'd met after I saw that robin. I felt the contagion of magical thinking. Life becomes a series of omens. I wanted them to imply the presence of some organizing spirit, or at least compose a story.

"Vaya con Dios," Leonora told me. "You should have a baby someday."

When Emerson lamented that "the material is degraded before the spiritual," he was referring to the ways we have "transferred nature into the mind, and left matter like an outcast corpse." The actual body of 52 Blue has become the outcast corpse, the matter left over once our machinations are done. This alchemy holds both violence and beauty. Emerson understood both parts. "Every spirit builds itself a house, and beyond its house a world; and beyond its world, a heaven," he wrote. "What we are, that only can we see."

Wondering aloud about the whale, Leonora once asked me: "How do you know that he wasn't sent here to heal us, and his song is a healing song?"

Maybe every song is a healing song if we hear it in the right mood—at the end of the right seven weeks, or the worst ones, the ones lost to us forever. Maybe desire and demand are just the same song played at different frequencies. At one point, Leonora told me, simply, "The whale is everything."

52 Blue suggests not just one single whale as a metaphor for loneliness, but metaphor *itself* as salve for loneliness. Metaphor always connects two disparate points; it suggests that no pathos exists in isolation, no plight exists apart from the plights of others. Loneliness seeks out metaphors not just for definition but for the companionship of resonance, the promise of kinship in comparison. Now there's an entire coterie gathered around this particular kinship, people tracking the same pulse of a minivan-sized heart. You might say it's a community formed around an empty center. When we pour our sympathy onto 52 Blue, we aren't feeling for a whale, exactly. We're feeling for what we've built in his likeness. But that feeling still exists. It still matters. It mattered enough to help a woman come back from seven weeks at the edge of death.

At one point during our conversation on Whidbey Island, I mentioned Leonora to Joe. At first I wasn't sure he'd heard me, but near the end of our visit he turned to me and said, "That woman you mentioned, the one who was in the coma." He paused. I nodded. "That's really something," he said.

Joe was right when he said that the whale is just a whale. And so was Leonora when she said the whale is everything. What if we grant the whale his whaleness, grant him furlough from our metaphoric employ, but still allow the contours of his second self—the one we've made—and admit what he's done for us? If we let the whale cleave in two, into his actual form and the apparition of what we needed him to become, then we let these twins swim apart. We free each figure from the other's shadow. We watch them cut two paths across the sea.

We Tell Ourselves Stories
in Order to Live Again

In April 2000, a Louisiana toddler named James Leininger started having nightmares about plane crashes. Whenever his mother came to his bedroom to comfort him, she would find his body contorted, his arms and legs flailing as if he were struggling to extricate himself from something. He repeated the same phrases again and again: "Airplane crash! Plane on fire! Little man can't get out!"

Over the next few years, an increasingly specific story emerged from these dreams. James eventually told his parents they were memories from another life. He said he'd been a pilot shot down by the Japanese. He started using proper nouns that his parents couldn't account for. He'd flown a Corsair. He'd taken off from a ship called the *Natoma*. His parents hadn't ever talked to him about World War II and couldn't imagine where these visions were coming from. James told them about his friends on the ship: a man named Jack Larsen, and guys named Walter and Billy and Leon, who had all been waiting for him in heaven. He named his G.I. Joes after them. His mom, Andrea, became convinced that James was remembering another life. His father, Bruce, was more skeptical.

But when Bruce started doing some research, he found pieces of information that made it hard for him to stay that way. An aircraft carrier called the *Natoma Bay* had been deployed near Iwo Jima in 1945. Its crew included a pilot named Jack Larsen and another named James Huston, who was shot down near Chichi-Jima on March 3 of that year. The crew of the *Natoma Bay* also included Walter Devlin and Billie Peeler and Leon Conner, all of whom perished not long before Huston himself. How would a little boy have known about these men, let alone the name of their ship and the sequence of their deaths?

In 2002, Bruce went to a *Natoma Bay* reunion and started asking questions. He wasn't about to tell anyone what his son claimed to remember; he told everyone that he was writing a book on the history of the ship instead. Andrea, meanwhile, wasn't worried about the military history. She just wanted to end her son's nightmares. She told James that she believed him but that his old life was over. Now he had to live this one.

Seeking closure was the idea behind a trip the family took to Japan when James was eight years old. The plan was to hold a memorial service for James Huston. They rode a fifteen-hour ferry from Tokyo to Chichi-Jima, then a smaller boat to the approximate spot in the Pacific where Huston's plane had gone down. That's where James tossed a bouquet of purple flowers into the ocean. "I salute you, and I'll never forget," he said. Then he sobbed into his mother's lap for twenty minutes straight.

"You leave it all here, buddy," his father told him. "Just leave it all here."

When James finally looked up and brushed away his tears, he wanted to know where his flowers had gone. Someone pointed to a distant spot of color on the water: there they were, far away but still visible, still floating, drifting away on the surface of the sea.

* * *

On a sunny January day in 2014, I visited the offices of a small research institute in Virginia called the Division of Perceptual Studies (DOPS). I was there to interview a child psychiatrist named Jim Tucker, who had spent the past fourteen years compiling a database of children who claimed to remember prior lives. By the time I met Tucker, his database included more than two thousand families, but he called James Leininger his strongest case.

I was interviewing Tucker on assignment for a glossy New York magazine, and I knew my editors expected a debunking. When I told people I was writing a story about the DOPS, whose research focused on past-life memories, near-death experiences, and extrasensory perception, they often said, "Wait, WHAT?" It lent itself to easy jokes. But I felt defensive of reincarnation from the start. It wasn't that I necessarily believed in it. It was more that I'd grown deeply skeptical of skepticism itself. It seemed much easier to poke holes in things—people, programs, systems of belief—than to construct them, stand behind them, or at least take them seriously. That ready-made dismissiveness banished too much mystery and wonder.

The beliefs themselves are hardly unusual. We've all wondered what happens after we die. A 2018 Pew study found that 33 percent of Americans believe in reincarnation, and a 2013 Harris Poll estimated that 64 percent believe in the more loosely defined "survival of the soul after death." Back home in New York, whenever I rode the subway, I saw photos of the thirteen-year-old autistic boy who had gone missing that October. The boy was from Queens; there was no Queens-bound train his face wasn't on. I was irrationally convinced they would find him, or that he was somehow safe, wherever he was—and if that conviction made me foolish, I wanted to be a fool.

When Tucker welcomed me into the DOPS offices, housed in a

stately brick building in downtown Charlottesville, he didn't seem like a kook or a mystic. He was a personable, lucid, clearly intelligent guy—middle-aged and losing his hair, but lithe and trim, like your high-school best friend's marathon-running dad. He was self-possessed, with a courtly formality. He chose his words carefully but unapologetically as he explained how mediums channeled the spirits of the dead and birthmarks could testify to injuries sustained during prior lives. It was a bit like listening to a geologist on acid matter-of-factly describe the composition of the soil.

Founded in 1967, the DOPS is technically affiliated with the University of Virginia but is financed mainly by private donations, including an original million-dollar bequest from the man who invented Xerox technology, Chester Carlson, whose wife believed she had some skill at ESP. After a cover story about its research ran in the University of Virginia alumni magazine in 2013, the online comments were full of reactions from readers who found its existence ridiculous, or were "appalled" to learn about its connection to the university.

As Tucker showed me around their offices, I scribbled a catalog of odd details in my notebook, the low-hanging fruit of institutional quirk. A framed photo showed one former director handing a copy of his book, *The Handbook of Near-Death Experiences*, to the Dalai Lama, who knew a thing or two about reincarnation himself. The bulletin boards were papered with inspiring quotes ("Our notions of mind and matter must pass through many a phase as yet unimaginable") and flyers describing ongoing research projects ("Investigation of Mediums Who Claim to Give Information About Deceased Persons," "Mystical Experiences in Epilepsy"). We passed the "shielded room," designed for experiments on extrasensory perception: a grim-looking cave with a La-Z-Boy recliner where subjects waited to receive messages from "senders" elsewhere in the building. Tucker explained the mechanics of the room as an afterthought—its walls covered in metal sheeting to block cell-phone cheating—as if I probably already knew how ESP chambers worked.

Touring the DOPS, I often felt like a teenager trying to keep from giggling in sex-ed class. But my humor reflex didn't feel entirely authentic. It felt more like channeling an internalized sense of collective judgment, some anonymous "sensible" perspective that told me I'd be a fool if I took any of this stuff seriously; or else like the nervous laughter that erupts from us in the face of what we can't entirely understand.

The DOPS library contained an impressive glass case holding weapons from all over the world—a Nigerian cutlass, a Thai dagger, a Sri Lankan sword—that corresponded to injuries supposedly transferred across lives. The placard beneath a gong mallet from Myanmar told the story of a monk who was struck on the head by a deranged visitor and allegedly came back a few years later as a boy with an unusually flattened skull. In a nearby aisle, stacks of pamphlets documented various DOPS studies, including one titled "Seven More Paranormal Experiences Associated with the Sinking of the *Titanic*." We passed two spoons mounted on the wall, one twisted as if it had been melted over flames. When I asked Tucker about them, his reply was nonchalant. "Those?" he said. "Bent-spoon experiments."

Then there was the lock. When Ian Stevenson, the founding director of the DOPS, died, in 2007, he left behind a lock whose combination was known only to him. The idea was that he'd find a way to send it back if his soul survived death. Tucker and his colleagues had received several call-in suggestions from strangers, but they hadn't gotten the lock open yet. When he told me about the lock, Tucker finally allowed a certain wry playfulness into his voice. But during most of our visit, he kept himself on limited rations when it came to reincarnation jokes. At dinner that night, he told me he'd once tried his hand at writing fiction, and when I asked if he'd ever thought about picking it up again, he smiled. "Maybe in another life."

Tucker told me that having a career as a credentialed child psychiatrist alongside his DOPS work made him feel like he was inhabiting a split self. "My child-psychiatry work has been my mild-mannered Clark Kent identity," he said. "But then there's a secret identity, completely connected to another world." He outlined the makeup of his database: Most of his cases were children between the ages of two and seven, and their memories, which often took the form of vivid dreams, were suffused with a wide range of emotions—fear, love, grief. Most were from foreign countries, and many were children Tucker himself had never met, though he regularly went to interview new families who contacted him with their claims. He referred to a case as "solved" whenever a plausible prior life had been identified, usually someone in the family; though occasionally it was a stranger, as it had been for James.

Tucker seemed like a sensible straight man who had somehow found himself playing Hamlet to the Horatios of the world: *There are more things in heaven and earth...than are dreamt of in your philosophy.* He'd grown up Southern Baptist in North Carolina and hadn't given much thought to reincarnation until his second marriage. His second wife, Chris, also academically trained, believed in psychic abilities and reincarnation, and being with her had opened him up to considering things he never had before. Tucker eventually grew to regard his child-psychiatry practice as "rewarding but not fulfilling." It was gratifying to see kids getting better with treatment, but ultimately it was just "one appointment after another. There was no big picture." His work with past-life memories felt more expansive. It was about following the hazy patterns of a picture that stretched far beyond the limits of his vision.

Weeks later, when I listened to recordings of our interviews, I was embarrassed to hear myself repeatedly declaring to Tucker my "openness to mystery." This insistence had been in earnest, but I could also hear in my voice the shrill and overeager tones of self-convincing, and the savviness of strategy. On some level, I'd been trying to persuade Tucker that I wasn't just another skeptic. Janet Malcolm has famously described the journalist as "a kind of confidence man, preying on people's vanity, ignorance, or loneliness, gaining their trust and betraying them without remorse." And in my interviews with Tucker, I could hear myself confessing to him in advance: "You can never tell the story about somebody that's precisely the story he would have told about himself."

By the time I visited Tucker at the DOPS, I'd been involved in 12-step recovery for more than three years. I'd found that its grace required extinguishing, or at least suspending, many forms of skepticism at once: about dogma, about clichés, about programs of insight and pre-fabricated self-awareness, about other people's ostensibly formulaic narratives of their own lives. In recovery, we were asked to avoid "contempt prior to investigation," and writing a piece about reincarnation— visiting the DOPS and its bent spoons—seemed like another test of this willingness to keep an open mind.

Coming of age as a writer, I had always loved Joan Didion's essay "The White Album," which famously begins, "We tell ourselves stories in order to live," and less famously ends in pretty much exactly the same place, with Didion reiterating her suspicions about all of these "stories" and their false coherence as if it wasn't a point she'd already made several times. Eventually, I started to have my doubts about her doubt. I hated its smugness—how she positions herself as a knowing skeptic in a world full of self-delusion. I started to believe there was an ethical failure embedded in skepticism itself, the same snobbery that lay beneath the impulse to resist clichés in recovery meetings or wholly dismiss people's overly neat narratives of their own lives.

In my own work, I found myself increasingly addicted to writing about lives or beliefs that others might have scoffed at: people who claimed to suffer from a skin disease most doctors didn't believe in, or self-identified outsiders who felt a spiritual kinship to an elusive whale. But if I was honest with myself, this affinity also carried the faint whiff of self-righteousness. Maybe I liked telling myself I was defending underdogs. Or maybe it was cowardice. Maybe I was too scared to push back against the stories people told themselves in order to keep surviving their own lives.

In this case, it wasn't that I was convinced by Tucker's ostensibly "physics-based" account of how reincarnation worked: a theory grounded in a series of experiments drawn from the history of physics that one physicist I interviewed called "cherry-picked" and selectively misinterpreted. Tucker was a psychiatrist, after all, not a physicist. It was more that I felt emotionally, spiritually, and intellectually allergic to a certain disdainful tone that implied it knew better, that it understood what was possible and what wasn't. It seemed arrogant to assume I understood much about consciousness itself—what it was, where it came from, or where it went once we were done with it.

D own in Virginia, I accompanied Tucker on interviews with two families. Both had teenagers who'd remembered prior lives as children. At a large house overlooking bare winter woods, a twenty-year-old college student named Aaron told me that when he was young he'd remembered being a tobacco farmer. He'd had visions of a farm, a mean sister, a fire. He pretend-smoked whatever he could get his hands on: twigs and straws and Popsicle sticks. He was obsessed with tattoos and motorcycles and wouldn't wear anything but cowboy boots. He even wore them to the pool with nothing but his bathing suit.

His mother, Wendy, told me that learning about Aaron's "old soul" helped explain why he often struggled to make friends his own age. She always wanted to throw him birthday parties, but never knew whom to invite. "Not to hurt your feelings, son," she told him, "but you never fit in anywhere." Aaron himself attributed his more recent dating troubles to the same old soul. While the girls around him seemed mainly interested in partying, he explained, he wanted to settle down and start a family. As we spoke, we could see a man through the window standing at the edge of the woods, throwing sticks for a bristling trio of dogs. When he turned around to come inside, Wendy asked me not to mention anything about reincarnation. Her boyfriend was a jet mechanic, she explained. He found all of this absurd.

At a smaller house in a more working-class neighborhood, with a lawn full of deflated plastic reindeer, a mother named Julie explained that her daughter Carol had started speaking late and didn't say much once she'd started. When Julie finally asked Carol why she was so quiet, at the age of four or five, Carol at last mentioned her other family: long-haired parents who grew herbs and owned a mint-green rotary phone. Carol found it confusing that she didn't live with them. She missed them. Julie recalled, "I felt like I had to tell her, 'I really am your mother.'" She worried Carol might share her past life with her classmates at show-and-tell and get teased for it.

More than a decade later, Carol—almost twenty—told me and Tucker that she had recently started culinary school to learn how to decorate cakes for people with food allergies, and Julie speculated that her daughter's creative tendencies may have also carried over from her prior existence. She explained that one of Carol's strongest past-life memories was of drawing at a kitchen table. The association felt charged with the willed electricity of a horoscope: almost anything can fit into the puzzle of your life if you want it to.

After a beat, Carol gently corrected her mother's story. In her memory, she hadn't been drawing at a kitchen table but painting at an easel inside a glass-walled skyscraper. The conversation paused. We all dwelled in the blurry zone between Carol's memories and the stories Julie had told herself about these memories—where the kitchen had replaced the skyscraper and the drawing had replaced the easel, where the kaleidoscope of memory had reshuffled its glimmering shards.

My flight home got canceled by a rare Virginia blizzard, and I spent two nights killing time at a corporate hotel near the airport, drinking seltzer after seltzer at the lobby bar. The bartender and I exchanged pained glances as the TV delivered endless doomsday news: corruption, molestation, dead dolphins bloodying the saltwater of a secret Japanese cove. In some deep unspoken part of my psyche, I'd convinced myself that agnosticism and acceptance were moral virtues unto themselves, but in truth I wasn't so sure. Maybe I wasn't doing anyone any favors by pretending that my belief system was tolerant enough to hold everything as equally valid. Maybe there were experiences I couldn't relate to and things I might never believe.

Why did I want to defend these tales of prior lives, anyway? It had less to do with believing I could prove that reincarnation was real and more to do with investigating why it was appealing to believe in it. If we told ourselves stories in order to live, what did we get from stories that allowed us to live again? It was about something more than buffering against the terrifying finality of death. It had to do with recognizing the ways we're shaped by forces we can't see or understand.

On the television screen at the airport hotel bar—in the middle of that blizzard, just before I went to bed—I saw the face of Avonte Oquendo, the missing boy from Queens. His remains had been discovered in the East River. Back when they thought they might still find him alive, the police had played a recording that his mother had made, in order to help him trust them: "Avonte. This is your mother. You are safe. Walk toward the lights."

*　　*　　*

Driving down Louisiana back roads a few weeks later, on my way to the Leiningers' home in Lafayette, I passed forests webbed with pockets of glistening water, and shotgun shacks collapsing under their own weight. The radio in my rental car spoke to me about demons. "I believe in the spiritual enemy," a man said. "He works by way of sub-stitution."

Before coming down, I'd interviewed a child psychiatrist named Alan Ravitz about the possibility of past-life memories, and he'd been less immediately dismissive than I'd expected. "Who the hell knows?" he said. "Anything is possible." He admitted that Tucker had found "certain sorts of phenomena that are just difficult to explain," and stressed that many of these reported past-life memories weren't "the typical kind of imaginative material that kids would come up with." But Ravitz posited that "past lives" like these could also emerge from a subtle process of reinforcement. When a kid tells a story—or recounts an odd memory or a weird dream that felt real—and gets any kind of attention for it, it's only natural for the child to keep expanding it.

These dynamics of reinforcement—maybe operating for parents and children alike—were part of what fascinated me about these cases. We tell stories about why we're lonely, or what we're haunted by, and these stories about absence can define us as fully as our present realities. Kids build identities around ghosts. A mother believes that her son has trouble making friends because the soul of an old man lives inside him. Stories about past lives help explain this one. They promise an extraordinary root structure beneath the ordinary soil of our days. They acknowledge that the realities closest to us—the rhythms of our lives, the people we love most—are shaped by forces beyond the edges of our sight. It's thrilling and terrifying. It's expansion and surrender at once.

Down in Louisiana, I was renting a cabin out in Arnaudville, past the daiquiri drive-through and the biker barn saloon on I-49, past the church marquee that said JESUS IS A HUGGER and the hand-painted sign advertising USED SUGAR KETTLES FOR SALE, past tiny streets with speed signs in bright purple: 7½ MILES PER HOUR. The cabin was a wooden shack set back among pecan and magnolia trees, with an old wooden sign for DR. KILMER'S SWAMP ROOT above the toilet and a brass lamp beside a bed where I imagined sleeping with all the men I wasn't sleeping with anymore. Their ghosts crowded the shack, vessels for all the selves I used to be.

The Leiningers lived in a modest house shadowed by river birches draped in Spanish moss. When Bruce answered the door, he offered me a cup of coffee and a slice of banana bread, then—almost immediately—offered to show me his gun collection. I could tell it made him wary to see me writing in my notebook. "I'm not a gun nut," he said, holding a gun in each hand. After I used the bathroom, I emerged to find a collection of bullets spread across his comforter. I didn't want to touch them, but I mentally recorded them as a "telling detail." The tattoo that ran along my arm was posing questions about this man, this moment, and these bullets. *Homo sum: humani nil a me alienum puto*, it said. "I am human: nothing human is alien to me." Had I been foolishly unwilling to acknowledge that some people *were* alien to me? Did I need to identify with all the gun-loving men of this world? Was it naïve or even ethically irresponsible to believe I should find common ground with everyone, or that it was even possible?

In preparation for my arrival, Bruce had pulled out his material about the *Natoma Bay* and its pilots—more than a decade's worth of research. The dining room table was covered with notebooks and folders, but it was "only a fraction," he said, of what he had in his closets. He had compiled a separate notebook for every single soldier who died on the ship, crammed with as much biographical information and as many military after-action reports as he could assemble. There was a wooden champagne crate full of microfiche reels that the ship's historian had sent him. Bruce freely admitted: "I was obsessed." Everything was labeled PROPERTY OF BRUCE LEININGER / RESEARCH MATERIAL FOR 'ONE LUCKY SHIP' ©. *One Lucky Ship* was the book that Bruce was writing about the *Natoma Bay,* the book that would finally make good on the story he'd told its veterans years earlier, in order to gain access to their inner circle. Now he sent the families of dead pilots any information he'd gathered about how their loved ones had fought and died, specifics they had almost never gotten from the military. Bruce told me he believed that James Huston had returned in the body of his son for a reason—so that he and Andrea could recover this sliver of American history, one that might otherwise have been lost to obscurity.

Bruce showed me the office closet that James had once pretended was his cockpit, jumping out wearing a canvas shopping bag on his back like a parachute. Then he brought out some of the artifacts he'd gathered over the years, including a vial of soil from Iwo Jima and a piece of melted engine from the kamikaze plane that flew into the *Natoma Bay* in 1945—a metal hunk coated in melted tar and bits of redwood from the ship's deck. Bruce handled it like a holy relic.

After years of research, Bruce had finally managed to locate Anne Huston Barron, James Huston's sister, whom he initially befriended under the auspices of his usual cover story. About six months after making contact, however, he and Andrea decided to tell Anne the actual reason for their interest in her brother. They were nervous. They started the phone call by suggesting that she might want to pour herself a glass of wine. They had the number of her local EMT service on hand in case the news was too much of a shock. As Bruce and Andrea shared these details—the glass of wine, the EMT number—I heard echoes of *Soul Survivor,* their 2009 book about James's past-life memories. Their witty asides had become part of a well-worn story. Even its grooves of self-deprecation held the uneasy echoes of lines performed effectively and often.

As for Anne? She wasn't sure what to make of their revelation at first—she was shocked—but eventually she came to embrace the idea that their son was her brother reincarnated. Perhaps there was something comforting about the possibility that her James was not entirely gone. Bruce showed me one of her letters. "All of this is still overwhelming," she'd written. "One reads about it, but never expects it to happen to you." And in her neat, orderly print, an unequivocal affirmation: "But I believe."

When I met James, he struck me as a pretty well-adjusted teenager. He seemed polite but vaguely bored, and evinced close to zero interest in talking to me. Here was yet another stranger curious about past-life memories that he hadn't remembered in years, not since that ceremony on the sea. It was easier to draw him out on other subjects: his commitment to jujitsu, his advice on how to tell if your gator meat had been decently prepared. He wasn't at all defensive, but I sensed he was a bit tired of the whole past-life production, and perhaps a bit sheepish about the publicity circus these memories had yielded— the book and the interviews—the way you might amiably tolerate the public antics of an embarrassing sibling. He no longer wanted to be a Navy fighter pilot like James Huston; now he wanted to be a Marine. But he also spent much of the afternoon playing a video game that involved shooting from a simulated cockpit, and his bedroom was still full of the model airplanes Bruce had built for him, dangling from the ceiling.

The hardest part about spending time with the Leiningers was how much I liked them. As we ate dinner together at a local creole restaurant, shadowed by a twelve-foot taxidermy alligator, I knew I wasn't writing the story they wanted me to write about their family. Once again, Janet Malcolm had articulated my guilt before I'd even felt it: "Like the credulous widow who wakes up one day to find the charming young man and all her savings gone, so the consenting subject of a piece of nonfiction writing learns—when the article or book appears—*his* hard lesson." And yet, it seemed too easy to narrate the Leiningers as hucksters of petty mystery, parents who had turned their son's alleged past life into something like a cottage industry: a best-selling memoir and another book in the works, a slew of television specials and speaking gigs. Their motives never struck me as entrepreneurial. It seemed more like they had encountered something genuinely mysterious in their son—a force they couldn't explain—and that their explanation had become a narrative engine of its own, a story that granted them a sense of purpose: to excavate one forgotten corner of human history, and—more broadly—to testify to the world that a soul could travel from one body to another.

Of course, the story of their son also gave them a way to be special: to sell a book, to be interviewed on television. I'd started to notice an abiding irony embedded in stories of reincarnation. Even as they replaced a belief in the uniqueness of the self with an idea of interchangeability—suggesting that your soul had belonged to others before it belonged to you—they also provided an extraordinary explanation for deeply ordinary things: a shy daughter, a son with no friends, a toddler with nightmares. They turned quotidian experiences into symptoms of an exotic existential phenomenon.

Near the end of our visit, the Leiningers offered to show me some of the television specials they had been featured in. Together we watched *The Ghost Inside My Child* and *Science of the Soul*. We watched a Japanese special with a voiceover that had never been translated; the

Leiningers still didn't know what it said. It was this TV special that had funded their trip to Chichi-Jima and its cathartic farewell. We watched the B-roll footage, in which the Leiningers sit in a boat for hours, waiting for the ritual. I would see James weep, his parents promised, almost as an implicit challenge: *Try not to believe after you've seen how hard he cried.*

Andrea left the house as we watched, insisting that she needed to buy a printer cartridge but also confessing that it made her too emotional to watch James weep. Bruce wanted to skip past his own "silly speech" on the boat, but I asked him not to. It turned out to be an earnest homage to the bravery of James Huston, and to the beauty of his final resting place—those blue waters off a remote Japanese island where, as Bruce said on camera, "my own son's journey began."

People on the show kept asking James how he was feeling. "Okay," he said. "Good."

I couldn't help wondering whether these initial responses had disappointed his family, or the filmmakers—if it had been frustrating to stage an elaborate memorial on the other side of the world, and have no tears to show for it.

On-screen, however, Bruce gave no sign of disappointment. "I'm glad you don't feel anything," he told his son. "You've suffered for so long."

It was only after the eulogy was done and the tribute paid, when Andrea finally said that it was time to say goodbye to James Huston, that her son started crying. And then he kept going. He just couldn't stop.

Offscreen—years after that day, on his living room couch—Bruce got quiet. He told me that it still upset him to consider what had been going through his son's mind that day. At one point, a camera guy crept into the frame to give James a hug. Then he embraced Bruce too.

"They were just in pieces," Bruce said, meaning the whole Japanese crew. At this point, their tears had become an inextricable part of the story, proof of their investment and belief. But I wondered what it must have been like for them, sitting beside the ostensible reincarnation of a soldier who'd fought against their country.

Andrea rejoined us later to watch some of the other documentaries. She said she especially liked the one that didn't make her look a million years old. The friendliest of the family's four cats climbed onto the couch with us, but turned away from the screen. I sensed that she, too, had seen these shows before.

Bruce mouthed the words he said on-screen before he actually said them. "Bullshit!" he whispered to himself, a moment before he barked out the word on the television. He had been re-creating his own skepticism for the interviewer, playacting an earlier version of himself from the days before he'd come to believe in James's memories. Bruce enjoyed performing his former disbelief because it wasn't something that ran counter to his current faith; it was actually a necessary part of the same narrative arc, suggesting to other skeptics that their doubt was perfectly reasonable but ultimately wrong.

For her part, Andrea seemed less interested in other people's relationships to James's memories and more interested in how James himself had experienced them. She showed me a stack of his young drawings: messy circles meant to show the motion of propellers, peppery dots meant to represent anti-aircraft flak, everything broken and splintered and covered with rashes of red-marker blood. She showed me his stick-figure parachutists falling through the sky. Some of their chutes had bloomed into arcs above their bodies; others, less lucky, had chutes collapsed into straight lines above them.

From across the room, where he was still watching the TV, Bruce mentioned that according to an after-action report he'd found, James Huston once shot down a parachuting Japanese pilot. Andrea was shocked; she hadn't known that. "I just got chills," she said. "That's probably why James was always drawing them—because he shot one down."

Meanwhile, on the TV screen, Bruce sat on a tiny boat and placed a hand on his son's back. "You're such a brave soul and spirit," he said.

In that moment, beneath the sensational story of reincarnation, there was a simpler story at work: a father trying to make his son feel better. These were two parents who wanted to believe their love could fill the gap between what they couldn't explain and the explanations they sought anyway. Love is not immune from the human hunger for narrative. It's a hunger I experience constantly myself. It's the hunger from which I make my living. For this family, that hunger had built an intricate and self-sustaining story, all of it anchored by the desire to care for a little boy in the dark.

Before I left, Andrea handed me a composition James had written in seventh grade called "Nightmares":

The burning torture of fire and smoke hit me every single night for five years... The nightmares were not dreams, but something that actually happened: the death of James M. Huston. His soul was brought back in the human form. He was brought back in my body and he chose to come back to Earth for a reason; to tell people that life is truly everlasting.

The specter of skepticism haunted this crescendo, and James was wise to it:

You can think I am a fool for knowing this, for believing these things. But when my parents wrote the book about me and my story, people who were deathly ill or had incurable diseases sent me e-mails that said, "Your story helped me and made me not afraid to die."

At the bottom of James's composition his teacher had written just one word, three times in red: *Wow. Wow. Wow.*

* * *

A few months after I returned from Louisiana, I got a letter from my aunt. She had just spent the afternoon with my grandfather, a former chemical engineer a few months shy of his hundredth birthday. They had been talking about the possibility of reincarnation. For my grandfather—the first in his family to go to college, and a deeply rational man his whole life—the question of what came next was no longer abstract. He and my aunt had eaten salmon and potatoes—solid foods, foods that reminded you that your body was still yours—while he sketched out his vision of living and dying: "We pick up a piece of consciousness when we are born, and when we die it goes back to where it came from."

That same week, a magazine fact-checker was filling my in-box with his skepticism every day. He informed me that more than one World War II aircraft carrier had a Walter and a Leon and a Billy on its crew, so the names were probably just coincidence, and that no Corsairs had ever flown from the *Natoma Bay*. Some part of me wanted to get into it, to tell him that maybe there never were Corsairs flying from the *Natoma*, but James Huston had been one of only twenty pilots flying Corsairs as part of an experimental team earlier in the war. "There's photographic evidence!" I wanted to shout, like a proper Bruce Leininger acolyte, but my defensiveness had never really been about the facts. It had always been about the vision.

The most compelling question for me had never been "Is reincarnation real?" It had always been "What vision of the self does reincarnation ask us to believe in?" I found something appealing about the vision of selfhood it suggested: porous and unoriginal. It was deeply related to what I loved about recovery—that it asked me to understand myself as interchangeable, to see my dilemmas as shared and my identity as something oddly and inescapably connected to distant strangers. Recovery was another story of reincarnation, after all: the sober self reborn from its drunken past. It was as if reincarnation made explicit the philosophical premise underneath recovery itself. If recovery said, "Your soul isn't this special thing," then reincarnation said, "Your soul isn't even yours." If recovery said, "You could have been this other person," then reincarnation said, "You actually *were* this other person."

And if reincarnation is a story some people find comforting, then it's also true that the soul is just a story, too: the notion of an essential, singular self in each of us. Reincarnation both buffers this belief and disrupts it: what we call our soul doesn't die, but perhaps it was never ours. Ultimately this is what appealed to me about the story of reincarnation, that it asked me to believe in a self without rigid boundaries—a self that had lived before and would do it again. In this way, it was a metaphor for what I was struggling to accept about living at all: that nothing we lived was unique, that we were always—in some sense—living again.

Reincarnation is an assertion of contingency: *I could have been anyone. Maybe I was a nurse or a hitman or a mean guy or a hero. Maybe I was a colonial explorer, a colonized subject, a queen or a sailor.* It's humble and it's the opposite of humility, the same way people can read my tattoo as empathy or arrogance: "Nothing human is alien to me." In all my wrestling with reincarnation, I'd been looking for a way to get humble in the face of consciousness, to be the teacher writing, "Wow. Wow. Wow," rather than giving a letter grade.

Reincarnation struck me as an articulation of faith in the self as something that could transform and stay continuous at once—in sobriety, in love, in the body of a stranger. This faith believes a thirteen-year-old boy in Queens might not be lost for good. This faith says, "Come back." Come back to Lafayette, to Virginia, to Myanmar. Come back with scars telling a story no one understands, to a lawn full of crumpled plastic reindeer or a house overlooking skeletal winter trees, to a jet mechanic throwing sticks for the dogs, a man who refuses to believe you were ever a lost boy in Long Island City. Come back to some suburb off the interstate, some condo, some row house. Come back remembering, so you can tell us where you've been. We want to know. We watch a little boy wear his cowboy boots to the pool. We watch a little man who can't get out. We watch the past fill the present like smoke: the memory of sisters and parachutes and flames. We say, *Wow*. We say it again. We stay humble. We can't know for sure until the body turns up in the river—and even then, it might not be the end. We walk toward the lights. We are safe, or else we aren't. We live, until we don't. We return, unless we can't.

Layover Story

This is the story of a layover. Who tells that story? I'm telling it to you now. One January evening, my flight got delayed out of Louisiana, where I'd been talking to people about their past lives, and I missed my connection in Houston. I had a night there. Trying to have a travel experience near the Houston airport is like trying to write a poem from the words on a yeast packet. Don't try to make it beautiful. Just let it rise. Let the freeways run like unspooled thread into the night. Blink against the neon signs of chain stores. Take shelter where you can.

I take shelter at the salmon-pink hotel where I am sent. On our shuttle from the airport, I hear the voice of a difficult woman coming from the front row. She can't believe the bus will run only hourly the next morning. She can't believe her dinner voucher is for so little money. She needs someone to take her bag into the lobby. She'll also need someone to fetch it tomorrow. Later, at the hotel restaurant, her voice is there again at the table behind me: She wants her bag placed where she can see it. She wants her water without ice. She doesn't want to be a pain but she really needs to know if the veggie wrap is absolutely 100 percent vegetarian. She wants to know about the other stranded people sitting around us, especially Martin the German, and the Penn State math major. The math major loves Pi Day. The woman with the voice wants to know if she bakes pie for Pi Day? No, she just eats pie for Pi Day. What kind of pie does she like? All kinds. What kind of math does she like? All kinds. Well, okay. She especially likes patterns and sequences. The woman with the voice wants to know how she feels about i to the i? The undergrad doesn't know about i to the i. "Oh, girlfriend," says the woman with the voice. "Go look up i to the i."

When she finally turns to me, the woman with the voice turns out to be a woman with curly black hair. She asks what I do for a living. She loves that I'm a writer. Turns out she's coming from a vacation in Cabo. Turns out she's on my flight back to Newark. She suggests we protest the hourly shuttles together. The 4:00 a.m. departure is too early for our flight, but the 5:00 a.m. is too late. We should campaign for a 4:40, or a 4:45. She is a difficult woman from New York trying to convince me that we should be difficult women from New York together. But I'm not a difficult woman from New York. I'm not any kind of person from New York. I just happen to live there. I just want to take the 4:00 a.m. shuttle and stop talking about it. It embarrasses me to be associated with her request, with her sense of entitlement, with these justifications—*I hurt more, I need more*—perhaps because I recognize myself in them.

It's only when the woman and I walk to the front desk to check on the shuttle that I notice how she walks. The woman with the voice is also a woman with a body. She's limping. Once I notice her limp, I feel guilty about leaving her to make the shuttle request alone—as if it would be an act of abandonment, in her hour of need, to refuse her my company. She tells the clerk she needs help with her bags, and in the morning she will need help again. She explains that she was in a wheelchair at the airport. I bet she has one of those nebulous pain conditions where the pain is always moving somewhere else. I bet she felt like a victim before she ever started hurting. I am actually thinking these things, and I am someone who has written indignantly about the world's tendency to minimize the pain of women in precisely these ways, for precisely these reasons.

We don't get our 4:40 shuttle. She's going to speak to a manager, she tells me. She'll call me when she gets this sorted out. She takes my number. We trade our names.

Back in my room, I google the name she's given me. It's fairly unusual and involves a body part. The first ten hits are all the same porn star; the next hit is an article about a stabbing spree in New York. A homeless man lunged at several strangers with a half scissors. The face of the woman with the voice is one of the five faces. I enlarge her on my screen. I try to remember her limp, which part of her was hurting.

When I see her in the morning, I won't tell her what I know. The etiquette of our era demands that we pretend we are still unknown to each other, though she will know I probably googled her, and I will know she probably googled me. But I find myself reframing everything I've seen her do—every complaint, every demand, every annoying attempt at small talk—as if a victim couldn't also be a solipsist. Now I want to read everything about her more generously, in order to compensate her for the indignity of becoming a character in my story, *the woman with the voice*, when she was already another kind of character, in another story entirely.

The next morning, I try to help the woman with the voice as best I can. I carry her bags through the Houston airport. I offer to stay with her while she waits for her wheelchair. I barely grimace when she speaks rudely to the airport staff. She's been *stabbed*. She asks me to preboard the plane with her and get her bag stowed above her seat. She asks if I'd help her get from Newark to the city, once we arrive—if I can get her through the airport train station in New Jersey, through New Jersey Transit, then through Penn Station itself, in New York—all those stairs and escalators and platforms and doorways and crowds and crowded baggage racks. I say *yes, yes, yes*. Yes to all of it! She has a story and now I'm part of it. I'm swollen with virtue. I'm so swollen with virtue I can hardly believe it when the man sitting next to me on the flight wants to have a conversation. Doesn't he understand? My virtue has already found its object; I have none left for small talk with strangers. The woman with the voice is sitting in the front of the plane, probably making someone wish they were sitting in the back.

The man next to me starts talking about driving his sister out to Texas, where she was moving for work. She's a traveling nurse and they drove through an ice storm in Atlanta and I really couldn't care less. This guy is just a kid, complaining about the Houston airport not having enough vending machines. I feel like his mother, as if I should offer him a snack. On the tiny monitors above us a nature documentary plays: a baby bison is getting cornered by a pack of wolves. What will happen next? Only one thing, we all know. Back home in Brooklyn, no one is waiting for me. I'm newly single and not-so-newly thirty and leaving lots of crumbs between my couch cushions from dinners made of crackers that don't seem like the dinners of an adult.

Now this guy is talking about his tour in Iraq. He says he got used to desert skies. *Oh.* His life is a little different than I'd thought. I don't know how to ask him about the war. But I ask him anyway. I ask him about the guys he was there with—that seems safe, possible. He shakes his head: the best crew of guys ever. "Now here I am," he says, nudging his duffel bag. "Flying home with an army bag full of hermit-crab shells." I ask how many are in there. Maybe fifty, he says. He has a daughter and she has four pet hermit crabs. I ask if they have names. "They've got so many names I can't keep track," he says. "Their names are always changing." Right now there is one named Clippers and the others are Peaches. All three of them? Yep. Just Peaches and Peaches and Peaches. He says they need a bottomless buffet of shells. They keep getting bigger, so they keep needing new ones.

So the shells in his bag aren't hermit-crab shells because they were made *by* hermit crabs, but because hermit crabs might someday use them? Yes, he says. That is correct.

Perhaps there is profundity in this. We claim something not by making it, but by making it useful. What we squat inside can begin to constitute us. And now he's saying something else, something about the new aquarium he's building for Clippers and the Peaches. He's using old shower doors from his construction company. He has over twenty large sheets of glass, he says, and more than fifty smaller ones. And I'm trying to run the meaning-making logic over this one too: *we have the big and the small; we have more than we can use.* But it doesn't yield; Houston all over again. And how big will his crab aquarium be, anyway? An entire city block? This guy can't decide whether to be interesting or not—like someone who is mostly late but every once in a while, unaccountably, on time. Why would I possibly believe he owed me interest, anyway? Other lives are shells I want to scavenge only when the mood strikes right, only when the shells are good enough.

For now, I want to know what these crabs eat. He says they'll eat pellets, but they prefer fresh fruit. What kind of fruit? Pineapples, he says. They love pineapples. He explains they have a lot of preferences. For example, they need salt water *and* fresh water.

What about when they live in the ocean? I ask. How do they get fresh water then?

He doesn't know. He says, "That's what I'm still trying to figure out."

This man punctures me. I felt like his mother until he said he was a father. I think of all the fear he's known—the guilt, and loss, and boredom—and how I don't know any of it. His endlessness is something I receive in finite anecdotes: big desert skies, a little girl poking crabs. Sometimes I feel I owe a stranger nothing, and then I feel I owe him everything; because he fought and I didn't, because I dismissed him or misunderstood him, because I forgot, for a moment, that his life—like everyone else's—holds more than I could ever possibly see.

It makes me think of that David Foster Wallace commencement speech, "This Is Water," the one that everyone finds inspiring except the people who think it's unbearably trite and find it pathetic that everyone else is so inspired by it. I'm so inspired by it. Wallace talks about the tedium of standing at a supermarket checkout counter, irritated by the other people in line, "how stupid and cow-like and dead-eyed and non-human they seem." But, he says, you can choose to see them differently. You can regard the woman who just yelled at her kid and admit that for all you know she might have just stayed up three nights straight with a husband dying of bone cancer. Maybe she just helped your spouse get through some tangle at the DMV. Maybe the annoying woman on the bus just got stabbed by a deranged stranger on her morning jog. If you learn to pay attention, he says, "it will actually be within your power to experience a crowded, hot, slow, consumer-hell type situation as not only meaningful, but sacred, on fire with the same force that lit the stars."

* * *

The Newark airport train station in the middle of a blizzard does not feel on fire with the same force that lit the stars. I am helping the woman with the voice and the injured body get onto a train headed into the city. We get hot chocolate at the tiny station café, and wait on the outdoor platform, in the Jersey cold, while the snow comes down. I'm tired of benevolence, ready for my own apartment. She tells me it was stupid, how she got hurt. It was her own fault.

I'm a little bit confused. Is this a confession of privilege guilt? Guilt at her complicity in the systems that oppressed the homeless man who stabbed her? Is she going to tell me that he had a story too? Because he did: untreated mental illness, a life spent moving from shelter to shelter. He got sentenced to more than twenty years in prison, where most likely his mental illness remains untreated still. One of his victims was a toddler. This is the kind of story with an easy victim and an easy villain; except maybe it's not so easy—maybe we are all the villains, maybe that's what the woman with the voice is trying to tell me. She is also telling me she is tired of standing, though I cannot make her a chair.

Anyway, she says, she was dancing down in Cabo, and her knee started hurting, but she kept dancing anyway. It was "Mamma Mia." How could she not keep dancing? That's how she hurt herself. She looks at me and I nod. How indeed.

But inside I'm feeling robbed, like something has been stolen from me: the story in which I carried the bags of a woman still recovering from a stabbing attack. Now I'm in a story about a woman who danced too hard on the Mexican Riviera. It's a story about putting bags in overhead compartments and waiting in the bitter Jersey cold, about getting to the ugliest train station in the world and weaving through its maze of underground tunnels with three suitcases to emerge into the grim bustle of a purgatory between Midtown and Koreatown.

In a way I can't explain, I've started to feel attached to this woman, weirdly protective. It's like we've been on some kind of odyssey together, and it has less to do with the night in Houston or the blizzard in Jersey and more to do with all her shapeshifting in my internal narrative. First she was a tyrant, then a saint, and finally just a tourist, dancing.

We part ways by the cabstand. The woman with the voice thanks me for my kindness. She'll take a taxi home. I'll take the subway to my empty apartment, where I'll read another article about the stabbing, full of eyewitness quotes. In another photograph of the woman with the voice, she's being carried by a police officer. She has one hand wrapped around his neck, the other hand pressed against her own throat. I will never hear what her voice sounded like when she was crying out, in broad daylight, for help; when she was just a difficult New York woman asking her city to save her.

This is how we light the stars, again and again: by showing up with our ordinary, difficult bodies, when other ordinary, difficult bodies might need us. Which is the point—the again-and-again of it. You never get to live the wisdom just once, rise to the occasion of otherness just once. You have to keep living this willingness to look at other lives with grace, even when your own feels like shit, and you would do anything to crawl inside a different one; when you would claw one Peaches out of the way, and then another, and then a third, just for a shot at some shell of respite. A 3:30 a.m. wake-up call in Houston isn't the respite shell. New Jersey public transit the day after a New Jersey Super Bowl isn't the respite shell. The blizzard is no respite shell for anyone; it makes the hurt knee throb harder.

Does graciousness mean you want to help—or that you don't, and do it anyway? The definition of grace is that it's not deserved. It does not require a good night's sleep to give it, or a flawless record to receive it. It demands no particular backstory.

You thought the story kept changing, but the most important part never did. She was always just a woman in pain, sitting right in front of you. Sometimes it hurts just to stand. Sometimes a person needs help because she needs it, not because her story is compelling or noble or strange enough to earn it, and sometimes you just do what you can. It doesn't make you any better, or any worse. It doesn't change you at all, except for the split second when you imagine that day when you will be the one who has to ask.

Sim Life

G idge Uriza lives in an elegant wooden house overlooking a glittering creek, its lush banks lined with weeping willows. Nearby meadows twinkle with fireflies. Gidge keeps buying new swimming pools because she keeps falling in love with different ones. The current specimen is a teal lozenge with a waterfall cascading from its archway of stones. Gidge spends her days lounging in a swimsuit on her poolside patio, or else tucked under a lacy comforter, wearing nothing but a bra and bathrobe, with a chocolate-glazed doughnut perched on the pile of books beside her. "Good morning girls," she writes on her blog one day. "I'm slow moving, trying to get out of bed this morning, but when I'm surrounded by my pretty pink bed it's difficult to get out and away like I should."

In another life, the one most people would call "real," Gidge Uriza is Bridgette McNeal, an Atlanta mother who works eight-hour days at a call center and is raising a fourteen-year-old son, a seven-year-old daughter, and severely autistic twins who are thirteen. Her days are full of the daily demands of raising children with special needs: giving her twins baths after they have soiled themselves (they still wear diapers, and most likely always will), baking applesauce bread with one to calm him down after a tantrum, asking the other to stop playing the *Barney* theme song slowed down until it sounds, as she puts it, "like some demonic dirge." One day, she takes all four kids to a nature center for an idyllic afternoon that gets interrupted by the reality of changing an adolescent's diaper in a musty bathroom.

But each morning, before all that—before getting the kids ready for school and putting in eight hours at the call center, before getting dinner on the table or keeping peace during the meal, before giving baths and collapsing into bed—Bridgette spends an hour and a half on the online platform Second Life, where she lives in a sleek paradise of her own devising. *Good morning girls. I'm slow moving, trying to get out of bed this morning.* She wakes up at half past five in the morning to inhabit a life in which she has the luxury of never getting out of bed at all.

What is Second Life? The short answer is that it's a virtual world that launched in 2003 and was hailed by many as the future of the internet. The longer answer is that it's a controversial landscape—possibly revolutionary, possibly moot—full of goth cities and preciously tattered beach shanties, vampire castles and tropical islands and rain-forest temples and dinosaur stomping grounds, disco-ball-glittering nightclubs and trippy giant chess games. In honor of Second Life's tenth birthday, in 2013, Linden Lab, the company that created it, released an infographic charting its progress: 36 million accounts had been created, and their users had spent 217,266 cumulative years online, inhabiting an ever-expanding territory that comprised almost seven hundred square miles composed of land units called "sims." People often call Second Life a game, but two years after its launch, Linden Lab circulated a memo to employees insisting that no one refer to it as that. It was a *platform*. This was meant to suggest something more holistic, immersive, and encompassing.

Second Life has no specific goals. Its vast landscape consists entirely of user-generated content, which means that everything you see has been built by someone else—an avatar controlled by a live human user. These avatars build and buy homes, form friendships, hook up, get married, and make money. They celebrate their "rez days," the online equivalent of a birthday: the anniversary of the day they joined. At church, they cannot take physical communion—the corporeality of that ritual is impossible—but they can bring the stories of their faith to life. At their cathedral on Epiphany Island, the Anglicans of Second Life summon rolling thunder on Good Friday, or the sudden illumination of sunrise at the moment in the Easter service when the pastor pronounces, "He is risen." As one Second Life handbook puts it: "From your point of view, SL works as if you were a god."

In truth, in the years since its zenith in the mid-2000s, Second Life has become something more like a magnet for mockery. When I told friends that I was working on a story about it, their faces almost always followed the same trajectory of reactions: a blank expression, a brief flash of recognition, then a mildly bemused look. *Is that still around?* Second Life is no longer the thing you joke about; it's the thing you haven't bothered to joke about for years.

Many observers expected monthly-user numbers to keep rising after they hit one million in 2007, but instead they peaked there—and have, in the years since, stalled at about eight hundred thousand. And an estimated 20 to 30 percent are first-time users who never return. Just a few years after declaring Second Life the future of the internet, the tech world moved on. As a 2011 piece in *Slate* proclaimed: "Looking back, the future didn't last long."

But if Second Life promised a future in which people would spend hours each day inhabiting their online identity, haven't we found ourselves inside it? Only it's come to pass on Facebook, Twitter, and Instagram instead. As I learned more about Second Life and spent more time exploring it, it started to seem less like an obsolete relic and more like a distorted mirror reflecting the world many of us actually live in. Perhaps Second Life inspires an urge to ridicule not because it's unrecognizable, but because it takes a recognizable impulse and carries it past the bounds of comfort, into a kind of uncanny valley: the promise of not just an online voice but an online body; not just checking Twitter on your phone, but forgetting to eat because you're dancing at an online club; not just a curated version of your real life, but a separate existence entirely. It crystallizes the simultaneous siren call and shame of wanting a different life.

In Hinduism, the concept of an avatar refers to the incarnation of a deity on earth. In Second Life, it's your body: an ongoing act of self-expression. From 2004 to 2007, an anthropologist named Tom Boellstorff inhabited Second Life as an embedded ethnographer, naming his avatar Tom Bukowski and building himself a home and office called Ethnographia. His immersive approach was anchored by the premise that the world of Second Life is just as "real" as any other, and that he was justified in studying Second Life "on its own terms" rather than feeling obligated to understand people's virtual identities primarily in terms of their offline lives. His book *Coming of Age in Second Life*, titled in homage to Margaret Mead's classic about adolescent girls in Samoa, documents the texture of the platform's digital culture. He finds that making "small talk about lag [streaming delays in SL] is like talking about the weather in RL," and interviews an avatar named Wendy, whose creator always makes her go to sleep before she logs out. "So the actual world is Wendy's dream, until she wakes up again in Second Life?" Boellstorff recalls asking her, and then: "I could have sworn a smile passed across Wendy's face as she said, 'Yup. Indeed.'"

One woman described her avatar to Boellstorff as a truer manifestation of her interior self. "If I take a zipper and pull her out of me, that's who I am," she told him. Female avatars tend to be thin and impossibly busty; male avatars are young and muscular; almost all avatars are vaguely cartoonish in their beauty. These avatars communicate through chat windows, or by using voice technology to actually speak. They move by walking, flying, teleporting, and clicking on "poseballs," floating orbs that animate avatars into various actions: dancing, karate, pretty much every sexual act you can imagine. Not surprisingly, many users come to Second Life for the possibilities of digital sex—sex without corporeal bodies, without real names, without the constraints of gravity, often with elaborate textual commentary.

The local currency in Second Life is the Linden Dollar, and recent exchange rates put the Linden at just less than half a cent. In the decade following its launch, Second Life users spent $3.2 billion of real money on in-world transactions. The first Second Life millionaire, a digital-real-estate tycoon who goes by Anshe Chung, graced the cover of *Businessweek* in 2006, and by 2007 the GDP of Second Life was larger than that of several small countries. In its vast digital Marketplace, you can still buy a wedding gown for 4,000 Lindens (just over $16) or a ruby-colored corset with fur wings for just under 350 Lindens (about $1.50). You can even buy an altered body: different skin, different hair, a pair of horns, genitalia of all shapes and sizes. A private island currently costs almost 150,000 Lindens (the price is fixed at $600), while the Millennium II Super Yacht costs 20,000 Lindens (just over $80) and comes with more than three hundred animations attached to its beds and trio of hot tubs, designed to allow avatars to enact a variety of bespoke sexual fantasies.

Second Life started to plateau just as Facebook started to explode. The rise of Facebook wasn't the problem of a competing brand so much as the problem of a competing model. It seemed that people wanted a curated version of real life more than they wanted another life entirely.

They wanted to become the sum of their most flattering profile pictures more than they wanted to become a wholly separate avatar. But maybe Facebook and Second Life aren't so different in their appeal. Both find traction in the allure of inhabiting a selective self, whether built from the materials of lived experience—camping-trip photos and witty observations about brunch—or from the impossibilities that lived experience precludes: an ideal body, an ideal romance, an ideal home.

Bridgette McNeal, the Atlanta mother of four, has been on Second Life for just over a decade. She named her avatar Gidge after what the bullies called her in high school. Though Bridgette is middle-aged, her avatar is a lithe twentysomething whom she describes as "perfect me—if I'd never eaten sugar or had children." During her early days on Second Life, Bridgette's husband created an avatar as well, and the two of them would go on Second Life dates together, a blond Amazon and a squat silver robot, while sitting together at their laptops in their study at home. It was often the only way they *could* go on dates, because their kids' special needs made finding babysitters difficult. When we spoke, Bridgette described her Second Life home as a refuge that grants permission. "When I step into that space, I'm afforded the luxury of being selfish," she said, invoking Virginia Woolf: "It's like a room of my own." Her virtual home is full of objects she could never keep in her real home because her kids might break or eat them—jewelry on dishes, knickknacks on tables, makeup on the counter.

In addition to the blog that documents her digital existence, with its marble pools and frilly, spearmint-green bikinis, Bridgette keeps a blog devoted to her daily "RL" existence as a parent. It's honest and hilarious and full of heartbreaking candor. Recounting the afternoon spent with her kids at the nature center, she describes looking at a bald eagle: "Some asshole shot this bald eagle with an arrow. He lost most of one wing because of it and can't fly. He's kept safe here at this retreat we visited a few days ago. Sometimes I think the husband and I feel a little bit like him. Trapped. Nothing really wrong, we've got food and shelter and what we need. But we are trapped for the rest of our lives by autism. We'll never be free."

When I asked Bridgette about the allure of Second Life, she said it can be easy to succumb to the temptation to pour yourself into its world when you should be tending to offline life. I asked whether she had ever slipped close to that, and she said she'd certainly felt the pull at times. "You're thin and beautiful. No one's asking you to change a diaper," she told me. "But you can burn out on that. You don't want to leave, but you don't want to do it anymore, either."

Second Life was invented by a man named Philip Rosedale, the son of a U.S. Navy carrier pilot and an English teacher. As a boy, he was driven by an outsized sense of ambition. He can remember standing near the woodpile in his family's backyard and thinking, "Why am I here, and how am I different from everybody else?" As a teenager in the mid-'80s, he used an early-model PC to zoom in on a graphic representation of a Mandelbrot set, an infinitely recursive fractal image that kept getting more and more detailed as he got closer and closer. At a certain point, he realized he was looking at a graphic larger than the Earth. "We could walk along the surface our whole lives and never even begin to see everything," he explained to me. That's when he realized that "the coolest thing you could do with a computer would be to build a world."

Just as Rosedale was beginning to envision Second Life, in 1999, he attended Burning Man—the festival of performance art, sculptural installations, and hallucinogenic hedonism that happens every summer in the middle of the Nevada desert. While he was there, he told me, something "inexplicable" happened to his personality. "You feel like you're high, without any drugs or anything. You just feel connected to people in a way that you don't normally." He went to a rave in an

Airstream trailer, watched trapeze artists swing across the desert, and lay in a hookah lounge piled with hundreds of Persian rugs. Burning Man didn't give Rosedale the idea for Second Life—he'd been imagining a digital world for years—but it helped him understand the energy he wanted to summon there: a place where people could make the world whatever they wanted it to be.

This was the dream, but it was a hard sell to early investors. Linden Lab was proposing a world built by amateurs and sustained by a different kind of revenue model—based not on paid subscriptions, but on commerce generated in-world. One of Second Life's designers recalled investors' skepticism: "Creativity was supposed to be a dark art that only Spielberg and Lucas could do." As part of selling Second Life as a world rather than a game, Linden Lab hired a writer to work as an "embedded journalist." This was Wagner James Au, who documented the digital careers of some of Second Life's most important early builders: an avatar named Spider Mandala (who was managing a Midwestern gas station offline) and another named Catherine Omega, who was a "punky brunette...with a utility belt" in Second Life, but offline was squatting in a condemned apartment in Vancouver. The building had no running water and was populated mainly by addicts, but Omega used a soup can to catch a wireless signal from nearby office buildings so she could run Second Life on her laptop.

Rosedale told me about the thrill of those early days, when Second Life's potential felt unbridled. No one else was doing what he and his team were doing. "We used to say that our only competition was real life." He said there was a period in 2007 when more than five hundred articles a day were written about their work. Rosedale himself loved to explore Second Life as an avatar named Philip Linden. "I was like a god," he told me. He envisioned a future in which his grandchildren would see the real world as a kind of "museum or theater," while most work and relationships happened in virtual realms like

Second Life. "In some sense," he told Au in 2007, "I think we will see the entire physical world as being kind of left behind."

Alice Krueger first started noticing the symptoms of her illness when she was twenty years old. During fieldwork for a college biology class, crouching down to watch bugs eating leaves, she felt overwhelmed by heat. One day while she was standing in the grocery store, it suddenly felt as if her entire left leg had disappeared—not just gone numb, but disappeared. Whenever she went to a doctor, she was told it was all in her head. "And it *was* all in my head," she told me, forty-seven years later. "But in a different way than how they meant."

Alice was finally diagnosed with multiple sclerosis at the age of fifty. By then she could barely walk. Her neighborhood association in Colorado prohibited her from building a ramp at the front of her house, so it was difficult for her to go anywhere. Her three children were eleven, thirteen, and fifteen. She didn't get to see her younger son's high-school graduation, or his college campus. She started suffering intense pain in her lower back and eventually had to have surgery to repair spinal vertebrae that had fused together, then ended up getting multidrug-resistant staph from her time in the hospital. Her pain persisted, and she was diagnosed with a misalignment caused by the surgery itself, during which she had been suspended "like a rotisserie chicken" above the operating table. At the age of fifty-seven, Alice found herself housebound and unemployed, often in excruciating pain, cared for largely by her daughter. "I was looking at my four walls," she told me, "and wondering if there could be more."

That's when she found Second Life. She created an avatar named Gentle Heron, and loved seeking out waterslides, excited by the sheer thrill of doing what her body could not. As she kept exploring, she started inviting people she'd met online in disability chat rooms to join her. But that also meant she felt responsible for their experiences, and eventually she founded a "cross-disability virtual community" in Second Life, now known as Virtual Ability, a group that occupies an archipelago of virtual islands and welcomes people with a wide range of disabilities—everything from Down syndrome to PTSD to manic depression. What unites its members, Alice told me, is their sense of not being fully included in the world.

While she was starting Virtual Ability, Alice also embarked on a real-life move: to the Great Smoky Mountains in Tennessee from Colorado, where she'd outlived her long-term disability benefits. ("I didn't know you could do that," I told her, and she replied, "Neither did I!") When I asked her whether she felt like a different version of herself in Second Life, she rejected the proposition strenuously. Alice doesn't particularly like the terms *real* and *virtual*. To her they imply a hierarchical distinction, suggesting that one part of her life is more "real" than the other, when her sense of self feels fully expressed in both. She doesn't want Second Life misunderstood as a trivial diversion. After our first conversation, she sent me fifteen peer-reviewed scientific articles about digital avatars and embodiment.

Alice told me about a man with Down syndrome who has become an important member of the Virtual Ability community. In real life his disability is omnipresent, but on Second Life people can talk to him without even realizing he has it. In the offline world, he lives with his parents—who were surprised to see he was capable of controlling his own avatar. After they eat dinner each night, as his parents wash the dishes, he sits expectantly by the computer, waiting to return to Second Life, where he rents a duplex on an island called Cape Heron. He has turned the entire upper level into a massive aquarium, so he can walk among the fish, and the lower level into a garden, where he keeps a pet reindeer and feeds it Cheerios. Alice says he doesn't draw a firm boundary between Second Life and "reality," and others in the community have been inspired by his approach, citing him when they talk about collapsing the border in their own minds.

When I first began working on this essay, I imagined myself falling under the spell of Second Life: a wide-eyed observer seduced by the culture she had been dispatched to analyze. But being "in-world" made me queasy from the start. I had pictured myself defending Second Life against the ways it had been dismissed as little more than a consolation prize designed for people for whom "first life" hasn't quite delivered. Instead I found myself writing, *Second Life makes me want to take a shower.*

My respect deepened intellectually by the day. I talked with a legally blind woman whose avatar had a rooftop balcony from which she could see the view (thanks to screen magnification) more clearly than she could see the world beyond her computer. I heard about a veteran with PTSD who gave biweekly Italian cooking classes in an open-air gazebo. I visited an online version of Yosemite created by a woman who had joined Second Life in the wake of several severe depressive episodes and hospitalizations. She used an avatar named Jadyn Firehawk and spent up to twelve hours a day on Second Life, devoted mostly to refining her curated digital wonderland—full of waterfalls, sequoias, and horses named after important people in John Muir's life—grateful that Second Life didn't ask her to inhabit an identity entirely contoured by her illness, unlike internet chat rooms focused on bipolar disorder that were all about being sick. "I live a well-rounded life on SL," she told me. "It feeds all my other selves."

But despite my growing appreciation, a certain visceral distaste for Second Life endured—for the emptiness of its graphics, its nightclubs and mansions and pools and castles, their refusal of all the grit and imperfection that make the world feel like the world. Whenever I tried to describe Second Life, I found it nearly impossible—or at least impossible to make it interesting—because description finds its traction in flaws and fissures. Exploring the world of Second Life was more like moving through postcards. It was a world of visual clichés. Nothing was ragged or broken or dilapidated—or if it was dilapidated, it was because that particular aesthetic had been carefully cultivated.

Of course, my aversion to Second Life—as well as my embrace of blemishes and shortcomings in the physical world—testified to my own good fortune as much as anything. When I moved through the real world, I was buffered by my (relative) youth, my (relative) health, and my (relative) freedom. Who was I to begrudge those who had found in the reaches of Second Life what they couldn't find offline?

One day when Alice and I met up as avatars in-world, she took me to a beach on one of the Virtual Ability islands and invited me to practice tai chi. All I needed to do was click on one of the poseballs levitating in the middle of a grassy circle, and it would automatically animate my avatar. But I did not feel that I was doing tai chi. I felt that I was sitting at my laptop, watching my two-dimensional avatar do tai chi.

I thought of Gidge in Atlanta, waking up early to sit beside a virtual pool. She doesn't get to smell the chlorine or the sunscreen, to feel the sun melt across her back or char her skin to peeling crisps. Yet Gidge must get something powerful from sitting beside a virtual pool—pleasure that dwells not in the physical experience itself but in its anticipation, its documentation, and its recollection. Whatever categories of "real" and "unreal" you want to map onto online and offline worlds, the pleasure she finds in going to Second Life is indisputably actual. Otherwise she wouldn't wake up at half past five in the morning to do it.

From the beginning, I was terrible at navigating Second Life. "Body part failed to download," my interface kept saying. Second

Life was supposed to give you the opportunity to perfect your body, but I couldn't even summon a complete one. For my avatar, I'd chosen a punk-looking woman with cutoff shorts, a partially shaved head, and a ferret on her shoulder.

On my first day in-world, I wandered around Orientation Island like a drunk person trying to find a bathroom. The island was full of marble columns and trim greenery, with a faint soundtrack of gurgling water, but it looked less like a Delphic temple and more like a corporate retreat center inspired by a Delphic temple. The graphics seemed incomplete and uncompelling, the motion full of glitches and lags. I tried to talk to someone named Del Agnos but got no response. I felt surprisingly ashamed by his rebuttal, transported back to the paralyzing shyness of my junior-high-school days.

On that first day in-world, I teleported to a deserted island where there was supposed to be an abandoned mansion and a secret entrance to a "bizarre circus in the sky," but all I found was a busted lifeguard station perched on stilts in the sea, where I was (once again!) ignored by a man who looked like a taciturn cross between a WWF wrestler and a Victorian butler, with a silver-studded dog collar around his neck. I ended up falling off a wooden ledge and bobbing in the gray rain-pocked waves, under a permanently programmed thunderstorm. This wasn't exactly the frustration of lived experience, in all the richness of its thwarted expectations, but something else: the imperfect summoning of its reductive simulation. It was like a stage set with the rickety scaffolding of its facade exposed.

Each time I signed off Second Life, I found myself weirdly eager to plunge back into the obligations of my ordinary life. Pick up my stepdaughter from drama class? Check! Reply to my department chair about hiring a replacement for the faculty member taking an unexpected leave? I was on it! These obligations felt real in a way that Second Life did not, and they allowed me to inhabit a particular version of myself as someone capable and necessary. It felt like returning to the air after struggling to find my breath underwater. I came up gasping, desperate, ready for entanglement and contact: *Yes! This is the real world! In all its vexed logistical glory!*

At my first Second Life concert, I arrived excited for actual music in a virtual world. Many SL concerts are genuinely "live" insofar as they involve real musicians playing real music on instruments or singing into microphones hooked up to their computers. But I was trying to do too many things at once that afternoon: reply to sixteen dangling work emails, unload the dishwasher, reload the dishwasher, make my step-daughter a peanut-butter-and-jelly sandwich before her final rehearsal for a production of *Peter Pan*. The concert was taking place on a dock overlooking an expansive bay of sparkling blue water. With my jam-sticky fingers, I clicked on a dance poseball and started a conga line—except no one joined my conga line; it just got me stuck between a potted plant and the stage, trying to conga and going nowhere. My embarrassment, more than any sense of having fun, was what made me feel implicated and engaged. In wondering what other people thought of me, I felt acutely aware—at last—of sharing a world with them.

When I interviewed Philip Rosedale, he readily admitted that Second Life has always presented intrinsic difficulties to users—that it is hard for people to get comfortable moving, communicating, and building; that there is an "irreducible level of difficulty associated with mouse and keyboard" that his team "could never make easier." Peter Gray, Linden Lab's director of global communications, told me about what he called the "white-space problem"—having so much freedom that you can't be entirely sure what you want to do—and admitted that entering Second Life can be like "getting dropped off in the middle of a foreign country."

When I spoke with long-term users, however, the stubborn in-accessibility of Second Life seemed to have become a crucial part of their assimilation narratives. They looked back on their early embarrassment with nostalgia. Gidge told me about the time someone convinced her that she needed to buy a vagina, and she'd ended up wearing it on the outside of her pants. (She called this a classic #SecondLifeProblem.) A Swedish musician named Malin Östh—one of the performers at the concert where I'd started my abortive conga line—told me about attending *her* first Second Life concert, and her story wasn't so different from mine. When she'd tried to get to the front of the crowd, she'd ended up accidentally flying onto the stage. Beforehand, she'd been sure the whole event would seem fake, but she was surprised by how mortified she felt, and this made her realize that she actually felt like she was among other people. I knew what she meant. If it feels like you are back in junior high school, then at least it feels like you are somewhere.

One woman put it like this: "Second Life doesn't open itself up to you. It doesn't hand you everything on a silver platter and tell you where to go next. It presents you with a world, and it leaves you to your own devices, tutorial be damned." But once you've figured it out, you can buy a thousand silver platters if you want to—or design the yacht of your dreams, or build a virtual Yosemite. Rosedale believed that if a user could survive that initial purgatory, her bond with the world of Second Life would be sealed for good. "If they stay more than four hours," he told me, "they stay forever."

Neal Stephenson's 1992 cyberpunk novel, *Snow Crash*, with its virtual "Metaverse," is often cited as Second Life's primary literary ancestor. But Rosedale assured me that by the time he read the novel he'd already been imagining Second Life for years. ("Just ask my wife.") The hero of *Snow Crash*, aptly named Hiro Protagonist, lives with his roommate in a storage locker, but in the Metaverse he is a sword-fighting prince and a legendary hacker. No surprise he spends so much time there: "It beats the shit out of the U-Stor-It."

In one study of reported life satisfaction among Second Life users, researchers concluded that because users reported such a large gap in satisfaction between their virtual lives and their real ones, it made sense that "some people may be strongly motivated to take refuge in digital life rather than try to change their real life." But if you inhabit a happier Second Life, does that make it harder to find satisfaction offline—if that actual life is constantly competing with a realm in which all fantasies are possible?

Hiro's double life in *Snow Crash* gets at some of the core fantasies of Second Life: that it could invert all the metrics of real-world success, or render them obsolete; that it could create a radically democratic space because no one has any idea of anyone else's position in the real world. Many residents of Second Life understand it as a utopia connecting people from all over the world—across income levels, across disparate vocations and geographies and disabilities—a place where the ill can live in healthy bodies and the immobilized can move freely. Seraphina Brennan, a transgender woman who grew up in a small coal-mining community in Pennsylvania and could not afford to begin medically transitioning until her mid-twenties, told me that Second Life had given her "the opportunity to appear as I truly felt inside," because it was the first place where she could inhabit a female body.

In his book *The Making of Second Life*, Wagner James Au tells the story of an avatar named Bel Muse, a classic "California blonde" who is played by an African American woman. She led an early team of builders working on Nexus Prime, one of the first Second Life cities, and told Au that it was the first time she hadn't encountered the prejudices she was accustomed to. In the offline world, she said, "I have to make a good impression right away—I have to come off nice and articulate, right away. In Second Life, I didn't have to. Because for once, I can pass." But this anecdote—the fact that Bel Muse found respect more readily when she passed as white in Second Life—confirms the persistence of racism more than it suggests the possibility of any liberation from it. Although many users see Second Life as offering an equal playing field, free from the strictures of class and race, its preponderance of slender white bodies, most of them outfitted with the props of the leisure class, simply reinscribes the same skewed ideals that sustain the unequal playing field in the first place.

Sara Skinner, an African American woman who has always given her avatars complexions similar to her own, told me the story of trying to build a digital black-history museum in a seaside town called Bay City. Another avatar (playing a cop) immediately built walls and eventually, ironically, a courthouse that blocked her museum from view. The cop avatar claims it was a misunderstanding, but so much racism refuses to confess itself as such—and it's certainly no misunderstanding when white men on Second Life tell Sara that she looks like a primate after she rejects their advances; when someone calls her "tampon nose" because of her wide nostrils; or when someone else tells her that her experience with bias is invalid because she is a "mixed breed." She plans to rebuild her museum somewhere else.

Au told me that though he was initially deeply excited by the premise of Second Life, particularly the possibilities of its user-generated content, he ended up disappointed by the fact that most people turned out to be primarily interested in clubbing like twentysomethings with infinite money. Rosedale told me he thought the landscape of Second Life would be hyper-fantastic, artistic, and insane—full of spaceships and bizarre topographies, Burning Man on virtual steroids—but what emerged looked more like Malibu. People were building mansions and Ferraris. "We first build what we most covet," he told me, and cited an early study by Linden Lab that found the vast majority of Second Life users lived in rural rather than urban areas. They came to Second

Life for what their physical lives lacked: the concentration, density, and connective potential of urban spaces—the sense of things *happening* all around them, and the possibility of being part of that happening.

Swedish entrepreneur Jonas Tancred joined Second Life in 2007, after his corporate headhunting company folded during the recession. Jonas was graying and middle-aged, a bit paunchy, but his avatar, Bara Jonson, was young and muscled, with spiky hair and a soulful vibe. What Jonas found most compelling about Second Life was not that it let him role-play a more attractive alter ego; it was that Second Life gave him the chance to play music, a lifelong dream he'd never followed. (He would eventually pair up with Malin Östh to form the duo Bara Jonson and Free.) Offline, Jonas might stand in front of a kitchen table covered with a checkered oilcloth, playing an acoustic guitar connected to his computer. But in Second Life, Bara would be rocking out in front of a crowd of supermodels and Mohawked bikers.

Before a performance one night, a woman showed up early and asked him, "Are you any good?" He said, "Yes, of course," and played one of his best gigs yet, just to back it up. This woman was Nickel Borrelly; she would become his (Second Life) wife and eventually, a couple of years later, the mother of his (real-life) child.

Offline, Nickel was a younger woman named Susie who lived in Missouri. After a surreal courtship full of hot-air-balloon rides, romantic moonlit dances, and tandem biking on the Great Wall of China, the pair had a Second Life wedding on Twin Hearts Island—at "12 p.m. SLT," the electronic invitations said, which meant noon Standard Linden Time. During their vows, Bara called it the most important day of his life. He did not specify which life he meant, or if the truth of his statement reached across both of them.

After he and Nickel got married, Bara's Second Life musical career started to take off. Eventually he was offered the chance to come to New York to make a record, one of the first times a Second Life musician had secured a real-life record deal. It was on that trip that Jonas finally met Susie offline. When their relationship was featured in a documentary a few years later, she described her first impression: "Man, he looks kinda old." But she said that getting to know him in person felt like "falling in love twice."

Susie and Jonas's son, Arvid, was born in 2009. By then Jonas was back in Sweden because his visa had run out. While Susie was in the delivery room, he was in his club on Second Life—at first waiting for news, and then smoking a virtual cigar. For Susie, the hardest part was the day after Arvid's birth, when the hospital was full of other fathers visiting their babies. What could Susie and Jonas do? Bring their avatars together to cook a virtual breakfast in a romantic enclave by the sea, holding steaming mugs of coffee they couldn't drink, looking at actual videos of their actual baby on a virtual television, while they reclined on a virtual couch.

Susie and Jonas are no longer romantically involved, but Jonas is still part of Arvid's life. He Skypes with them frequently and visits the States as often as he can. Jonas believes that part of the reason he and Susie have been able to maintain a strong parenting relationship in the aftermath of their separation is that they got to know each other so well online before they met. In this framing, Second Life wasn't an illusion but a conduit that allowed them to understand each other better than a real-life courtship would have. Jonas describes Second Life as a rarefied version of reality, rather than a shallow substitute for it. As a musician, he feels that Second Life hasn't changed his music but "amplified" it, enabling a more direct connection with his audience, and he loves the way fans can type their own lyrics to his songs. He remembers everyone "singing along" to a cover he performed of "Mmm Mmm Mmm Mmm" by the Crash Test Dummies, when so many people typed the lyrics that their *Mmm*s eventually filled his entire screen. For Jonas, the reality and beauty of his creations—the songs, the baby—have transcended and overpowered the vestiges of their virtual construction.

O f the more than thirty-six million Second Life accounts that had been created by 2013, only an estimated six hundred thousand people still regularly use the platform. (Approximately two hundred thousand more people try out the platform each month but don't come back.) That's a lot of users who turned away. What happened? Au sees the simultaneous rise of Facebook and the plateau in Second Life users as proof that Linden Lab misread public desires. "Second Life launched with the premise that everyone would want a second life," Au told me, "but the market proved otherwise."

When I asked Rosedale whether he stood behind the predictions he'd made during the early years of Second Life—that the locus of our lives would become virtual, and that the physical world would start to seem like a museum—he didn't recant. Just the opposite: he said that at a certain point we would come to regard the real world as an "archaic, lovable place" that was no longer crucial. "What will we do with our offices when we no longer use them?" he wondered. "Will we play racquetball in them?"

I pressed him on this. Did he really think that certain parts of the physical world—the homes we share with our families, for example, or the meals we enjoy with our friends, our bodies leaning close across tables—would someday cease to matter? Did he really believe that our corporeal selves weren't fundamental to our humanity? I was surprised by how rapidly he conceded. The sphere of family would never become obsolete, he said, or the physical home, where we choose to spend time with the people we love. "That has a more durable existence," he said. "As I think you'd agree."

* * *

Alicia Chenaux lives on an island called Bluebonnet, a quaint for-ested enclave, with her husband, Aldwyn (Al), to whom she has been married for six years, and their two daughters: Abby, who is eight, and Brianna, who is three, although she used to be five, and before that she was eight. As a family, they live their days as a parade of idyllic memories, often captured as digital snapshots on Alicia's blog: scouting for jack-o'-lantern candidates at the pumpkin patch, heading to Greece for days of swimming in a pixilated sea. It's like a digital Norman Rock-well painting, an ideal of upper-middle-class American domesticity—an utterly unremarkable fantasy, except that Abby and Brianna are both child avatars played by adults.

When Alicia discovered in her early thirties that she couldn't have biological children, she fell into a prolonged depression. But Second Life has offered her a chance to be a parent. Her virtual daughter Abby endured a serious trauma in real life at the age of eight (the specifics of which Alicia doesn't feel the need to know), so she plays that age to give herself the chance to live it better. Brianna was raised by nannies in real life—her parents weren't particularly involved in her upbringing—and she wanted to be part of a family in which she'd get more hands-on parenting. Perhaps that's why she kept wanting to get younger.

Alicia and her family are part of a larger family-role-play community on Second Life, facilitated by adoption agencies where children and potential parents post profiles and embark on "trials," during which they live together to see whether they are a good match. Sara Skinner, the would-be founder of a virtual black-history museum, told me about parenting a four-year-old son played by a man deployed in the armed ser-vices overseas. He often logged on with a patchy connection, just to hang out with Sara for a few hours while his service flickered in and out.

Sometimes adoptive parents will go through a virtual pregnancy, using "birth clinics" or accessories called "tummy talkers," package kits that supply a due date and body modifications, including the choice to make the growing fetus visible or not; as well as play-by-play announcements ("Your baby is doing flips!") and the simulation of a "realistic delivery," along with a newborn-baby accessory. For Second Life parents who go through pregnancy after adopting in-world, it's usually with the under-standing that the baby they are having is the child they have already adopted. The process is meant to give both parent and child the bond of a live birth. "Really get morning sickness," one product promises. "Get aches." Which means being informed that a body-that-is-not-your-corporeal-body is getting sick. "You have full control over your pregnancy, have it EXACTLY how you want," this product advertises, which does seem to miss something central to the experience: that it subjects you to a process largely beyond your control.

In real life, Alicia lives with her boyfriend, and when I ask whether he knows about her Second Life family, she says, "Of course." Keeping it a secret would be hard, because she hangs out with them on Second Life nearly every night of the week except Wednesday. (Wednesday is what she calls "real-life night," and she spends it watching reality television with her best friend.) When I ask Alicia whether she gets different things from her two romantic relationships, she says, "Absolutely." Her boyfriend is brilliant but he works all the time; Al listens to her ramble endlessly about her day. She and Al knew each other online for two years before they got married (she says his "patience and persistence" were a major part of his appeal), and she confesses that she was a "total control freak" about their huge Second Life wedding. In real life, the man who plays Al is a bit older than Alicia—fifty-one to her thirty-nine, with a wife and family—and she appreciates that he has a "whole lifetime of experiences" and can offer a "more conservative, more settled" perspective.

After their Second Life wedding, everyone started asking whether Alicia and Al planned to have kids. (Some things remain constant across virtual and actual worlds.) They adopted Abby in 2013 and Brianna a year later, and these days their family dynamic weaves in and out of role-play. When Brianna joined their family, she said she wanted more than "just a story," and sometimes the girls will interrupt role-play to say something about their adult lives offline: guy trouble or job stress. But it's important to Alicia that both of her daughters are "committed children," which means they don't have alternate adult avatars. While Alicia and Al share real-life photos with each other, Alicia told me, "the girls generally don't share photos of themselves, preferring to keep themselves more childlike in our minds."

For Christmas a few years ago, Al gave Alicia a "pose stand," which allows her to customize and save poses for her family: she and Al embracing on a bench, or him giving her a piggyback ride. Many of Alicia's blog posts show a photograph of her family looking happy, often accompanied by a note at the bottom. "Btw, if you want to buy the pose I used for this picture of us," one says, "I put it up on Marketplace." In another post, beneath a photograph of her and Al sitting on a bench, surrounded by snowy trees, cuddling in their cozy winter finery, Alicia admits that she took the photo after Al had gone to bed. She logged his avatar back on and posed him to get the photo just as she wanted.

To me, posing illuminates both the appeal and the limits of family role-play on Second Life. It can be endlessly sculpted into something idyllic, but it can never be sculpted into something that you have not sculpted. Though Alicia's family dynamic looks seamless—a parade of photogenic moments—a deep part of its pleasure, as Alicia described it to me, seems to involve its moments of difficulty: when she has to stop the girls from bickering about costumes or throwing tantrums about coming home from vacation. In a blog post, Alicia confesses that her favorite time each evening is the "few minutes" she gets alone with Al, but even invoking this economy of scarcity—appealing for its suggestion of obligation and sacrifice—feels like another pose lifted from real-world parenting.

Last year Alicia and Al adopted two more children, but found it problematic that the new kids wanted "so much, so fast." They wanted to call Alicia and Al "Mom" and "Dad" right away, and started saying "I love you so much" from the very beginning. They had a desire for intense, unrelenting parenting, rather than wanting to weave in and out of role-play, and they constantly did things that demanded attention—losing their shoes, jumping off the roof, and climbing trees they couldn't get down from. Basically they behaved more like actual kids than like adults pretending to be kids. The adoption lasted only five months.

There's something stubbornly beautiful about Alicia's Second Life family, all four of these people wanting to live inside the same dream. And there's something irrefutably meaningful about the ways Alicia and her children have forged their own version of the intimacies they've been denied by circumstances. But their moments of staged friction (the squabbling, the meltdowns) also illuminate the claustrophobia of their family's perfection. In their ability to court the ideals of domesticity too easily, Second Life families effectively short-circuit much of the difficulty that constitutes domestic life. Your virtual family will never fully reach beyond your wildest imagining, because it's built only of what you can imagine.

One evening during the earliest days of my Second Life exploration, I stood with my husband outside a barbecue joint in (offline) Lower Manhattan and asked him: "I mean, why isn't Second Life just as real as 'real life'?" At first, he said nothing. He just reached over and pinched my arm. (Quite hard, actually.) Then he said: "That's why it's not as real."

His point wasn't just about physicality—the ways our experiences are bound to our bodies—but about surprise and disruption. So much of lived experience is composed of what lies beyond our agency and prediction, beyond our grasp, beyond our scripts. So much dwells in surprise, in otherness, in missteps and unforeseen obstacles and the textures of imperfection: the grit and grain of a sidewalk with its cigarette butts and faint summer stench of garbage and taxi exhaust, the possibility of a rat scuttling from a pile of trash bags, the lilt and laughter of nearby strangers' voices. Second Life promises another reality but can't fully deliver the rifts and fissures that give reality its grain. In Second Life, landscapes often look like Thomas Kinkade paintings, sex exists in the imagination, parenting happens when you choose to log on. A 2011 study found that people attributed more idealized personality traits to their Second Life partners than to their offline partners—ranking them higher in extroversion, conscientiousness, agreeableness, and openness. Intimacy between two avatars isn't "unreal," but its reality is different from what happens when two people find themselves enmeshed in a relationship in the physical world—when the self has to stand behind the words she has spoken or the secrets she has disclosed, when she has to inhabit the daily constancy of her home.

In the perfected landscapes of Second Life, I kept remembering what a friend had once told me about his experience of incarceration. Having his freedom taken from him meant not only losing access to the full range of the world's possible pleasures, but also losing access to the full range of his own possible mistakes. Maybe the price of a perfected world, or a world where you can ostensibly control everything, is that much of what strikes us as "experience" comes from what we cannot forge ourselves, and what we ultimately cannot abandon. Alice and Bridgette already know this, of course. They live it every day.

In Second Life, as elsewhere online, *afk* stands for "away from keyboard," and during the course of his ethnographic research, Tom Boellstorff sometimes heard residents saying that "they wished they could 'go afk' in the actual world to escape uncomfortable situations, but knew that this was not possible; 'no one ever says "afk" in real life.'" This sentiment inspired what Boellstorff calls the "afk test": "If you can go 'afk' from something, that something is a virtual world." Perhaps the inverse of the afk test is a decent definition of what constitutes reality: something you can't go afk from—not forever, at least. Philip Rosedale predicted that the physical world would become a kind of museum, but how could it? It's too integral to our humanity ever to become obsolete, too necessary to these imperfect, aching bodies we use to lumber through it.

Did I find wonder in Second Life? Absolutely. When I sat in a wicker chair on a rooftop balcony, chatting with the legally blind woman who had built herself a house overlooking the crashing waves of Cape Serenity, I found it moving that she could see the world of Second Life better than our own. When I rode horses through a virtual Yosemite, I knew that the woman leading me through the pines had spent years on disability, isolated from the world, before she found a place where she no longer felt sidelined. That's what is ultimately liberating about Second Life—not its repudiation of the physical world, but its entwinement with that other world, their fierce exchange. Second Life recognizes the ways that we often feel more plural and less coherent than the world allows us to be.

Some people call Second Life escapist, and often its residents argue against that. But for me the question isn't whether Second Life involves escape. The more important point is that the impulse to escape our lives is universal, and hardly worth vilifying. Inhabiting any life always involves reckoning with the urge to abandon it—through day-dreaming; through storytelling; through the ecstasies of art and music, hard drugs, adultery, a smartphone screen. These forms of "leaving" aren't the opposite of authentic presence. They are simply one of its symptoms—the way love contains conflict, intimacy contains distance, and faith contains doubt.

— II —

LOOKING

Up in Jaffna

I t was early evening when I arrived in Colombo. We'd leapfrogged a day from New York, and everything felt half-dreamed. On my first flight, to Dubai, old men had peered out the bulkhead windows to check for the first lines of dawn, then dropped to the cabin floor in prayer. Dessert was apricot cake draped in cream. A teenage girl wore a bright pink T-shirt that read NEVER LOOK BACK. The *Gulf Times* was full of Middle Eastern justice—"Woman to be lashed for insulting morality police," "Arrest of atheist bloggers urged"—and chilling dispatches from my own country: "Tear gas and baton rounds can't keep the peace in Missouri."

I'd come to Sri Lanka on assignment for a travel magazine. The premise of the feature was that the magazine paid you to fly somewhere for a week but told you only twenty-four hours in advance where you were going. It was the kind of assignment that made other people jealous, but there was also something a bit shameful about it, as if it had distilled a certain colonial arrogance into a jaunty journalistic lark: *I'll just show up ignorant and narrate this place!* But had I turned down my free trip halfway around the world? I had not.

The next morning, I was planning to head north to the Jaffna Peninsula along the A9 highway, through the vast northern scrublands known as the Vanni. This was the territory controlled for many years by the Liberation Tigers of Tamil Eelam, better known as the Tamil Tigers, until they were finally defeated by Sri Lankan government forces, in 2009, near the shores of the Nanthikadal Lagoon. Thousands of civilians died during that final siege. One U.N. report put the number at forty thousand.

It's impossible to understand what it means to go north in Sri Lanka without a basic map of the fault lines that catalyzed the civil war—a Sinhalese Buddhist majority in the south; a Tamil minority concentrated in the north, with the Tigers fighting for a separate state—and some sense of that war's enduring aftermath: the damaged infrastructure and persistent ethnic tensions in a territory still thick with military presence.

In frantic preparation, I'd been reading deeper into the conflict. Every time I thought I'd found its beginning, I found another beginning that came earlier. Maybe the war started with Black July, in 1983, when anti-Tamil ethnic riots killed as many as three thousand in Colombo; or it began when the Tigers killed thirteen Sri Lankan soldiers in the ambush that prompted those riots; or it began in the 1950s when Sinhalese was designated the country's only official language. Every beginning was preceded by an earlier beginning, and the civil war itself had an ending that seemed, to many, like no ending at all. Two things became increasingly clear: there had been tremendous brutality that the government was not fully willing to own, and the country's ruptured populations did not agree on the narrative of their rupturing.

That first night in Colombo, I went to dinner with a Sri Lankan journalist. He picked me up at my hotel, the Galle Face: an old-school affair on the water, all teak angles and verandas, overlooking the restless slate-gray sea beyond. It was a room the magazine had booked for my first night, and I felt self-conscious about staying there, with its whiff of corroded English power. I told the journalist I was going north and asked him what he thought of how the government had been re-building since the war. He said the simplest way to put it was this: they hadn't done anything right. Government attempts to investigate war-time civilian disappearances had been largely token efforts. The Tamils were still carrying the burden of the struggle: military surveillance, a population of war widows. But he also told me, more than once, that it was dangerous to think of these citizens in the north exclusively or primarily as victims. They were also survivors, actively rebuilding their lives and communities.

He told me that Sri Lankans from the south were increasingly travel-ing north to visit parts of their country they'd never seen, and that the army had started running its own resorts, including a converted prison fort and a villa on the shores of the same Nanthikadal Lagoon where so many civilians had died. Later that night, I found the resort's Facebook page: "Enjoy a soothing holiday and the cool breeze of Nanthikadal Lagoon."

The journalist told me it bothered him to hear the way travelers talk about the north, especially its beaches—*pristine, unspoiled, undiscov-ered*. Those beaches aren't unspoiled, he told me. There are skeletons in the sand.

I asked how recently he'd been up there himself, and he just shook his head. Not recently, he said. He didn't have to go. He already knew. He wouldn't go just to *look*, he said. That would make him uncomfortable. He'd go only if he thought he could be useful.

About a year before I landed in Sri Lanka on assignment, I'd saved up enough adjunct-teaching money to travel to Cambodia on my own dime so I could visit a good friend living there. One of the first things I did in Phnom Penh was visit Tuol Sleng, the old Khmer Rouge prison: three concrete buildings whose box rooms still held rusting metal bed frames, old shackles, voltage boxes used to deliver electric shocks. It had been a school before it became a prison, or before it became whatever you call a place where fourteen thousand people came and seven survived. There were stains on the floors, but no plaques to tell us the names of the people whose bodies had bled there. Barbed wire gleamed from upper-level balconies. Many tuk-tuk drivers didn't like coming around at night, because they thought the place was thick with ghosts.

My guidebook had said: "No visit to Phnom Penh would be complete without a visit to Tuol Sleng." I wondered what they meant by *complete*. It seemed to suggest that you needed to pay your dues to history—to the wounds of the land—before you could earn the right to drink rum from wooden buckets on the umbrella-studded beaches of Sihanoukville, or shoot sepia-stained Instagram albums at Angkor Wat.

When I visited, everyone was snapping photos of the palm trees and the barbed wire. Everyone was sweating. It was a thick heat and the soda stand was doing good business. I was thirsty but refused to carry a Diet Coke through those halls of death. Whether I bought the soda or not, there was no escaping the inevitable affront. We were all going to look at these things, and then stop looking, and then keep on living just like we ever did. Genocide tourism turns public history into private commodity. The past is parceled into ticket stubs and photographs, into the souvenir of experience itself, so it can be taken home.

The Khmer Rouge documented their own practices obsessively, which made it easier to expose their atrocities. They'd effectively built themselves in effigy: all these photographs; the cisterns where prisoners had been dunked with their heads underwater; the gallows where they had been hanged. I told myself that it was better to have seen this place than it would have been to move over this land with no knowledge of its wounds at all; that it was better to see the slanted wooden plank studded with shackles, and the watering can beside it, to remember Christiane

Amanpour arguing with one of George W. Bush's speechwriters about whether waterboarding counted as torture. I told myself it was better to see the rows of photographs mounted on poster board on the ground floor of Building A: faces of people just after arriving, and then—thinner, gaunter, hollow eyed—just before dying, or leaving, which usually meant transport to the killing fields, which just meant dying somewhere else. After the graves became too full around Tuol Sleng, prisoners were loaded onto buses in the middle of the night and driven to a place called Choeung Ek, on the outskirts of town: the killing fields.

Choeung Ek was essentially a meadow and a generator and a toolshed full of ways to kill someone. By the time I visited, it was a meadow full of bones. This was not lyrical truth but literal fact. I watched my own shoes picking between and stepping over them. The dead were not done with us yet. There was a recognizable kind of reverence summoned by the experience of approaching the stupa, a Khmer burial monument— a glass tower full of skulls and femurs and ribs—when I removed my shoes and bowed my head, my body on one side of the glass, those bones on the other. That was a ritual whose rules I knew how to follow. But walking among bones was something else—stepping between the shards of a dead man's ribs, between scraps of old clothing and shoe rubber. It felt disrespectful to walk over the dead but also honest. We are always doing it anyway.

It wasn't particularly easy to get to Jaffna, the largest city in the north and the cultural center of the Tamil minority. Though the train lines bombed out by the Tamil Tigers had been largely rebuilt, the final leg to Jaffna wasn't open yet. I could have taken a plane from Colombo for a lot of money, or an overnight bus for much less, but I didn't want to travel by air or by night. Because I didn't want to see just Jaffna; I wanted to see the Vanni itself, the shift from south to north, the landscape of the war and what had been built since its end.

I found a driver who could take me all the way from the capital, an eight-hour journey by car. He seemed confused about why I was headed north, though he was eager to assure me I'd be safe there. "Danger before," he said. "One hundred percent okay now." He repeated this a few times over the course of the day: *One hundred percent okay, one hundred percent okay.* He was from a town on the southern coast, Ambalangoda, where he had been staying with his mother when the 2004 tsunami hit. He survived by holding on to a coconut tree. His mother died.

The early drive took us past bustling commercial towns, Kurunegala and Dambulla, and smaller, single-industry villages: a village full of pineapples, a village full of cashews, a village full of hubcaps. We passed tuk-tuks with their Che Guevara stickers—HE LOVE YOUR REBEL—weaving through the heavy traffic of all this capitalism: True Lover Shop, Hotel Cool Bar, Hotel Tit 4 Tat. Farther north on the A9, past the district capital of Vavuniya, the shops grew more scarce and ramshackle, makeshift huts strung with bags of potato chips, and the land opened up—more like plains, less like jungle. We passed shelled-out buildings, one after another, roofs blown off and walls blown ragged. Many had been people's homes. Now they were naked to the sky. My driver explained that Tigers had been hiding inside them; that's why they got bombed. *One hundred percent okay.* We seek narratives that will make it so. Violence becomes a necessity, or gets turned into a resort, a soothing holiday.

In Kilinochchi, the old Tiger capital, we stopped at an overturned water tower: ruins tall as a house, concrete cracked and crumbling, rebar jutting out, a tiny DANGER sign hanging off the side like a punch line in poor taste. We passed fields marked by faded skull-and-crossbones signs, where little concrete mounds covered unexploded mines. We hit the bleak expanse of Elephant Pass, a thin strip of land connecting the Jaffna Peninsula to the rest of the island, and stopped at an improvised tank, an armored bulldozer, enshrined in honor of Gamini Kularatne, who died thwarting a Tiger suicide mission. We watched a busload of visitors   presumably up from the south   buy orchids to place before his statue, flanked by soldiers standing as still as the bronze itself. Nearby display cases held Gamini's old uniform, his dishes, his sheets.

At a war memorial a few kilometers farther on, there was no one but me and my driver and a soldier who explained what the sculpture meant: its exploding shell with a lotus blooming from it, the two hands below shaking in peace. These meanings were offered in fragments of skewed translation, and they rang hollow. Whatever you might say about the end of the war—were there war crimes? how many? what kind? by whom?—it certainly wasn't a peaceful handshake. It wasn't anything like that.

I n Jaffna there were soldiers everywhere. There were soldiers by the gleaming white library with its sculpted domes, and soldiers by the hardware stores, and soldiers by the cricket field. There were soldiers at every intersection. The journalist had told me Jaffna had recently gotten its first stoplight, but I didn't see it. I saw only soldiers directing traffic.

I stayed in a single bed in a white room just down the road from the Nallur Temple, where barefoot worshippers walked circular paths around the premises. There were soldiers here, too, though they stood barefoot in the sand as well. I'm not sure I saw another tourist anywhere. Schoolgirls slowed on their bikes to say hello. Each time I left the hotel, I encountered the same boy in a wheelchair who wanted to shake my hand. Every time we shook, I smiled wide enough to feel the stretch and strain of my own skin. I owed him more than a smile. I owed him something I couldn't name. I kept thinking of what the journalist had said: "I would go there only if I felt I could be useful." I kept thinking of the Elizabeth Bishop poem "Questions of Travel": "Is it right to be watching strangers in a play / In this strangest of theatres?" I kept thinking of my tattoo. I'd gotten it with heartfelt intentions the year before, as an expression of kinship and curiosity, but now my own arm admonished me. Perhaps it was better to accept that not everything human was something I could know.

People like me—which is to say, people who've had the privilege to travel, and to think of traveling as a part of their identity—often like to travel where others like themselves haven't already gone, often like to think of this travel as more "authentic" and less "touristic." But in Jaffna, being away from other tourists didn't make me feel *less* like a tourist. Just the opposite. I was looked at, sussed out, wondered about, and rightly so, because what was I doing there, anyway? I felt my own lack of use.

In my room, there was a can of Pringles on the mini-fridge and three mangoes in a basket on the desk. Nathan, the de facto concierge, was eager to manage my experience. He kept calling the phone in my room: *You have had dinner? You have had lunch? You are going where today?* Nathan showed me pictures of his daughters. He said his Hindu family no longer spoke to him, because he'd converted to Christianity for his wife.

Walking through the buildings east of the old fort, I saw where the war damage was thickest: crumbling walls, empty chambers full of shrubs and climbing tendrils. Pink walls with strips of peeling paint enclosed stairs leading straight to the sky. A little boy chased a kitten into the damage. The roads by the water were a tight grid full of fishermen's shacks with blue mesh nets flung over their fences. A man squatted in the dusty road, mending one of them with twine. Baby goats were suckling outside the fuchsia doors of a tiny hospital. I tried to walk with purpose but clearly didn't have one. I ended up at the end of a cul-de-sac where a rainbow-colored house was pulsing noise from some interior boom box. I turned around, still trying to look purposeful, still failing. A round of firecrackers startled me—not because of what it was but because of what it wasn't. Men said *hello hi how are you*, asked where was I from, was I lost, what did I want, what did my arm say, pointing at my tattoo.

I skirted the barbed-wire edges of an army enclosure, long barracks with flung-open windows showing bare cots and racks of well-ironed uniforms. A man holding a machine gun watched me scrape bird shit off my shoe with a waxy green leaf. His smile said what he wasn't saying: *Where was I from, was I lost, what did I want?* In the courtyard behind him, another soldier was throwing big stones at a little dog. She held her ground. He kept throwing. The other soldier kept holding his gun. Birds kept shitting, above me and everywhere. I bent down again to keep wiping. After a few more minutes, the dog skulked away beneath the barbed wire.

I'd begun to feel increasingly frustrated by the nature of my own assignment. There's a notion that spontaneity permits authenticity, liberating us from the freight and tangle of too much context, too much research, too much intention. But this kind of spontaneity didn't seem to permit anything but ignorance. Looking at this place without knowing its history wasn't any kind of vision at all. Seeing the Jaffna library—its regal white spires, its security guard so proud to show me the second floor—would have been hollow without knowing it was rebuilt from the ruins of its predecessor, burned in 1981 by an anti-Tamil mob. It had been one of the largest libraries in Asia. Manuscripts were destroyed in that fire that existed nowhere else, that the world will never have again. The ghost of that destruction haunted the white spires I saw. What kind of authenticity comes from looking at a library and knowing nothing about the wreckage it emerged from? That's nothing but deficit. At least I knew enough to know how little I knew.

I had started reading about the war on my flight to Dubai, and kept reading as we touched down in Colombo—as I fell asleep on hotel beds, as I ate my breakfast of egg hoppers, their quivering yolks cupped by thin pancakes of fermented rice, as I described this "local specialty" in my notes before returning to descriptions of field-hospital amputations during the war. Was I blocking the place out when I read my book instead of walking through town? Or was I blocking it out when I walked through town without having read the book? The first was what I'd been trained to believe, but the second was starting to seem more like the truth.

On the overnight bus back to Colombo, I sat perfectly still while the elderly woman beside me arranged her orange sari carefully around her seated body. The bus was supposed to leave at 7:30. We got out of Jaffna around 10:00. We stopped to pick people up; we stopped to drop people off; we stopped to let someone purchase a television; we stopped so our driver could walk into a roadside Hindu shrine, place his palms together, and bow in worship. He came back clutching two fistfuls of flower petals. I wondered if he'd been praying for our journey, and I hoped so, because we kept screeching to avoid hitting things—a tractor piled high with rusty machinery, a van creaking along, turtle-slow and determined. As we finally rolled out of town, we passed one last soldier standing with his machine gun silhouetted against the clouds, and then a graveyard full of headstones catching the moonlight on their broad faces.

Around three in the morning we stopped for half an hour in the middle of the road while our conductor ran his flashlight over one side of the bus. Who knows what was getting fixed, or wasn't. We kept moving through the dark until it was finally dawn. We left the north behind: the hero and his orchids, the lagoon and its skeletons. What good had it done, in the end, that I'd seen anything at all? I was still an outsider to the damage.

True statement: Sri Lanka is paradise. Also true: every paradise is made possible by blindness.

Getting from New York to Dubai to Colombo had taken twenty hours, and getting from northern Sri Lanka to its southernmost point took seventeen: an overnight bus and then a coastal train past the Galle Fort—beside the pulsing green hills of the interior, not just green but *greens,* lime and mint and deep sage darkening into brown—and then a tuk-tuk ride to the town of Mirissa, where the bright blue sea flashed into view between wooden stands piled with glistening stacks of silvery fish.

Mirissa was where I did the things my magazine wanted in my article, exotic experiences to string like miniature anecdotes on a charm bracelet: swimming in a teal pool on a stone terrace, smelling roti sizzling on a griddle in the shadows, watching monkeys chase each other around the edges of ponds full of floating lotus blossoms. Mirissa was where I whale-watched in the rain, or whale-*sought* in the rain, while our boat hit waves as tall as houses and their spray left me storm-drenched and salt-soaked and blinking against the sting, sitting in the prow beside a woman who clenched the railing with one hand and a plastic baggie of her own vomit with the other. Mirissa was where I found the Sri Lanka you see in guidebooks, with white sand beaches and palms swaying in the rain, sweet lime water by candle-light and vanilla ice cream drizzled with treacle from the trees, passion fruits sliced open to show their bright pink flesh. Mirissa was where I ate dal so good I wanted to travel back in time and tell prior versions of myself, versions of myself that thought I'd eaten dal, that I'd never eaten dal at all. Not really.

The war was nowhere to be seen. But it was everywhere. The dead were everywhere.

What else can I tell you about the south? On the train, I sat next to a boy who was headed home to Matara. He seemed fifteen, maybe sixteen. He wanted to know about the phrase on my arm, what did it say? *Nothing human is alien to me,* I would have told him, except I couldn't, because some things are alien to me, like the Sinhalese language. He offered me his spicy peanuts and wanted to know if maybe I had a local mobile-phone number, which was amusing to me because I felt old enough to be his mother. He wanted to switch seats with me because maybe I wanted the window? He could tell I was hungry for beauty, that this was my role in the landscape—to consume it, to admire the plural greens. His smile was so big it showed his gums. I asked if he was a student somewhere.

He shook his head. "I am a soldier," he told me. "Up in Jaffna."

Then he showed me his tiny military portrait—no gums in sight. Just his green fatigues. I smiled, thumbs-up, and gave it back to him.

No, he said. He wanted me to keep it.

No Tongue Can Tell

On October 20, 1862, a year and a half into the Civil War, the *New York Times* reviewed the first public display of photography from the conflict: an exhibit of Mathew Brady's prints documenting the carnage at Antietam. "Mr. Brady has done something to bring home to us the terrible reality and earnestness of war," the *Times* reported. "If he has not brought bodies and laid them in our dooryards and along the streets, he has done something very like it." This praise implies a faith in photography's ability to offer immediate access, but it's an anxious faith, haunted by the persistent gap between actuality and representation: *something very like it.* The loss can be brought closer, but never close enough to touch. As Emerson once wrote about the death of his son: "I cannot get it nearer to me."

"No tongue can tell, no mind conceive, no pen portray the horrible sights I witnessed," a Union captain named John Taggart wrote to his brother after Antietam. His assertion of futility isn't the refusal of expression so much as its fiercest realization: insisting that it's impossible to describe war becomes the best way of describing it. The bodies can *never* arrive in the dooryards, Taggart suggests, at least not by the old means of expressive transport: text, language, tongue.

When a massive exhibition of Civil War photography opened at the Metropolitan Museum of Art a century and a half later in 2013, it was bracketed by these two sentiments: the *Times*'s assertion that Brady's photography had managed to evoke the "terrible reality and earnestness of war," and Taggart's denial that any mind could conceive of it. One voice insisted on the potential of representation, the other on its limits. By marking the beginning and the conclusion of the exhibit, they worked like conceptual bookends, making explicit the questions lurking behind portraits of rouge-cheeked soldiers and vistas of bloody battlefields: Can photographs offer what other forms of expression cannot manage? Can they offer what the mind can't fully hold? Are there certain kinds of horror that cannot ever be fully known?

America's war with itself marked a singular intersection of aesthetic experimentation and national trauma: a new art was being deployed to document an unprecedented tragedy. The Civil War changed the history of photography by giving it an unimaginable task, and photography, in turn, changed our very notion of war by giving it a previously inconceivable level of representation.

The rooms of the Met's exhibit, *Photography and the American Civil War,* held photos showing the brick skeletons of ravaged Southern factories and the outlined ribs of starving soldiers. They showed the lush grassy ravines of deep Virginia valleys, and "the scourged backs" of runaway slaves, another kind of landscape, where the whip had created its own lines and furrows. These juxtapositions suggested unspoken, unbearable stories: a group of young recruits eating dinner at camp, holding their forks high around a campfire, and then the bloated bellies of bodies on a battlefield. One could feel how quickly the boys became the corpses, how easily their bodies slid from one photograph to the next. Soldiers posing proudly with their weapons for studio portraits became the faceless amputees in clinical medical shots two rooms away. Private Robert Fryer, a teenager recently returned from battle, is shown holding his hand over his chest, with three fingers missing; it looks eerily like the way a younger boy might turn his hand into a make-believe gun, two longest fingers as barrel, to play at war.

War photography acknowledged death and protested it at once. Studio portraits of departing soldiers were meant to grant them several kinds of immortality: as talismans, they might prevent them from dying; as relics, they could preserve their memory once they were dead. Other images were plucked from the middle of the fray: photographers set up shop on battlefields still fuming with smoke or studded with rotting bodies. The forward march of technology—the desire to utilize new techniques and new effects, to make everything as real as possible, even *realer than real*—meant that some photos verged into various shades of the surreal. Soldiers wore the garish blush of hand-tinted color on their cheeks; stereoscopes created the crude 3-D effect of corpses emerging from rubble. These effects feel less like realism and more like the performances of actors trying too hard, their effortful urgency like a plea: *here, please, look at this dead man*—another body almost delivered to the dooryard, limbs pressed close to a pair of eyes pressed close to the stereoscopic viewer.

I n *Regarding the Pain of Others,* Susan Sontag articulates the shame of finding beauty in horror:

> That a gory battlescape could be beautiful—in the sublime or awe-some or tragic register of the beautiful—is a commonplace about images of war made by artists. The idea does not sit well when ap-plied to images taken by cameras: to find beauty in war photographs seems heartless. But the landscape of devastation is still a landscape. There is beauty in ruins.

There is certainly beauty in the ruins of these Civil War photographs—ruined industry and ruined woods and ruined bodies, crumbling factories against Georgia skies, fog lifting off corpse-riddled fields—but it's a dangerous beauty if it distracts us from the brute fact of all that death, and the long-standing structural brutality that gave rise to it: the institution of slavery itself.

The beauty of these photographs is more ethically productive as a kind of Trojan horse. It seduces us with awe, then lodges inside us as enduring horror. It also reminds us that the photo was once framed by someone. The ghost of the photographer looms. We are seeing everything through his eyes.

That sense of being haunted is part of what accounts for the appeal of what Sontag calls "anti-art" photography: "For the photography of atrocity, people want the weight of witnessing without the taint of artistry, which is equated with insincerity or mere contrivance." They want the weight of witnessing without the ghost of the witness, without his fingerprints obscuring their view.

That desire for witnessing without artistry was part of why people felt betrayed when they learned that certain photos from the Civil War had been staged: props placed, bodies moved, limbs arranged. Alexander Gardner's *Home of a Rebel Sharpshooter, Gettysburg*—which shows a Confederate corpse tucked into his ironic "home" between boulders—became the most famous object of this ire, after it came to light that Gardner most likely moved the corpse away from the battle-field and into the more "scenic" framing of this rocky ravine. As Sontag notes, the "odd" thing isn't that this photograph may have been staged, "it is that we are surprised to learn [it has] been staged," and not only surprised, but "disappointed." Our desire for the absolutely *un*altered photograph testifies to a collective delusion that the unmoved body would somehow offer an unmediated vision of reality.

Conspicuous forms of distortion, however, only force us to confront the truth that all photos are inevitably mediated, inevitably constructed, inevitably distancing. Once the bodies arrive in the dooryard, they aren't bodies anymore: they've been run through chemical solutions; they've been flattened, framed, and fitted.

If the taint of artistry is all over these photographs of the war, this taint is also the residue of something deeply authentic—the longing to glorify, to immortalize, to preserve. There's a way to look at the so-called taints of mediation and artistry not as traces of deception—the body wasn't *really* there, the soldier didn't *really* use that gun—but as truthful records of a ferocious desire to convey the courage and horror of war as powerfully as possible. It's the honesty of exaggeration, the truth of whatever desire—to command awe or indignation or sympathy—made us exaggerate in the first place. Perhaps the part of us that feels betrayed by prop guns and relocated bodies is continuous with, rather than betrayed by, the desire to move those bodies at all. Both rearrangement and its indignant backlash grow from a shared anxiety about the limits of representation. There is no way to photograph the soldier's body—moved or unmoved—that will communicate the whole truth of his life, and of his death.

Once you have peeled away the fantasy of photography as unconstructed truth, you can start to explore the fascinating story of its construction. "The camera is the eye of history," Mathew Brady once said, but behind the eye of the camera there was always the eye of a man (often Brady himself), and behind the man there was usually a team, and behind the team there was always some funding. Civil War photography was spurred and nourished by the marketplace: competing galleries funded photographers in the field, eager for the best shots, and profit-driven studios sold portraits to ordinary civilians. Emancipated slave Sojourner Truth sold her own portrait to raise money for other freed slaves. As she put it: "I Sell the Shadow to Support the Substance." For Truth, photography inverted the terms of ownership she had always suffered under. She "used to be sold for other people's benefit," she wrote; now she sold herself, for her own.

At the Met, guards kept saying "No photographs" inside hallways full of photographs, but people kept trying anyway, slyly lifting their cell phones, Instagramming all those captured corpses. The same hungers that made people take the photographs in the first place now made other people—strangers living a century and a half later—want to photograph them all over again: the desire to preserve and to possess, to carry forth, to hold close.

In a photograph called *Woman Holding Cased Portraits of Civil War Soldiers,* the young woman's face is stoic, unflinching. Her cheeks have been rouged so brightly—tinted in a studio, after the fact—that they no longer belong to her expression. She holds a double-sided frame displaying the faces of two men: one looks overexposed, the other shadowed. She grips the photos tightly. She wants something from those faces—and I wanted something from hers, when I stood before her portrait. I studied her expression to find out *what.* What did I want? Some feeling from her image, long faded but not yet gone. A trim curatorial label can't tell us what we're seeking from images of the dead. We want to remember things that never happened to us. We want to sense grief we never felt.

A friend who came with me to the exhibit—a photographer, incidentally—struggled to feel anything about its photographs of war. He wondered: How could you feel saddened by images that were supposed to make you feel sad? Didn't this expectation of pathos deaden their impact? How could we find ourselves overwhelmed by a feeling we know we are supposed to have? And when I spent hours in the exhibit, scrutinizing its photographs, maybe I was trying to get around that problem by thinking myself into grief. But you can't *think* the bodies through the dooryard gates. They can truly arrive only when you're surprised by their arrival.

For me, it wasn't a battlefield panorama that ended up delivering them. It wasn't a splay of corpses bloated on the grass, their pockets turned out by robbers. It wasn't even a shot of soldiers before battle: their forks stuck into crocks of beans, their crooked smiles, the sharp sting of their aliveness when I knew that many of them would soon be dead.

For me, it was a studio shot. The bodies arrived in the dooryard as three men posed in suits, with sleeves folded and pinned at the elbows: two standing, one seated, all stiff. In the photo, their faces are regal and stoic, two gazing into unknown middle distances, while the third has two black hollows—empty sockets—where his eyes should be. His face is also regal, also stoic. He is staring at nothing; he'll never stare at anything again.

When I saw this photograph, all the fascination that had been carrying me through the exhibit parted suddenly, like some great sea, to make way for feeling. It had something to do with the solemnity of its staging, how that care suggested a hunger for order amid the great chaos of war. And it had something to do with the expressionless faces of those men, how their refusal to show sadness invited me to fill the gap, make up the difference, obey the hydraulics of compensatory sympathy. It had something to do with the blind man's *mouth*, in particular, set in a rigid line whose affect I couldn't parse—determined? angry? hopeful?—because I couldn't read the expression in his eyes, because he had no eyes to read.

All these dissections of my sudden sympathy are accurate, but it would be more honest to say simply: Something *happened*. When I looked at that photo, something happened. A body arrived. It had no eyes. It belonged to William R. Mudge, Union soldier. Before the war, in Massachusetts, he worked as a photographer.

Make It Scream, Make It Burn

In the summer of 1929, after completing his freshman year at Harvard, James Agee headed west to spend a few months working as a migrant farmhand. As he wrote to Dwight Macdonald—his fellow Exeter alum, longtime friend, and eventual boss at *Fortune* magazine—he had grand visions for what the summer would hold:

> I'm going to spend the summer working in the wheat fields, starting in Oklahoma in June. The thing looks good in every way. I've never worked, and greatly prefer such a job; I like to get drunk and will; I like to sing and learn both dirty songs and hobo ones—and will; I like to be on my own—the farther from home the better—and will.

It's an amusing letter. Agee has never worked, but knows he'll enjoy it. He *has* gotten drunk, and he knows he'll enjoy that too. There's a sense of manifest destiny in his hypnotic syntax, a grammatical insistence on the fulfillment of desire: *I like to . . . and will; I like to . . . and will; I like to . . . and will.* He fantasizes about camaraderie and distraction. He wants to be delivered from his own interior life. He's done too much hard time with too many sonnet writers in Harvard Yard. He wants out. The thing looks good in every way. As it turned out, it wasn't.

"Kansas is the most utterly lousy state I've ever seen," he wrote Macdonald on "maybe August 1st." He continued: "Am now working at hauling and scooping grain on a 'combine' crew...I rammed a pitchfork into my Achilles tendon." Agee paints a vivid portrait of himself suffering under the heartland heat—hobbling along a dusty road, raising grain-dusted fingers to put scare quotes around his newly inherited life—but it's also clear he took pleasure in the hardship he described, or at least he took pleasure in describing it. He signs off: "Have to tackle a load now, Jim."

At that point in his life, Agee's manual labor didn't have much to do with his creative work back home. At Harvard in the fall, he'd been focused mainly on getting elected to the editorial board of the *Advocate,* the campus literary magazine, and composing dubious love lyrics to his long-distance girlfriend, to whom he was (painfully, it seems) trying to remain faithful: "I murdered joy, that your love might abide; / A precious skeleton lies at my side."

It was largely anxiety about this girlfriend—and their joy-murdering relationship—that had made Agee so eager to work the fields in the first place. "It will be hellishly bad work," he wrote, "so for once I won't have a chance to worry and feel like hell all summer." His letter imagines hard labor as liberation. It's absurd, of course, but Agee acknowledges his own absurdity before anyone else could possibly call him out on it. "I'm afraid it sounds a little as if I were a lousy bohemian and lover of the Earth Earthy, but I assume I'm nothing so foul, quite, as that." He is aware of how naïve he sounds as soon as he sounds that way. This preemptive self-excoriation would eventually become one of his hallmarks.

Agee's early letters bear so many traces of his later voice: a fascination with worlds far removed from his own; an anguished reeling between judging and valorizing his encounters; and an abiding obsession with the relationship between hard labor and interior life. How does feeling reside inside a body that works all day long? Does that kind of brutal monotony banish consciousness? Is it degrading to suggest that it does? To deny it?

The thing looks good in every way. Seven years later, Agee would indict the thing from every angle possible.

Researched in 1936 and eventually published in 1941, *Let Us Now Praise Famous Men*—Agee's sui generis work of sprawling lyric reportage—wrestles with the material lives of three sharecropper families in rural Alabama. The book describes their homes and the necessities of their daily labor. It catalogs their clothes and meals and physical possessions, their illnesses and their expenses. But it also forces us into the anguish of Agee's attempt to do this describing, as if his attempt were another house, a labyrinthine architecture of thwarted narratives and self-sabotaging journalism, built of convoluted syntax and tortuous abstractions, charged by feelings of attachment and—beyond and beneath all else—guilt. The book is exhaustive and exhausting. It is tormented about what it finds beautiful. Sometimes it doesn't even want to exist. "If I could do it, I'd do no writing at all here," Agee announces at the start of the book. "It would be photographs; the rest would be fragments of cloth, bits of cotton, lumps of earth, records of speech, pieces of wood and iron, phials of odors, plates of food and of excrement...A piece of the body torn out by the roots might be more to the point." He'd do no writing at all, besides the four hundred pages he ended up writing. He hadn't worked, but knew he'd like it. Now he *had* worked—at writing this book, a thankless job—and knew he didn't like what his labor had made, but offered it anyway, because what else could he do? This was what he'd done.

The project of *Praise* began when *Fortune* sent Agee to Alabama on assignment during the summer of 1936. He traveled with Walker Evans, whose accompanying photographs would become as famous as Agee's words. "Best break I ever had on *Fortune*," Agee wrote in a letter. "Feel terrific personal responsibility toward story; considerable doubts of my ability to bring it off; considerable more of *Fortune*'s ultimate willingness to use it as it seems (in theory) to me." Evans described how this sense of "terrific personal responsibility" shaped Agee's research: "Agee worked in what looked like a rush and a rage. In Alabama he was possessed with the business, jamming it all into days and the nights. He must not have slept."

Agee's doubts about his "ability to bring it off" only deepened once the business itself was done. As he wrote to Father James Harold Flye, a teacher at his Episcopal boys' school in Sewanee and one of his great lifelong mentors: "Everything there was unpredictable from day to day, I was half crazy with the heat and diet... The trip was very hard, and certainly one of the best things I've ever had happen to me. Writing what we found is a different matter. Impossible in any form and length *Fortune* can use; and I am now so stultified trying to do that, that I'm afraid I've lost the ability to make it right in my own way."

Agee was on staff at *Fortune*, outfitted with an office in the Chrysler Building back in Manhattan, where he went on all-night whiskey benders turning out copy about cockfighting and the Tennessee Valley Authority. But he was right to doubt their "ultimate willingness" to publish. The magazine killed the piece in late 1936. At that point, Agee began looking for other ways to write and publish the material. He applied for a Guggenheim grant, calling his project "An Alabama Record" and describing it as an attempt "to tell everything possible as accurately as possible [with] as total a suspicion of 'creative' and 'artistic' as of 'reportorial' attitudes and methods," and (humbly) "likely to involve the development of some more or less new forms of writing." He didn't get the grant. Eventually he got a small advance from a publishing house, so he holed up in New Jersey and began expanding his original article into the glorious sprawl that would eventually become *Praise*. The book was published to little fanfare in 1941, sold about six hundred copies, a few hundred more in remainders, and was, in Macdonald's words, "a commercial failure in every sense."

Not until its 1960 rerelease did the book catch fire, fueled by the energy of the civil rights movement and appreciated by a readership primed for the rich narrative texture of the New Journalism. Lionel Trilling would eventually call *Praise* "the most realistic and most important moral effort of our American generation," arguing not only for its cultural stature but also for the ways in which it could shift our expectations about what "realism" might mean, and the kinds of messy emotive texture that "realistic" portraits of human existence might require. In the meantime, it was generally believed that the original manuscript of Agee's magazine article had been destroyed, or lost for good—until his daughter discovered it in a collection of manuscripts that had been sitting in his Greenwich Village home for years: a thirty-thousand-word typescript titled simply "Cotton Tenants."

Reading this carefully structured original draft, alongside the un-spooling book it eventually became, offers a split-screen glimpse into the process of witnessing itself. How does the morally outraged mind begin to arrange its materials? And then—once it begins to doubt itself—how does it rearrange them all over again?

At first blush, it's tempting to understand "Cotton Tenants" and *Praise* in binary opposition: the unpublished article and the published book; one bound by capital, the other liberated by form. But there were no binaries in Agee's process, only the unfolding and self-frustrated quest to capture what he had seen, to do it justice—which he knew he would never do, and which he kept attempting anyway. *Praise* deploys more swollen syntax, more convolution, more metaphoric opacity, more soaring upsurges into song, but these differences are ultimately symptomatic of a deeper divergence in subject. The article documents the lives of others, while the book documents the process of documentation itself.

In some sense, *Praise* is nothing but an endless confession of everything Agee felt and thought and questioned as he tried to tell the story of these Alabama families. We see much of the material in the original article reproduced, but its nodes of physical particularity—descriptions of houses and objects and clothing and meals—are hopelessly enmeshed in the overpowering dilemma of a tyrannical narrative consciousness: Agee's bottomless but ever-thwarted desire for proximity. Imagine a director's cut five times as long as the film itself, with the camera constantly turning to gaze at the face of the director himself—explaining how it felt to film each scene, how he'd hurt the actors' feelings or how even the extended film you're watching now isn't nearly as good as the one he'd imagined.

While a glance at the table of contents in *Cotton Tenants* suggests a framework whose rules are already familiar—chapters titled "Shelter," "Food," "Health," and so on—the table of contents in *Praise* throws up its hands from the start, its sections odd and disordered. Three "Parts" are interspersed with unparallel sections: "(On the Porch: 1" and "(On the Porch: 2," both cupped by mysteriously unclosed parentheses—as if half-parenthetical, half-included—alongside a section called "Colon" and a section called "Intermission: Conversation in the Lobby," all of these preceded by several attempts at throat clearing: opening prologues called "Verses," "Preamble," and "All Over Alabama." This table of contents calls itself "Design of the Book," suggesting an inescapable self-awareness: this artifact is the product of much hand-wringing about how such an artifact could or should be put together, its various sections can't ever claim a full view, and its refusal to streamline them into consistency is an insistence on making the difficulty of its own construction legible.

The two texts offer starkly different visions of journalistic access: in *Tenants* it's implicit, while in *Praise* it's understood as constantly polluted. In *Tenants* we sense the physical bodies of Agee's subjects—wide-eyed and weary, sorghum-stuffed and boil-strewn—but in *Praise* we have to contend with Agee's body as well. An outraged and outrageous "I" is giving us everything we see, and giving it slanted, awed. We hear about Agee's emotional relationship to his subjects ("I am fond of Emma, and very sorry for her"), and we hear declarations of personality that often feel gratuitous. When Agee confesses, "I am the sort of person who generalizes," we think, *Yes, we know.* We recognize the Agee who went "half-crazy with the heat and diet," whose throat and gut protested the food he was served, whose skin protested the bed he was offered. When he describes spending the night with one of his families, sleeping on their porch, he lapses into the second-person "you," as if speaking to a separate self who slept there:

> Waking, feeling on your face the almost slimy softness of loose cotton lint and of fragile, much washed, torn cotton cloth, and immediately remembering your fear of the vermin it might be harboring, your first reactions were of light disgust and fear, for your face, which was swollen and damp with sleep and skimmed with lint, felt fouled, secretly and dirtily bitten and drawn of blood, insulted.

This visceral reeling is typical of the narrative voice in *Praise*. The speaker emerges as a set of nerve endings, disgusted and disgusted by his own disgust, cataloging physical particularity anyway, unafraid of banality and repetition in his descriptions ("loose cotton lint...torn cotton cloth"), feeling violated by the very place he wants to enter.

He understands himself as fouled and faraway at once. He begins the sentence with something external, the texture of linens, and ends up deep inside his own interior life, "insulted," the declaration isolated at the end of the sentence—a moment of pause, an experiential cul-de-sac.

The shape-shifting "I" of *Praise* was foreshadowed by a wobbly "you" in *Tenants* that shifts from reader to writer to subject. It often works as an imperative invitation. "It's a very unusual year when you do well with your most important crops," Agee writes, making farmers of his readers. Here, he describes a plague of pests: "They web up in the leaves and become flies; the flies lay eggs; the eggs become army worms by the million and you can hear the rustling of their eating like a brushfire." You can hear them eating—not just *can* but *must*. It's a moral command by way of pyrotechnic sorcery. The fire rages all around you.

Elsewhere, Agee uses "you" to make his readers occupy another position: his own. Observing the sharecroppers' children, he seems to shy away from the force of his reaction: "You will possibly get the feeling that they carry around in them like the slow burning of sulphur a sexual precocity." It is, of course, not *you* but Agee himself who has noticed this "sexual precocity," but Agee isn't ready to confess the sexual charge of his own attention. He isn't ready to own the "I" just yet.

When he finally does inhabit this "I" in *Praise,* he is often punishing it or pointing out its failures. Part of the claustrophobia of *Praise* is its suggestion that every strategy of representation is somehow flawed or wrong. It's a kind of paralysis. What to say if nothing will be good enough? We see an interesting prefiguration of this skepticism in *Tenants,* where Agee continually imagines problematic ways someone else could react to the same material. He keeps defining his voice by articulating what it's not. He spots a tinted photograph of Roosevelt in a frame on a mantel and imagines that a "Federal Project Publicizer" could "flash out some fine copy about the Ikon in the Peasant's Hovel"; he disputes a "stupid" but widely believed "exaggeration about child labor in the cotton fields"; he describes a "'rustically' bent" settee but puts "rustically" in ironic quotes. All of these dismissals evoke ways another witness might have witnessed wrongly: by flashing copy, exaggerating tragedy, or romanticizing poverty. Agee wants to establish that his documentary work isn't doing PR for Roosevelt or his New Deal; he wants to push back against the beautification of poverty; he wants to avoid sensationalizing the brutality of agricultural life so that its actual brutality can be better appreciated.

Here we find another important difference between article and book: In *Tenants,* Agee projects problematic reactions onto hypothetical observers; in *Praise,* he claims them as his own. He discards one sense of realism—the illusion of presenting truths unmediated and unaltered—and replaces it with another: confessing all mediation, all doctoring, all artifice and subjectivity, the inescapable contagion of the one doing the documenting—himself.

If Sontag wondered at the public hunger for "the weight of witnessing without the taint of artistry," then Agee measures the "weight of witnessing" in every way possible. He rails against the fantasy of objectivity. He maps the "taint of artistry" by exposing himself as an author disgusted and betrayed by his own representational materials. He rejects the strategies of both narrative fiction (plot, character, pacing) and standard journalism (the illusion of objectivity, or an "I" submerged to invisibility). Agee resists turning his characters into glorified archetypes by suggesting that poverty is "inevitably destructive" of consciousness as we understand it. He resists dramatic narrative by continually stressing the monotony of his subjects' lives. And amid his thousand-and-one metaphors, he suggests the inadequacy of metaphor itself.

Describing the departure of Emma—a young married woman to whom he has become attached and attracted, who is moving away with her husband—he gives us a paragraph-long sentence that recedes from comprehension just as Emma recedes from sight. We lose Emma just like Agee does. Starting midstream, we find Agee watching Emma's truck disappear into the distance:

> ...steadily crawling, a lost, earnest, and frowning ant, westward on red roads and on white in the febrile sun above no support, suspended, sustained from falling by force alone of its outward growth, like that long and lithe incongruous slender runner a vine spends swiftly out on the vast blank wall of the earth, like snake's head and slim stream feeling its way, to fix, and anchor, so far, so wide of the strong and stationed stalk: and that is Emma.

The closing beat reads like mockery: *and that is Emma*. But what is *that*? Is Emma the *slender runner*, the *snake's head*, the *slim stream*, the *strong and stationed stalk*? Is the *stationed stalk* the family she's being removed from? Does her departure hold hope or simply loss? If she is a *snake* and a *slim stream* and a *slender runner* all at once—the sibilance itself spreading like a long and lithe thing across the tongue—this heap of figurations suggests a kind of frantic clutching, layer upon layer, as if they will never be enough to bring Emma back, or to settle on the *that* of who she is, the *that* of any life.

At times, Agee invokes photography as a counterpoint to the failures of language and its inevitable distortions, suggesting that photos are "incapable of recording anything but absolute, dry truth," though this is just another straw-man mythology: all photographs are constructed by framing and selection. For the photographs he took with Agee in Alabama, Evans removed and rearranged objects in the sharecroppers' cabins, placing rocking chairs in natural light or removing clutter to coax a pleasing austerity from others' hardship, the same way Gardner moved the body of a Rebel sharpshooter to create a more aesthetically powerful tableau of tragedy. The cabins were rough drafts that Evans revised into iconic tableaux: a pair of boots standing picturesque on soil, a spare kitchen framed by angled wooden planks, a hanging white washcloth echoing bits of bright light reflected off the glass bulb of an oil lamp.

In a review of Evans's photographs called "Sermon with a Camera," the poet William Carlos Williams—who was himself, by his own declaration, "obsessed by the plight of the poor"—praised Evans's work not for its "absolute, dry truth" but for the ways it summoned universality by drawing eloquence and despair from its raw materials. "It is ourselves we see, ourselves lifted from a parochial setting...ourselves made worthy in our anonymity," Williams writes. "What the artist does applies to everything, every day, everywhere to quicken and elucidate, to fortify and enlarge the life about him and make it eloquent—to make it scream, as Evans does."

A re things 'beautiful' which are not intended as such, but which are created in convergences of chance, need, innocence, or ignorance?" Agee asks. In letters, he worries continually about his tendency to glorify poverty, troubled by his own "form of inverted snobbery...an innate and automatic respect and humility toward all who are very poor." Sometimes he confesses this snobbery ("I cannot unqualifiedly excite myself in favor of Rural Electrification, for I am too fond of lamplight") and sometimes he simply enacts it, noticing a "pure white mule, whose presence among them in this magic light is that of an enslaved unicorn." Agee's voice is full of sentiment and its backlash. He means his unicorns and doesn't. His eye for beauty turns his stomach, but he honors it anyway, insisting that "the partition wall of the Gudgers' front bedroom IS importantly, among other things, a great tragic poem."

Though it might be intuitive to assume that the lyrical excess of *Praise* became possible for Agee only once he had been unmoored from the financial anchor of *Fortune* and its straitlaced aesthetic, this isn't actually true. In fact, *Fortune* generally encouraged a certain brand of metaphoric abandon. Its owner, media magnate Henry Luce, founded the magazine on the belief that it would be easier to teach poets how to write about business than it would be to teach businessmen to write. Agee devoted plenty of real estate to melodramatic lyricism in his original unpublished article, describing flies "vibrating to death in the buttermilk" and vegetables "cooked far beyond greenness to a deep olivecolored death." Dinner isn't just *fatty*, it's *sepulchral*. Collard greens aren't just *fried*, they're *martyred*.

Only in *Praise* do we see Agee explicitly question his own lyrical excess. But if *Praise* questions the metaphoric prerogatives of poetry and resists the aesthetic techniques of narrative fiction, it openly deplores the strategies of journalism. As the Guggenheim committee already knew, Agee had a "suspicion" of creative, artistic, and reportorial methods alike. In *Praise* he critiques many isms—capitalism, consumerism, Communism, optimism—but his critique of journalism feels most pointed. It carries the sense of a spurned child rejecting his absentee parents. "The very blood and semen of journalism," Agee writes, "is a broad and successful form of lying." Elsewhere, his critique is more specifically pointed at *Fortune:*

It seems to me curious, not to say obscene and thoroughly terrifying, that it could occur to an association of human beings drawn together through need and chance and for profit into a company, an organ of journalism, to pry intimately into the lives of an undefended and appallingly damaged group of human beings, an ignorant and helpless rural family, for the purpose of parading the nakedness, disadvantage and humiliation of those lives before another group of human beings...and that these people could be capable of meditating this prospect without the slightest doubt of their qualification to do an "honest" piece of work, and with a conscience better than clear.

While *Praise* is still doing exactly what it condemns the journalistic establishment for soliciting—this "parading" of "nakedness, disadvantage and humiliation"—it certainly doesn't orchestrate this parade with a "conscience better than clear." It's in his deliberately muddied conscience that Agee distinguishes himself from the journalistic establishment. It's as if he accumulates moral debt by writing about a vulnerable population, then wants to repay it by confessing his own trespass. The strong emergence of the "I" in *Praise* is perhaps less a failure to get outside the self, or an unwillingness to grant textual real estate to otherness, than it is a deliberate formal choice to avoid the moral failures of journalism. And the drama of Agee's vexed relationship to the possibility of moral failure, more than the plight of the families themselves, is the closest thing to a plot that his book ever attempts.

The documentary "I" rarely documents without doing some damage. *How the Other Half Lives,* that classic text of social exposé, recounts a time when Jacob Riis, one of Agee's godfathers in the American poverty canon, breaks from civic sermon to make room for a brief revelation of ineptitude: "Some idea of what is meant by a sanitary 'cleaning up' in these slums may be gained from the account of a mishap I met with once, in taking a flash-light picture of a group of blind beggars in one of the tenements down here. With unpractised hands I managed to set fire to the house."

Riis published *How the Other Half Lives* in 1890, just a few years after the emergence of the portable (so-called "detective") camera. But instead of simply celebrating this new tool, Riis's narrative confesses a moment in which taking photos threatened to destroy what they were trying to capture. We imagine the bumbling witness igniting flash-lights on a frying pan and firing cartridges from a revolver, so eager to save these people that he almost kills them. "I discovered that a lot of paper and rags that hung on the wall were ablaze," Riis continues. "There were six of us, five blind men and women who knew nothing of their danger, and myself." Riis's confession carries the stink of paternalism even as it admits fault: he makes it clear that he "smother[ed] the fire" himself "with a vast deal of trouble." He is the agent of trouble, but he's also the only one who can see it—and the only one who has the power to repair it. He elucidates. He makes it scream. He makes it burn. He puts it out.

Agee never burned down any houses, but his prose betrays a constant preoccupation with the possibility of doing harm—more specifically, with the possibility that his reportage might betray his subjects, the ones whose pain he spins into lyric. He always felt the force and peril of his own intrusion. One of Evans's photographs shows the sign hanging above a fireplace mantel: *PLEASE BE quite Every body is Welcome*. And Agee did his best to stay quiet. He describes listening to the Gudger family waking at dawn:

> When at length I hear the innocence of their motions in the rear of the hall, the noise of the rude water and the dipper, I am seated on the front porch with a pencil and an open notebook, and I get up and go toward them.
>
> In some bewilderment, they yet love me, and I, how dearly, them; and trust me, despite hurt and mystery, deep beyond making of such a word as trust.
>
> It is not going to be easy to look into their eyes.

Here, Agee's guilt attaches to the "innocence" of his subjects and to the threat of his own pencil—the open notebook like a confessional between them—and his invocation of something "deep beyond making of such a word as trust" betrays his fear that trust itself can't ever apply, and neither can love. No matter how close he feels to his subjects ("how dearly"), Agee also confesses the shadow-side of this intimacy. It is not going to be easy to look into their eyes.

If he can't look into their eyes, Agee wants to do other things to them. He wants to eat their food and sleep on their beds. He wants to "embrace and kiss their feet." He wants to know them, and understand them, and explain them, to be loved by them and love them back; he even wants—at times—to make love to them. At one point, he imagines having a multiday orgy with Emma, the young bride who eventually disappears down a long dirt road:

> If only Emma could spend her last few days alive having a gigantic good time in bed, with George, a kind of man she is best used to, and with Walker and with me, whom she is curious about and attracted to, and who are at the same moment tangible and friendly and not at all to be feared, and on the other hand have for her the mystery or glamour almost of mythological creatures.

The fantasy of an orgy is so striking in its own right that it can be easy to gloss over its timing—"her last few days alive"—which seems to suggest that Agee cannot imagine a different kind of life for Emma, only a different kind of role she might play in his. Agee not only confesses his own desire but also projects this desire onto Emma, imagining what she thinks of him, betraying an amusing sliver of humility in placing "almost" before "mythological creatures."

For Agee, this orgy represents an alternative to grim procreation (he calls every conception in a sharecropper marriage a "crucifixion of cell and whiplashed sperm") and a consummate journalistic closeness: subject and object of the portrait finally joined. Agee fantasizes that this consummation could grant Emma, cloistered and degraded by circumstance, some liberty and bliss. "Almost any person, no matter how damaged and poisoned and blinded," Agee writes, "is infinitely more capable of intelligence and of joy than he can let himself be or than he usually knows." Sex represents the ultimate access. It resurrects capacity. It blooms against damage. But sexual intimacy also summons its opposite: the peril of defilement. It's no mere coincidence that Agee found deception in the "semen" of journalism. If Agee conjures the orgy as a fantasy of reciprocity and closeness, he also fears that journalism is more like onanistic spillage, an observer getting off at the expense of his subject.

When Agee finally does spend a night at the home of his subjects, it's not much of an orgy at all. "I tried to imagine intercourse in this bed," Agee writes, and (unsurprisingly), "I managed to imagine it fairly well." But this sexual fantasy quickly gives way to bodily reality: "I began to feel sharp little piercings and crawlings all along the surface of my body." This is something closer to the "insult" of violation, in which he is the one being preyed upon.

Imagination and insult are never far apart for Agee. The latter haunts the former as guilt and specter. After the impossible orgy, he knows, everyone would still be separated by the old subject/object divide, and Agee can't bring himself to imagine the "gigantic good time" without imagining what would happen once it finished: "how crazily the conditioned and inferior parts of each of our beings would rush in, and take revenge." Whatever fleeting pleasure or closeness an orgy could provide, it would inevitably be followed by the betrayal of returning context. Agee would once again be the journalist; Emma would once again be the subject. They couldn't stay in bed forever.

* * *

Jacob Riis describes how he once fought the impulse to cry out at a city-planning meeting when a builder called for designing more humane apartments. "I wanted to jump in my seat at that time and shout Amen," Riis writes. "But I remembered that I was a reporter and kept still." He wrote *The Other Half* instead. It was his way of trying to make the world a place that could deserve an *Amen*—an accusation and an exhortation, a prayer directed at the entire city.

Praise is a prayer, but it is also an admonishment. To read it, says writer William T. Vollmann, "is to be slapped in the face." Agee wasn't thinking just about himself—his own guilt, his own love, his own arms flung hopelessly around his subjects—he was thinking about you, reading his words, what you could see and what you couldn't. He wanted to throw a pile of excrement on your open notebook and let you figure it out. The dilemma of impotence—the quest to keep speaking, and the inability to ever say enough—is one of Agee's great legacies. It choked and spurred his speech.

But Agee's legacy isn't merely his sublime articulation of futility. His legacy isn't just journalistic skepticism. It is his attempt to find a language for skepticism and to rewrite journalism in this language—to insist upon a sincerity that lies on the far side of self-interrogation. In the four hundred–odd pages of *Praise* we find a lot of guilt, but we also find a lot of research. The rough draft of *Tenants* helps us remember this. It lets us witness what Agee made first, and examine it alongside the epic it became once it got digested by the organs of an endless self-loathing.

In *Tenants* we have the first failure in a long line of failures—all of them filled with rush and rage, all of them beautiful. We have the first record of eloquence before it learned to scream. *Tenants* summons a *you*, and it extends an invitation that becomes a command: You can look. You must. Look at what Agee wrote when he remembered he was a reporter, and wouldn't keep still, wouldn't keep *quite*. Look what happened when he sought an *Amen* and found these words instead. Now look closer. You can feel him getting restless. You can hear the rustling of his guilt like the beginning of a brushfire.

Maximum Exposure

O n a warm autumn day in 1993, two women met near a shanty-town in Baja California. Annie was an American photographer on vacation, staying in a friend's trailer with her girl-friend. María was hiking up a hill in the noon heat with her two young daughters, bringing lunch to her husband, Jaime, a bricklayer, who was digging clay from the hillside. She was nearly eight months pregnant. Her girls had just found a discarded sketchpad in the bushes. Annie gave them her pencils. She felt an immediate connection to María that had something to do with her warmth and her energy with her daughters, and also something to do with the jarring splendor of the land around them: their shantytown against the glim-mering Pacific, that jolt of poverty alongside beauty, neither canceling the other.

Annie had brought only a point-and-shoot camera with her on the trip, but she asked María if she could take a few photos of her anyway. María said yes. This part might not seem important: the asking, and the saying yes. But that tether of request and consent was the core of everything that unfurled between these two women over the decades that followed. *Can I take this moment of your life and make my art from it?* Annie photographed María standing with her daughters against the brown, grassy horizon, and then the whole family at the door of their two-room adobe house—parents weary, kids grinning.

Annie wasn't the first white woman who had asked to photograph María. But she was the first one who returned. Back home in Los Angeles a few weeks after they first met, stuck in gridlock traffic on her way to a gig taking school photos, Annie had a realization. It took the form of a panic attack. It wasn't just about the fact that she was going to miss the school job—one of her first paying jobs as a photographer—it was that the world seemed to be falling apart. The radio was talking about ethnic cleansing in Bosnia. Her best friend from art school had recently been killed in a hit-and-run after returning from taking photographs in Kuwait. Everything seemed fragile and heavy at once. On that congested highway, pounding the steering wheel in frustration, Annie was determined not to waste any more time. She found her mind traveling back to the family she'd met in Mexico. She promised herself—on that day, in that rush-hour traffic—that she would keep photographing them for ten years.

Ten years became fifteen, then twenty, then twenty-five, until Annie had made twenty-six trips over the course of the next quarter century.

The first time Annie returned to Baja, María came to the door of their adobe in a panic, saying her baby was sick. She had diarrhea and a fever. María was afraid she'd die. This was Carmelita, whom she'd been carrying when she and Annie met on the hill. Annie didn't understand María's panic until she learned that another one of her babies had died after being ill with diarrhea several years before.

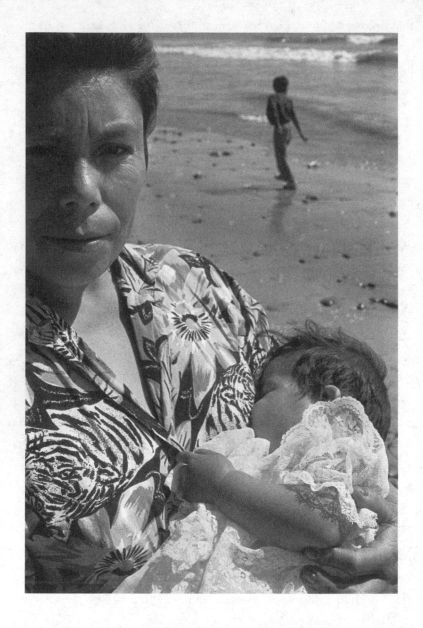

María and Carmelita on the beach, 1994

It would be like this whenever Annie returned—she was plunged right into the stream of their lives. Proof sheets from her early visits show all the detritus and glory of everyday existence: a wheelbarrow full of dirty dishes, a box spring propped up as a fence, two girls sitting atop a tower of bricks as tall as a two-story house, a boy waiting behind a market table full of screwdrivers. Her photos excavate the vexed feelings simmering beneath ordinary moments: a mother laughing, inadvertently showing a glimpse of the rotten teeth she is ashamed of; a father lighting his cigarette against the wind off the ocean, laying bricks at four o'clock in the morning; the same father bathing himself with a mug and a plastic bucket, looking sheepish, or nuzzling his infant daughter's neck, punch-drunk with love.

During one early visit, Annie watched the kids do their homework by candlelight after the neighbor had cut off their illegal electricity, then bartered prints of her own photos to coax that neighbor to restore the wiring. During another trip, Jaime was helping Annie jump-start her Oldsmobile—the one they all called the red donkey, *burro rojo*—when the cops arrived, frisked Jaime, and put him in their van. When Annie protested, saying he'd only been helping her, they said they knew exactly who he was. Taking photos was the only way Annie knew how to protest his arrest, but her photos didn't keep the police from hauling him away.

"Don't take pictures of us, little bird," they told her over their car speakers, as they drove past the edge of her frame. But she took them anyway, for twenty-five years.

You could call Annie committed, or you could call her obsessed. Obsessed with seeing María and her family evolve across the decades, and obsessed with the elusive horizon of a complete gaze. She kept visiting as the toddlers became children, then teenagers, and then parents with toddlers of their own. She kept visiting as Jaime started drinking more and hitting María; after a fire ravaged their two-room adobe and Jaime switched from booze to heroin; after María left him and moved to the city where her mother lived; after she found a new partner and a new home, a new job in a factory making sandals.

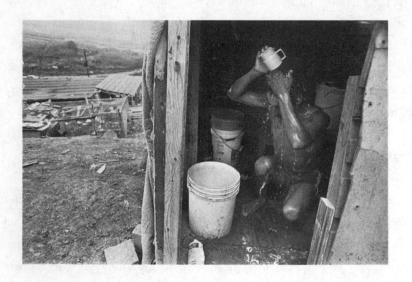

Jaime, washing, 1995

Twenty-five years was long enough for humanity and too long for sainthood. It was long enough for children to slough off the snakeskins of their innocence—to get booze habits, get into fights, get pregnant, get across the border. Over and over again, Annie was forced to see her subjects in more complicated terms. The day that Jaime was arrested, for instance, Annie raced up the hill to tell María he'd been taken away, and María told her that she had been the one who called the cops. Jaime had struck her across the face with his belt buckle during an argument about Carmelita's baptism.

Annie's documentary work is a process of intimate entanglement. When she says, "I photograph from where my heart lives," her phrasing is built upon decades of road trips and plane flights and time off her day jobs; decades of fleabites and bellyaches and fevers and sleeping on floors and learning slingshot strategy from four-foot experts; decades of counseling a woman through two abusive relationships; decades of finding the right moment, the right dusk light, the right gaze from mother to child; or not finding the right moment and showing up again anyway. "Now that I think about it," she told me once, "this work has survived and thrived almost twice as long as my longest love affair."

Annie Appel isn't famous, but her work is part of a powerful documentary tradition. It's a lineage that extends from W. Eugene Smith's seminal 1951 photo-essay in *Life*, about a black South Carolina midwife ministering to rural patients, to Mary Ellen Mark's photographs of homeless teenagers in 1980s Seattle. It stretches back to the "folk studies" of North Carolinian Bayard Wootten, a single mother who borrowed a camera in 1904 to take photos to support her two sons, and reaches forward to the contemporary portraits that Galician photographer Lua Ribeira has taken of spice addicts on the streets of Bristol. "I have become close to some of them," Ribeira said of her subjects, "but...that clash, it is painful and complicated." These are all photographers who take ordinary people as their subjects and insist on the importance of "ordinary" lives, who are not interested in telling fairy tales about their photographs as redemptive or their gazes as objective, who forge intense emotional relationships with their subjects and create images shaped by that intensity. Ribeira once remarked of her homeless subjects, "In this structure we exist in, they have to be *there* for us to be *here*," and her photographs momentarily collapse that distance—not to pretend that it has been bridged, but to insist on looking across it.

In many ways, Annie claims the identity of an outsider artist with pride. Her work has been exhibited mainly at small galleries around

San Pedro, the Los Angeles port town where she lives in an apartment tucked behind the storefront dance studio in which her wife teaches tango lessons. For a decade, Annie has had a day job as the supervisor of a photo lab in order to support her projects: traveling across the country to make portraits of Occupy protesters; photographing a cloistered nun in a Hollywood monastery; setting up a portable studio on the grass of Pershing Square in downtown Los Angeles—inviting anyone to sit for portraits, including the homeless, persuading the police to let her stay when they arrived to send her away—then coming back twenty-three years later to repeat the project. But for nearly three decades, the cornerstone of her creative life has been the Mexico project. Every time Annie calls her mother to say she's heading back to Mexico, her mother asks, always gently, some version of the same question: "Again? Don't you have enough pictures of that family yet?" Always following up with a mother's concern: "Is anyone paying you?"

The fact that Annie hasn't gotten substantial institutional support for her work only brings her own investment into sharper focus. She has not only devoted herself to her Mexico project for a quarter century in the absence of serious official recognition, she has also devoted herself to funding it—and to fighting for her work, over and over again.

When the Smithsonian acquired a series of her Occupy portraits for its permanent collection in 2015, it was a powerful lifeline of affirmation. Annie flew the photographs to Washington, D.C., herself, committing to memory how it felt to carry her portfolio into the museum, and the giddy, floating sensation of carrying an empty portfolio out the door. It meant so much to her that the world had finally said: *Your work matters.*

Her work does matter. It matters because her photographs are full of human life in its mess and complexity, because they illuminate intimacy as a compost heap smoldering with layers of fear and distance and longing. Her work matters because it evokes the ways that daily life simultaneously holds tedium and astonishment, drudgery alongside sudden surges of wonder.

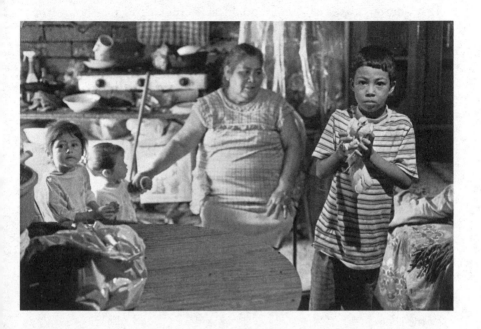

Doña Lupe caring for grandchildren, 2003

In a 2003 photo of Doña Lupe, María's mother, sitting with three of her grandchildren, so much is visible at once: the strain of caring for these children, and the love that fuels her care. Lupe sits on a stool, holding her youngest granddaughter's wrist, with a pile of dishes on the counter behind her. The features of the children's faces are lit by sunlight, exposed in their ordinary holiness. Lupe's grandson Joelle looks gangly and hopeful in a striped shirt and baggy jeans, holding a pigeon in both hands, its feathers peeking out between his fingers. It's as if he's offering this bird to the person behind the camera as a gift, something precious squirming in his hands that might fly away at any moment. His expression is full of fragile hope and tentative uncertainty. He is poised just at the far edge of youth, not yet ashamed to find the world wondrous.

But what makes the photo truly extraordinary is precisely what feels *un*-wondrous about it. A more predictable cropping of the shot might have been framed more fully around Joelle and the bird—making the image more lyric, more iconic, and more symbolic, the young boy with this symbol of hope and flight—but Annie's composition does something else. She frames the photo so that it includes not just Joelle and the bird but also his grandmother and two of his young cousins, alongside the mess of the kitchen behind them: a bag of trash blurry in the foreground, a broomstick drawing our eyes toward a corner of the frame; all of these visual elements making it hard for the eye to know where to land. It's akin to what we might have seen if Walker Evans had not rearranged the homes of his sharecropper subjects to evoke from their poverty an uncluttered restraint, all clean lines and simplicity. Annie refuses to do that. She insists on letting the clutter of daily life into her frame alongside the soulful surges. She insists that each is part of the other.

Many of her images are compositionally off-kilter, as the photographer Ryan Spencer pointed out to me, in a way that makes them more visually surprising, caught in a purgatory between being centered and uncentered. It's a visual manifestation of Annie's interest in capturing in-between moments, not necessarily moments of high drama but moments of ordinary humanity. This jarring quality summons the French aesthetic of *jolie laide:* the idea that something is beautiful because of its imperfections, not in spite of them. In one photo of María's daughter Angelica and her four kids, the composition vibrates with humanity not despite the fact that Angelica's youngest baby is crying, but *because* he is crying. The frame is electrified by that disruption.

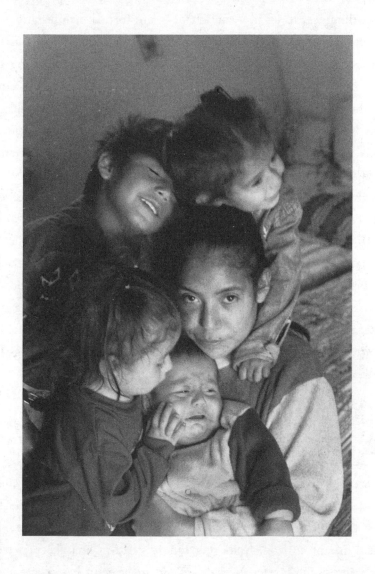

Angelica and her four children, 2007

These elements of Annie's work—her irregular compositions and her willingness to let in visual chaos—are formal manifestations of her commitment to portraying life in all its complexity, just as the duration of her project manifests her commitment to allowing the human complexity of her subjects to unfold across decades. Once you become obsessed with documenting, it can seem impossible to stop. No ending feels honest or defensible. What does it mean to make art from other people's lives? What distinguishes exploitation from witnessing, and when is that witnessing complete? Is it ever? It's the problem of Borges's imagined map: In order to show every detail of the world, a map would have to be as large as the world itself. It would have no edges. It would never be done. Which is to say: A family keeps living; you keep witnessing. A woman keeps getting older. Her kids keep getting older. Her kids have kids of their own. You keep witnessing. The woman you're witnessing gets upset with you. You keep witnessing. Her life seems like it's falling apart. Your life feels like it's falling apart. You keep witnessing. It's endless. That's the problem, and the point.

Annie grew up in El Paso during the 1960s and '70s, directly across the border from Ciudad Juárez. "Born and raised in twin cities divided by a river," as she describes it. From her childhood home on Thunderbird Drive—way up the mountain on the west side of town, in one of the wealthiest parts of the city—Mexico was a distant horizon. Nana, her family's live-in housekeeper, went back across the border every weekend to be with her own family. Whenever Nana got detained on her way back to El Paso, she'd be gone for days. If she was outside when the green immigration car cruised down Thunderbird Drive on a weekday, she would duck into the house.

The border was always there, and Annie was always aware of being on one side of it—her life built on the guilt of privilege, the abiding shame she calls "my age-old apology for being born into a well-to-do household in El Paso." Whenever Annie's relatives visited from the East Coast, they all went across the border to buy embroidered dresses and cheap liquor. Annie and her brother crossed the border to buy a bag of what turned out to be loco weed—the stuff gringos got tricked into paying for. Annie didn't know that girls were disappearing from Juárez when she rode across the border as a fourteen-year-old tomboy, with a group of older friends, to get drunk on tequila in bars where all you had to do to get a drink was be tall enough to reach the counter. One of Annie's teachers explained that El Paso had the highest traffic-fatality rates in the nation because of immigrants running across the highway. During driver's-ed lessons, Annie was told to watch for them. As soon as she turned sixteen, she started driving housekeepers in her neighborhood to the bus stop on Fridays for their weekend trips across the border.

As a child, Annie would squint at Juárez across the river whenever her family drove down the interstate, hoping to see an actual person amid its cardboard-roofed shacks. But it was too far away. The scale wasn't right. "At night, without electricity, the darkness on their side of the river was complete," she remembers. "It was as if I were staring into the empty horizon over open seas." But the horizon wasn't empty. Annie knew that as a kid, and she has spent twenty-six trips and twenty-three thousand frames rejecting that delusion. She's been forcing exposures instead.

For the entirety of her Mexico project, Annie has carried the same three cameras: all Nikon, all fully manual; one loaded with color film, two with black-and-white. She never uses zoom or telephoto lenses. For a close-up, she has to get close. She never uses a flash, only ambient light. She never crops her images in the studio, which means forcing herself to trust the way her eye composes the photo in the moment of its capture.

Annie's rules function like formal constraints in a poem, supplying generative boundaries that animate her creative impulse. But they also evoke the procedures of ritual. For Spencer, photographers are "the art-world equivalent of pitchers on the mound," because all their super-stitions about process remind him of baseball players wearing unwashed hats or kissing their gold crosses, chewing a particular brand of tobacco or drawing lucky figures in the dirt with their toes.

Annie's formal constraints create the texture of immediacy in her compositions, but they wouldn't be possible without the emotional commitments embedded in her process: her deep immersion in the lives of her subjects, the long-term arc of building these relationships. Annie only learned the phrase *participant observer* after she'd already been one for years. She can't plan her photos; she just has to be there when the right moment shows up—which means being there for all the other moments, too. Every great shot isn't just about its particular light or angle or composition, it is also about all the years that came before, the ones that delivered Annie and her subjects to that instant in time.

What do her photos show? A boy holding a pigeon. A girl holding her grandmother's hand. A group of kids playing tag with bloody hands, after sticking their fingers in a still-wet bull skull perched on a wheelbarrow, its dead tongue lolling. Her photos show Carmelita as an infant, as a sullen schoolgirl, then as a teenager at her first job—putting up a market stall, its orange tarp filtering the sunlight like the veined skin of an internal organ. Annie's photos don't remove her subjects from their circumstances, but they don't reduce them to their circum-stances, either. She doesn't conscript them into serving easy moralizing arguments about inequality or guilt. She lets their faces occupy her frames in many different ways: sometimes so large that their particular features blur their background entirely, sometimes vague in the dim light, sometimes pushed partially out of view.

In one photo of María's son Carlos, taken on a bus in Mexico, Carlos is looking straight at the camera—his gaze disarming and penetrating, his face in crisp focus while those of his fellow passengers are blurred. This composition captures the essence of Annie's whole project because it highlights the way she observes her subjects in situations of anonymity, like an ordinary bus ride, in order to dramatize the illumination of their particular humanity—in this case, Carlos's gaze brought into startling clarity.

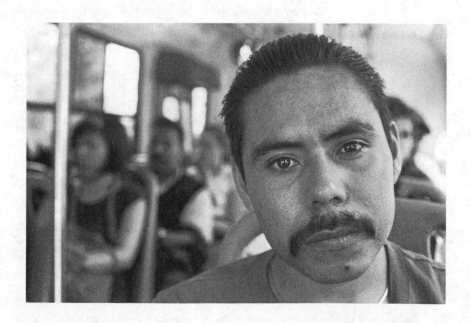

Carlos on the bus, 2007

*　　*　　*

One early photograph from 1995 shows Annie sitting with María and Jaime at their kitchen table. Jaime is eating, his hand hovering over the beans. There's a stack of tortillas in the foreground, a bottle of Coke mostly drunk, a portrait of Jesus regarding everyone. On the wall behind Jaime, eight holes are visible from nights he punched through the plaster during drunken rages. Annie looks exhausted, a bit bleary, but not nervous or uncomfortable. She isn't putting on a performance of affection or closeness. Two of her cameras rest beside her on the table.

What strikes me most about the kitchen-table photo is the fact that these three people aren't looking at each other. They are looking past one another, in a way that suggests both familiarity and slippage. Annie's photos are interested in making room for these unvarnished moments, for the ways people see past each other—how they can't quite make eye contact because they are too tired to connect, too wary to trust fully, too depleted to reveal themselves. Her photos refuse reductive tales of connection that elide these sly, persistent, constitutive gaps between people. Instead, they claim the world of what *is*—in which these ruptures are as much a part of intimacy as an embrace.

This kitchen-table shot is also, of course, a photograph of the photographer—her cameras resting on the table. Another photo shows Annie's shadow falling across a stack of bricks, and this image feels like a confession: I was *there*. She was part of it. Her photographs insist upon the mess of subjectivity, the tangle of caring and caring *for*, of getting angry and coming back. In a 2000 photograph taken at Doña Lupe's house, Annie crouches in front of Carlos with a camera held up to her face as he laughs and the rest of the family watches. She is at the center of the frame, but of all the people in the photo, hers is the only face you cannot see—as if she is confessing her desire to erase herself, as well as her understanding that this cannot ever fully happen.

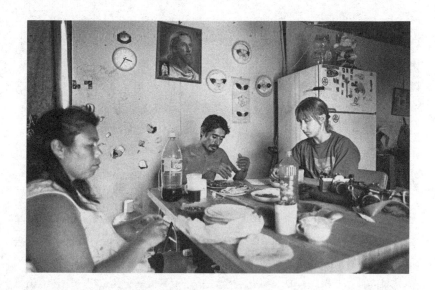

Self-portrait with María and Jaime, 1995

Annie has transcribed her Mexico journeys in a series of diaries that now total more than a thousand pages. They describe long naps on the couch with the youngest baby, Viviana, sleeping on her chest, feeling her tiny heart beat twice as fast as her own; or sweltering afternoons spent at the river with Carlos, watching him catch a two-inch fish in an empty can of Orange Fanta, letting him sling green algae at her forehead and then getting him back by smearing it between his shoulder blades. These diary entries are a reminder that the documentarian was also, always, a woman drying her socks on the windowsill and getting eaten alive by the "night shift" of mosquitoes, a woman who got irritated and tired, who drank cold beers alone when she was exhausted by the relentless communion she craved, who was heartbroken by a lover's betrayal back in California or by her father's death in

Texas—who brought those griefs with her. They soften the diary pages like humidity.

Annie always knew how absurd it was to arrive in Baja or San Martín or Tijuana and complain about her "grumpy boss" alongside everything María and her kids were facing. Her journals confess how the lens sometimes felt like a necessary buffer between their lives and her own guilt: "No electricity, for some reason, at Lupe's tonight, so I was officially excused from picture-taking, and couldn't stomach hanging out in her house without the distraction of work to keep me from thinking too much about how impossible the way they live is." It wasn't always romantic to watch the kids do homework by candlelight.

Getting involved never felt sufficient, but it started to seem necessary. After María's youngest brother, Guillermo, came across the border with his family, Annie kept taking photographs of their new life in the States. And when Guillermo faced deportation, Annie wrote a letter on his behalf and helped his wife, Gloria, look for a house to rent in a different town. After taking photographs of Gloria at work—picking grapes in a vineyard, her scarf-wrapped face almost hidden among the vines—Annie purposefully tracked muddy footprints across the floor of the vineyard's upscale tasting room. She wanted to bring dirt into a room that had forgotten the hands picking the grapes outside, or had never cared at all—had never cared about the woman who'd crossed a desert pregnant, who supported an infant daughter with a chronic lung disease while living with the daily terror that her husband might get deported. Annie understood her own muddy footprints as an act of insistence, the ways her photographs were an act of insistence: that this woman existed, that her life mattered.

It can be easy to believe that a documentary project requires absence in order to do its work most effectively: that the writer or photographer or filmmaker should step out of the frame in order to leave room for her subjects. Early in her Mexico project, Annie fantasized about this kind of invisibility: "relinquishing self 100% so as to become a blank canvas of sorts, on which I can record the true colors of the situation at hand." But for me, Annie's work succeeds because it fails at making her absent. She's at the kitchen table. Her shadow falls across the bricks. Her photos are saturated by the full range of her feelings: admiration of Jaime's curiosity, rage at his drunken violence. Her presence isn't cumbersome baggage, but part of the work itself. "Self" and "other" are not forces caught in a zero-sum game. Annie's failure to remove herself entirely doesn't obstruct what she documents, it widens the scope of what she's documenting: not just her subjects but the emotional complexity of photographing them. She confesses her own residue. She owns the taint of artistry.

Self-portrait with the family at Doña Lupe's house, 2000

*　　*　　*

The language of photography conjures aggression and theft: You *shoot* a picture. You *take* a photograph. You *capture* an image or a moment. It is as if life—or the world, or other people, or time itself—has to be forcibly plundered, or stolen.

If you take a photograph, what do you give in return? In the early years, Annie knew that a single paycheck from her day job could pay for a year of textbooks for María's kids, or even a few months' rent. She gave what she could: cash, art supplies, backpacks, new shoes, bananas, beans. Her budgets list the pesos she spent on each trip: for a waterpark trip with María's sons, for jicama and toothpaste, for mangoes and tortillas, for a birdcage for Doña Lupe, for tickets to the hypnotist and popcorn at the show. Each time she returned, she brought back prints for everyone in the family, giving them back to themselves.

When María needed to get one of her rotten front teeth pulled—it made her too self-conscious to smile—she asked Annie for the money to get it done. Annie said she would give her the money to fix her teeth if María would start smiling for her photographs. It was a joke, and also something more complicated than a joke—an acknowledgment of the ongoing transaction that framed their deepening intimacy.

When Annie finally gave María the money, María didn't use it for her teeth. Five years later, María asked again, and got the money again, and didn't use it for her teeth again. Annie felt betrayed both times, and judged herself—both times—for feeling that way.

What did María use the money for? Clothes for the kids. Tortillas. Propane.

After Jaime switched from tequila to heroin, and his abuse grew intolerable, María asked Annie for the money to leave him. Years later, Annie recalled their talk this way:

María called to ask me for help after she'd finally decided to flee Jaime's violence against her and the children. One hundred dollars for six bus tickets and a thirty-six-hour bus ride home. Was it right? And if I'd denied her request for help? A different life for them all. I've wondered if I did the right thing for ten years now. Looking at photos from that time, I identified a bottle in Jaime's hand for a majority of the images. I'd forgotten that part, like the feeling of fear when he beat her in front of me that time.

Once Annie had gotten close enough to María and her family, *not* doing anything started to feel like doing something, too. When María's elder daughters accused her second partner, Andres, of beating them when they refused his sexual advances, Annie thought about giving María a month's rent so she could get a place of her own. "Discovered that a house the size of María's current place runs $30 U.S. a month," Annie wrote in her journal. "Thought I could pay her rent in advance if she wants to leave this abusive man...What should I do? What shouldn't I do?" She didn't end up offering rent for a new place, but she did tell Andres she was aware of his abuse, and willing to defend María: "I stood a foot away from him, and face to face I whispered, 'Should I hit you with my new belt? Which end should I use—the metal buckle, or the smooth side? Show me how to do it properly, Andres.'"

In one journal entry, Annie instructs herself, "Always say yes," but her diaries also confess the times she didn't: the time she didn't pay for Doña Lupe's propane tank, the time she didn't give María her favorite green sweater, the times she needed to be alone for the day. She never gave anyone in the family her address because she knew if they ever crossed the border and showed up at her home, she wouldn't be able to turn them away.

When photographer Mary Ellen Mark and her husband, Martin Bell, were making their 1983 documentary *Streetwise*, centered on a thirteen-year-old Seattle prostitute named Tiny, they were constantly torn about how much help to offer. It can feel inhuman to document pain without trying to ameliorate it. But a documentary project can become unsustainable when it claims the additional responsibility of aid. And it's also true that for some subjects no amount of aid will ever feel like enough. Mark and Bell never gave the kids they were filming money, but they did give them food, jackets, and shoes. When they went back to New York after they were done shooting, they offered to take Tiny with them—"to adopt her, essentially," as Bell put it. The only condition was that she go to school, which she didn't want to do, so she didn't go with them. They stayed in touch with her for decades, and nineteen years later, she told them: "I think about it all the time. The fact that I didn't come."

In 1993, while South African photojournalist Kevin Carter was taking photographs of the rebels in Sudan, he captured an image that would become famous: a skeletal toddler crawling on the dirt toward a feeding station while a vulture perched behind him. Carter crouched down carefully—not wanting to disturb the bird, so he could get the best possible shot—then waited twenty minutes for the bird to fly off; when it didn't, he shooed it away and let the boy continue on his journey. Carter didn't bring the boy food. He didn't take him to the feeding station. He simply sat under a tree, and smoked, and wept. "He was depressed afterward," one friend reported. "He kept saying he wanted to hug his daughter." Fourteen months later, the photograph won him a Pulitzer Prize. "I swear I got the most applause of anybody," he wrote to his parents after the ceremony, but two months later he killed himself at the age of thirty-three. In the note he left behind, he said: "The pain of life overrides the joy to the point that joy does not exist."

In her diaries, Annie interrogates all the mythic versions of herself that she has wanted to believe in. "What truths shall I tell?" she wonders. "Paint myself as savior?" For decades, she has struggled against her desire to become one. In one entry she describes herself as a "naked, vulnerable, egotistical, self-absorbed artist masquerading as a well-intentioned 'do-gooder,' such an effective mask I'd even convinced myself." After years, she finally told herself, "Not my job to play karma cop."

I first discovered Annie's work five years ago, when she wrote me an email saying she felt a kinship between her photographs and my writing—in particular, an essay I'd written about James Agee and his expansive, relentless, guilt-ridden book about sharecropper families in Alabama. When Annie described the duration of her own documentary project, I felt humbled. At that point, it already comprised more than twenty visits. It made me ashamed of the ways I'd written about the lives of others after knowing them for a year, or even a month. How meager that seemed in the face of Annie's ongoing gaze. The ethical divide between showing up and coming back loomed large; it made me feel accused. This was respect, I thought: to look and *keep* looking, not to look away as soon as you'd gotten what you needed. Respect meant letting your subjects get older, letting them get more complicated, letting them subvert the narratives you'd written for them. It meant having enough stamina and humility to say: *I'm not done. I haven't seen enough.* In one diary entry, nine years into her project, Annie wrote: "I understand nothing."

From the beginning, Annie's Mexico project struck me as a spiritual descendant of *Let Us Now Praise Famous Men,* not only because both projects involved privileged white artists documenting impoverished families, but because both projects were fueled by a persistent sense of their own incompleteness. When it came to on-goingness, Annie had Agee beat. While he'd reported for months, she'd been coming back for decades. But both of them were hounded by the suspicion that no matter how much they said or showed, it would never be enough to conjure their subjects fully. The part of Annie that confessed she understood nothing could have been speaking directly to the part of Agee that worried his efforts would be failures, or at least wanted that confession contained within his project; the part of him that worried his words were not enough, that wanted to offer broken plates and excrement instead of sentences and paragraphs.

As I kept corresponding with Annie, I frequently felt flooded by her desire for connection and communion. For every note I sent to her, I got three back; for every reply, three more. (After I mentioned that to her, I got an email from her with the subject line *My third reply.*) It didn't feel foreign to me, her hunger, but deeply intuitive: it spoke to the part of me that had stayed on the phone with my high-school girlfriends for hours each night, even though we'd already spent the entire day together; that thrill of feeling no borders between us, the futile attempt to reach a saturation state of closeness in which there was nothing we hadn't shared.

The first time Annie and I met in person, it was for coffee in a hotel lobby, and I arrived to find she had brought two huge suitcases and started unloading their contents across several coffee tables. It was an array of her own prints alongside a spread of books that had inspired her. She'd set up a light stand so she could take my portrait. It was excessive. It was taking up room. I loved it. She was an agile, quick-moving woman with sandy blond hair cropped short around her ears. She radiated momentum and appetite.

In one of her letters to me, Annie said she missed in herself "a sense of inner boundaries that I have longed to understand since childhood." Over the years, I've started to suspect that whatever force prevents these boundaries from finding purchase inside her—her unquenched curiosity, her porousness, her hunger for fuller exchange—is also precisely what carries her back to Mexico over and over again. She once told me about her fascination with the construction crew that perpetually painted and repainted the Long Beach bridge. She could see them from her studio window. They would spend a year repainting one side, then a year repainting the other, in a never-ending loop. "All these years later I can see my early obsession with the idea of 'process' taking shape," she told me, remembering her fascination with those painters and their endless job. "Little did I know at the time this would one day describe me too."

When I finally wrote about Annie's work, in a brief essay to accompany a magazine portfolio of her Mexico photos, the piece upset her. I wondered if the critical distance of writing about her rather than *to* her felt like a boundary erected between us. She said the writing had made her feel betrayed and exposed, and she articulated that reaction as a kind of abandonment, as if I'd left her by removing too much of my own subjectivity. "Where are you in this, Leslie?" she wrote. "It does not even sound like your voice." Apologizing a few months later, she said: "It was my own inability to handle the intensity of your gaze, and the naked truth."

I have spent much of my life as a writer chasing poet C. D. Wright's suggestion that we try to see people "as they elect to be seen, in their larger selves." But it's an impossible dream. Making art about other people always means seeing them as *you* see them, rather than mirroring the way they would elect to be seen. And yet I felt defensive of Annie. In the face of the ways others might dismiss her obsessiveness as pathology or excess, I felt protective of her relentless drive toward connection and her compulsion to make herself vulnerable, to communicate fully, to say *everything*, to document everything, to capture every nuance, every complexity. At a certain point, I started to suspect that my ongoing obsession with Annie's obsession stemmed partially from a savior complex of my own—my attempt to defend an outsider artist who was almost stubbornly uncool in her methods and her affect, who was gloriously unrestrained and sentimental, who didn't apologize for being earnest. Sometimes the relationship between artist and subject can get messy and overwhelming. Agee knew it, and so did Annie, and so did I.

Annie's impulse to keep expanding her project plays out a certain fantasy I've felt in my own work: to put no boundaries around my evocation of my subjects, to make them infinite, to let them keep going forever. Representing people always involves reducing them, and calling a project "done" involves making an uneasy truce with that reduction. But some part of me rails against that compression. Some part of me wants to keep saying: *there's more, there's more, there's more.* It's why I often write ten thousand more words than I was assigned.

It's back to the Borges problem: in order to do justice to the world, the map has to reproduce the world in its entirety. But does more of a thing always make it truer? If the average length of a photographic exposure is one-sixtieth of a second, Spencer observed, that means Annie has cumulatively captured only about six minutes of her subjects' lives. But the force of Annie's work isn't the achievement of a complete gaze. It's the yearning for completion. Her work succeeds most fully not as a comprehensive account of a family but as an account of her longing to know them—as a testimony, more broadly, to the human desire to witness other people.

There is something contagious about her obsession. It has certainly infected me—her sense that no account can ever be complete, or *enough*. If Annie feels it about María and her family, then I've come to feel it about her. Her appetite has started to seem ecstatic, her drive toward connection almost Whitmanesque: a generative superpower. And I'm convinced that the fulfillment of her longing would only take away the engine of her art.

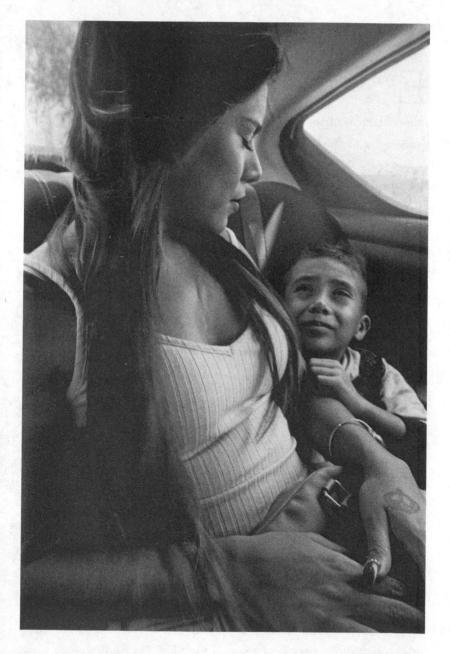

Carmelita and Diego, 2017

* * *

Every time I hear from Annie, she tells me that the Mexico project has gotten larger: another trip, another set of photographs, another series of entries in her ever-expanding diary. In recent years many of these trips have involved visiting María's brother Guillermo and his family in the various American cities where they have lived, and on each trip she plunges right into the grain of their lives: going to church with Guillermo to pray he won't get deported, helping Gloria straighten out a tax reimbursement, listening to their daughter tell stories about her Tinker Bell doll and to their son talk about wanting to go to medical school because he has been so deeply affected by his younger sister's lung disease. Even though Annie initially decided it wouldn't be wise to give Guillermo her home address, she eventually ended up not only giving him her address but inviting him to visit her in San Pedro.

When I called Guillermo to ask him directly about his relationship with Annie, I reached him in the midst of work. He'd just purchased a van to start up a portable mechanic's shop and was headed to a junkyard to pick up an engine. He could still remember the first time he'd met Annie, back in the early '90s, when he'd come home to find a stranger standing outside his house, taking photographs, and had no idea what she was doing there. He hadn't seen a lot of Americans. The first thing he ever said to her was "Someday, I'm going to get to your country."

Now that Guillermo was here, he still insisted that—even under Trump—it was a better life for his children. "We are a little bit afraid," he told me, and then I heard Gloria say something in the background, and he corrected himself: "We are a lot afraid." Whenever he left the house, he said, Gloria would make the sign of the cross for his safety, and he would tell her, "If I don't come back, you'll know why."

When I asked Guillermo how his relationship with Annie had

evolved over the years, he paused for so long I wondered if the connection had dropped. But eventually he said, "I think...too much," and I realized he was struggling to describe a relationship that felt so encompassing. Annie had photographed his entire life. "When I don't remember something about my life," he told me, "I ask Annie, because she has probably photographed it."

On her visits, he explained, she was constantly taking photographs. "When we are eating, she photographs us eating. When we are working, she photographs us working. All the time. All the moments." He could look at her photographs and see his children as infants, or himself as a child, living in poverty in San Martín. When he was just a teenager, Annie gave him the money he needed to move away from his hometown. She had always been there for him to talk to. She had always told him he would be able to live his dreams. As we spoke, I kept waiting for darker notes to creep into his voice—for any suggestion that perhaps sometimes he felt invaded by Annie's attention, or betrayed by it. But I never heard those notes. Those were simply the tensions I'd conjured when I'd imagined the narrative for myself.

When I asked Guillermo what single thing he would want someone to know about Annie and her relationship with his family, he said: "She is a good person." And then: "She is my sister." Not *like*, but *is*. And to his kids, she is *Tía Anita. Tía Anita.* He didn't say it once, but several times. He wanted me to understand.

Annie calls her work a form of love, and considers love a form of focused attention. In the academic programs where I've studied and taught, where bromides are kryptonite and emotion is expected to footnote its own presence, it is always risky to use the word *love* without cautionary quotes. But that's part of why I keep coming back to Annie: there's no room for scare quotes in how she speaks. She owns the heart in her work. It's another kind of transgression.

And if Annie's work is fueled by love, then it's a form of love that doesn't blunt or distort her gaze. Her love sharpens her sight. Her work has helped me trust that an enduring emotional investment—even in all its mess and mistakes, *because* of its mess and mistakes—can help you see more acutely. It can sensitize your gaze to the competing vectors of emotion churning beneath ordinary moments: the particular angle of a woman's body over her laundry; a father's bewilderment as he stares down at his crying daughter; the posture of a man at the doorway of his new home, grinning as he holds his tired son, right before carrying him across the threshold.

When I look at Annie's early proof sheets, from her first visits to Baja, I see some version of what she saw then: a mother with her infant, a father with his encyclopedias and his tequila bottles and his towering stacks of bricks. But I also see the long shadows cast by everything that hasn't happened yet: years of day jobs and rejected grant applications and ruptured love affairs; fights with mothers and unexpected pregnancies; addictions and fires and bus rides to new lives. I see the lurking horizons of a project that would keep leaving Annie humbled, more confused than when she'd begun. After nine years: *I understand nothing.* In those early negatives, I see cornflakes and cigarettes and stubborn wind and sudden laughter. I see everything the photos knew alongside everything they didn't know yet, and this unknowing is one more definition of love: committing to a story you can't fully imagine when it begins

— III —

DWELLING

Rehearsals

Weddings are holiness and booze, sweat under the dress, sweet icing in the mouth. A whaler's church in the afternoon, sunlit and salted, gives way to the drunken splendor of a barn, and an entire island is suddenly *yours*, yours and everyone's. You feel the lift of wine in you, you feel the lift of wine in everyone, and you're all in agreement—not to believe in love, but to want to. This, you can do. You dance with a stranger and think, *We have this in common, this wanting to believe.* In what, again? In the possibility that two people could actually make each other happy, not just today but on ten thousand days they can't yet see.

Weddings are hassle. Hassle is spending money you don't have to celebrate the lives of people who have more money than you do. Hassle is finding yourself booked on a round-trip flight, Boston to Tulsa, and wondering, *How did this happen?* Hassle is driving to an Oklahoma conference center in the middle of the night. Hassle is getting stuck in traffic on the Brooklyn Bridge and listening to your friend's boyfriend talk about getting his pilot's license. Hassle is taking the PATH train to Hoboken at two in the morning, shoulder to shoulder with the drunkest bridge-and-tunnel crowd, thinking, *"Bridge-and-tunnel" is such a demeaning phrase*, and also, *These people are really drunk!* Weddings are taking a plane, a train, a bus, a ferry, and then setting down your bulky backpack in a little internet café to check your email and finding a note from your new boyfriend saying he just talked about you with his father for the first time. This makes the wedding ahead feel swollen with possibility. You're someone who might someday be loved. You're in the game.

Weddings are getting dropped at a post office on a dusty road in the middle of the Catskills and waiting for a ride to the lodge. There's always a lodge. There's always cocktail hour at the lodge, and group activities at the lodge, and a hurried hunt for a bridesmaid's missing shoes at the lodge. We go distances to celebrate the love of people we love, but sometimes it hurts the heart to stand alone on an empty road and think, *What am I doing here?*

Everyone talks about weddings as beginnings but the truth is they are also endings. They give a horizon of closure to things that have been slowly dissolving for years: flirtations, friendships, shared innocence, shared rootlessness, shared loneliness.

Weddings are about being single and wondering about being in love, and being in love and wondering about being in love—what it's like for other people, and whether it hurts as much as it sometimes does for you. At every wedding, all of a sudden, all bets are off and everyone is asking when your boyfriend is planning to propose, and you are watching your boyfriend talk to the girl at the cheese table, and the wine in you wants to fight, and the wine in you thinks, *You will never love me like I need you to.*

You thought you knew drunk crying before you went to weddings. You'd gotten tipsy on cheap wine in the middle of the afternoon, alone, and cried rereading emails ex-boyfriends sent before they were ex-boyfriends. But you didn't know this kind of drunk crying: alone in the bathroom at your brother's wedding, or your other brother's wedding. And you couldn't even explain it properly, because you were happy for them, you were, but you were also feeling something else, only you'd gotten too drunk to remember what it was. You learned there was a kind of crying that was okay, and another kind of crying that wasn't—a violent, angry crying—and without quite noticing, you'd crossed from one to the other.

Sometimes the best weddings are the weddings of strangers. You are only a date. No particular feelings are required. You cry as a groom remembers his mother, who died of cancer years earlier, and even though you've never met this guy, he'd once been in a band with your boyfriend, you can see the way he looks at his wife, and you think his mother must have loved him well. When you step outside the barn, it's sunset in early June and there are fields of something under the light, and you think of that Sting song, the one you were always embarrassed to love, except maybe it's not embarrassing to love it here. You have a little quiche in your palm, and you feel your boyfriend's arms wrap around you from behind—he has only one suit, you know its crispness well—and this moment might be a little too sweet, like wedding cake, but it's yours. You summon your most primal, shameful dreams—for some kind of life you learned to love in magazines—and feed them tiny quiches, these dreams, and hope that these will be enough.

You wonder what they feel, people who get married, at the precise moment they commit to their vows. Is it only bliss, or also fear? You hope for fear. Because mostly you can't imagine feeling anything else. Except when you can summon the edge of a man's suit against your back, familiar, his hand on your arm, his voice in your ear.

By *you*, of course, I mean *I*. I wonder about fear. I don't want to be afraid.

At thirteen I took a flight from Los Angeles to San Francisco and wondered what my father loved in the woman he was about to marry, and what he'd loved in my mother, and if there was anything he *still* loved in my mother, and how these circles might overlap, if laid across one another. At the airport my mother hugged me and tried her best to pretend she didn't feel betrayed that I'd chosen to go, that she wasn't buckling under the weight of thirty years ending. Or maybe she was going to buckle once I left. I could see it. I took it with me.

At the wedding I cried what my mother hadn't cried in front of me. I cried in a room full of the relatives of my father's new wife. I was that terrible stepdaughter, the one from terrible movies, *making a scene* in front of everyone. I sat in the corner of a dim banquet hall and my brothers patted me on the back so I wouldn't feel so fully out of place, so fully without an anchor. They didn't have wives yet then. I didn't want anyone to look at me. That was part of why I started crying even harder, which of course must have seemed like just the opposite: a plea for everyone's attention.

When my parents first separated, my father had moved into a dark apartment in a corporate-looking building facing a grove of eucalyptus trees. I remember he got an ice-cream maker so we could make ice cream together. I remember the ice cream tasted like ice crystals. I remember finding a photograph of a beautiful woman with a blurry face on his dresser. I remember thinking the whole place felt incredibly lonely. I remember feeling sorry for him.

Months later, when he told me he was getting married, to a woman I hadn't yet met, I thought of the woman in the photograph and realized that his loneliness had lied to me. It wasn't his but mine, my own loneliness reflected in the cage of his new life, a space in which I felt I had no place.

When I cried at his wedding, I cried for the betrayal of that dim apartment—how I'd imagined him lonely when in fact he was happy, and how my sympathy had made a fool of me in the end.

The Long Trick

When my grandfather died, I lost a man I'd never really known. I was nearly thirty and I'd seen him maybe three times in my life. He existed mainly as legend: a drunk and a pilot. He was a colonel in the Air Force, stationed in Brazil during World War II, and for the rest of his life he claimed that country as a second home: bought a tract of land in the jungle, off the grid, and eventually got sober in Natal. He raised my father and my two aunts before he quit drinking and started taking lithium; after doing these things he got married again and had two more daughters. Over the years, I came to realize he'd been a very different father to them.

When I was young, my father used to tell me stories about going to the airfield with his dad when he was a boy. He loved watching Marshall inspect his plane, circling the tires and checking the glass canopy for cracks. These stories didn't make me feel close to my grandfather so much as they made me feel close to my father. They brought me into his awe. Once, I asked my dad if he'd been proud that his dad knew how to fly a plane. He was quick to specify: not just a *plane*, a bomber jet. That meant yes, he'd been proud. That meant he still was.

His voice got soft when he spoke about the way Marshall held his helmet case like a briefcase in his hand, like any regular businessman going to work, except his office was an airfield, and his business was in the sky.

My father never learned to fly a plane, but he spent a lot of time in flight. For my whole childhood, his work took him all over the world. The casual ease with which he mentioned a round-trip to Beijing was thrilling, his voice gravelly with authority and elusiveness, his presence electrified by the fact that he always had commitments elsewhere. His passport was a patchwork of entry stamps and visas. He always had to order extra pages.

I grew up worshipping the men in my family, my father and my two older brothers, but once I turned nine, they all started leaving. My brothers went to college. My father moved across the country for work. I don't remember being angry about it. He was gone so often anyway. I knew his work was important, but I didn't know why. I didn't know why my parents got divorced when he got back. I didn't get angry about that either. Instead, I got angry that my middle brother, Eliot, went to college, two years after Julian, my oldest. These ordinary departures carried the full weight of betrayal. They made me realize I wasn't as central to their lives as they were to mine.

The house was very quiet in those days. It was just me and my mother. A few months into Eliot's freshman year, I made a drawing on our computer, using an early-'90s graphics program that made everything look like an Etch A Sketch. It was a self-portrait of me sitting on his bed with big fist-sized teardrops pasted under my eyes. I called it *Jealous Sorrow*.

I used to call Eliot in his faraway dorm room and refuse to get off the phone until he told me he loved me. *I love you*, I'd say. *I love you I love you I love you*. I'd say it until he said it back. Sometimes he did. Sometimes he didn't. Sometimes there was just silence. I felt so wronged. Really, of course, I felt wronged by my father. Really, of course, pleading to that quiet line, I was talking to my father.

Before my brothers were gone, and before my father was gone, my grandfather was gone. He was the original absent man. The distance between him and my father—the fact that they saw each other so rarely—was almost never discussed. But decades later, when my grandfather was dying of cancer, my father asked me to come to the small fishing town on the Chesapeake Bay where Marshall lived with his second wife. Eliot and I sat with our father at a seafood shack about a ten-minute drive from the house where his own father was dying. He'd camped out there over a dish of crab cakes because he wanted to grant his stepmother and his half sisters their privacy. It made me sad to think my father thought he would be intruding on his own father's death.

Marshall died with his youngest grandson, just one month old, tucked into the crook of his arm. When I saw his body an hour later, still lying on the bed, he looked frail and jaundiced: a smooth wax statue, yellow face capped with a pale blue beanie, eyes partway open.

During the days after his death, life in his house felt physical and proximate: soft blankets on chairs, soup on the stove, babies crying. My father's stepmother, Linda, and his half sisters, Danica and Kelda, were gracious in their grief. They welcomed us into a home that smelled like shampoo and cooking oil and diaper cream. They read us the poem they had read to Marshall as he was dying: *I must go down to the seas again, to the vagrant gypsy life, / To the gull's way and the whale's way where the wind's like a whetted knife*. Both of my aunts had newborn sons who remained oblivious in the face of mortality: they got hungry, got gassy, got confused and amazed by every little thing. Danica told me that for days life in that house had been all about bodies: nursing her son, turning her father in bed so he wouldn't get sores, helping him get to the bathroom when he was able to walk, then changing his bedpan when he wasn't.

Eliot was reserved—he was almost always reserved—but he was comfortable holding the babies. His posture with them summoned his whole life back home: everything he had built, the kind of father he had chosen to become. Back in Vancouver, he had a wife and two young sons and a split-level house and a job in infrastructure: bridges and railroads and highways. Nothing in the air. He hit suburban playgrounds on weekends. He wasn't afraid of presence. That's what I told myself back then. Now I think maybe he was afraid of presence, just like the rest of us, and kept showing up anyway. He carried a briefcase but it held no helmet. He stayed on land.

On the other side of the continent, in Connecticut, I was smoking cigarettes on my stoop and feeling sorry for myself by replaying arguments I'd had with my boyfriend before we broke up. At the tail end of my twenties, newly sober and newly single and still regularly commuting to other people's weddings, I had just broken the lease on the apartment I'd shared with my ex and moved into a one-room studio with a fridge full of seltzer water and a dryer whose indoor vent laced the humid air with tiny particles. It always smelled like mint from the extract I'd sprinkled everywhere to repel the mice that kept coming back anyway. The loneliness of that apartment seemed like apt punishment for fleeing my relationship instead of working on it harder—for being fickle, unstable, and uncertain; for being needy but unable to reciprocate the love I needed. My mother wanted me to have children, and some part of me wanted that also—a part of me buried deep beneath the fear of being constantly accountable to another person.

It was bracing to show up at this old wooden house in Virginia where two people had been married for decades, settled here in a little fishing town at the tip of a peninsula. The local catch was Atlantic menhaden, which was not a kind of fish that people ate but a kind of fish that people ground into chicken feed. The local processing plant was called Omega Protein. Eliot had learned all this on Wikipedia. We joked about the name *Omega Protein*. It sounded sinister. But it moved me, somehow, that Eliot had gone to the trouble of looking up this town. He wanted to know something about this place besides *someone died here*. I got that. I wanted to know something about my grandfather that wasn't about his death, or the mythology of his life. And it wasn't just him I wanted to know better, but also the traces of him left in the men of my family. His ghost seemed like a way of understanding those parts of them that had always been mysterious and opaque—that had always felt far away, even when they were right in front of me.

The Portuguese word *saudade* is infamously untranslatable, but I've always loved how it describes something more mysterious than sheer nostalgia. It's a longing not for what you've lost but for what you've never had. It's something like homesickness, but it could mean homesick for a place you've never been. It's at home in Brazil, where Marshall went when he wasn't with his family. It usually takes a grammatical construction that suggests possession or company: you have *saudades*, or you can be with them. As if longing could become a kind of company. As if it could compensate for absence itself. *Saudade* is a name for the ache I feel when I conjure that image of my father and his father on the airfield: a little boy in awe of the sky-bound pilot kneeling next to him, eager to help him check the cockpit for cracks. I miss that airfield, even though I've never been there. It's a memory that pulses inside me, even though it's not mine. It glows with my desire to know the man and boy who live inside it.

* * *

W hen I was six years old and couldn't fall asleep at night, Eliot started to sleep on my empty bottom bunk. We called it sleep insurance. It helped just to know that his body was in the darkened room with mine.

I can't remember a time when I wasn't obsessed with Eliot's life. He told me so little about it. I kept his senior-prom photo framed on my bureau for years, his date in a gold lace dress with gold pumps. (This was 1992.) It was endlessly fascinating to me, the question of what kind of woman he found beautiful. Bruce Springsteen was his favorite singer, so I listened to "Human Touch" on repeat for clues about his inner life. (It wasn't until years later that I realized it *might* not be his favorite song.) He played on the varsity tennis team and I loved to watch him practice with his doubles partner, Amir, while I called out commentary from the sidelines. "Eliot rips a winner down the line!" I'd say, or, "Amir slaps another unforced error into the net!" I remember Amir asking, "Is she going to do this all day?" I left his actual tennis matches with my palms covered in red crescents from where I'd dug my nails into the skin from game-point nerves.

My mom once told me that when I was a baby, Eliot often cried when I cried. He was nine years old. He couldn't calm down until I did. As an adult, he'd come to keep his feelings studiously private, as if he'd already done all the crying he planned to do in his lifetime. But I needed to remember: he had once cried for me. It was proof that I had the power to move him.

W hen my parents fell in love, my father was already engaged to another woman. He and my mother were working together in Brazil—a research project my grandfather had put together, focused on rural education—and my childhood vision of their affair gleamed with the luster of myth: kissing on rugged Brazilian beaches, swimming in the wild, frothing Atlantic. I even loved the part of the story about my father's fiancée getting so angry she threw the birthday cake she'd baked for him in his face. When I was a kid, I focused on Brazilian beaches because it was easier to imagine those postcard vistas than it was to imagine my father's fiancée asking herself what she could have done to make him love her enough to stay. I wanted to imagine the story of my own origins as an epic passion rather than an ordinary betrayal. In truth, of course, it was both. I identified with my mother in the story, because she was my mother. But for years I would be the one wondering—with my father, my brothers, my boyfriends—*What can I do to make him love me more?*

For a long time, I was angry at my father for his restlessness, his absences, and his countless infidelities. But by the time Marshall died, I'd begun to acknowledge how many similarities existed between us. We both liked our work. We both liked our wine. I was not entirely unlike him in what I sought from the world—what I felt I was owed, or didn't owe anyone. I had always sworn I wouldn't repeat the mistakes that had run roughshod over my family, but I found myself more than capable of cheating on boyfriends—there I was, the first time, mouth tasting like cigarettes and orange soda and liquor, waking up next to an Irish guy who had just ridden his motorcycle all the way across Latin America. It was almost liberating that I could no longer judge my father for all the times he'd done something like this too. It's not that seeing yourself becoming your parents doesn't mean you can't still be angry at them. In fact, it can make you even angrier. *You made me this way!* But it nagged at my judgment like a hair caught on the back of my tongue.

If I spent my twenties becoming more like my father, Eliot had already spent his twenties becoming his opposite: a committed monogamist with a career in investment banking and designs on a house with a white-picket fence. I saw Eliot's identity as an inverted inheritance—this desire to become the things his father had not been.

A month before Eliot's wedding—when he was in his early thirties, and I was in my early twenties—we had a conversation about relationships, one of the most revealing talks we'd ever had. I told him my white-room theory: I wanted to find a guy with whom I could spend three days in an empty white room and not get bored. I'd just ended a relationship in the way I had begun to end relationships, the way I would keep ending relationships: getting out once I got bored. Once I wanted out of the white room. My invitation to Eliot's wedding had my ex-boyfriend's name on it, because we'd been together when it was sent, but I was going to the wedding alone—and *proud* of going alone—because going alone meant I wasn't settling, and I thought settling was one of the worst things that could happen to a human being.

That day we talked, before Eliot's wedding, I asked him what he wanted. Why was he marrying the woman he was marrying? He said they had similar visions for the life they wanted to build; they had compatible values and like-minded approaches to practical things like finances. When I was twenty-one, that sounded like the opposite of romance: *similar visions for the life we wanted to build.* Looking back, at thirty-five, it seems like everything.

They had their wedding in Yosemite, and I ended up delaying the ceremony by half an hour because my bridesmaid's corset tore as I was zipping it up. My future sister-in-law was gracious. We'd fix it, she said. And we did. Another bridesmaid was a seamstress; I was literally sewn into my outfit. Even though I told everyone I was mortified at delaying the ceremony, secretly I was a little proud. I was a force for chaos, for disruption, for whatever the opposite of settling was. I was unsettled, hard to contain, recently single, breaking seams.

In truth, the ceremony was beautiful. I remember seeing how happy my brother looked, and my sister-in-law; realizing how little I knew of other people's hearts, how little I knew of my own. At their reception they served apple pies instead of wedding cake because they both preferred pie. Another shared vision. When I cried that night, brimming with vodka and chardonnay, I kept mentioning my ex's name in conversation just so everyone would know that coming alone was a choice I'd made. I used the toe of my sparkly party shoes to grind cigarette butts into the redwood planks of a deck that overlooked rippling green meadows gone dusky in the twilight. It was so beautiful. I was so drunk.

Back then, life existed most forcefully for me in evenings like those: bleary nights when I confronted the difficulty of love—my broken heart! my ex's broken heart!—and felt existentially alone, and drank enough Absolut to tell everyone I was feeling that way. But as the years unfolded, life started to seem less like something that crystallized in these cinematic moments—weeping in bathrooms, or gesticulating with a glowing cigarette tip against the backdrop of a darkening summer sky—and more like something that accumulated across broad swaths of ordinary days: morning commutes, school pickups, the heat of my little nephews' bodies pressed against mine on couches, listening to *The Lorax*, asking for apple pie instead of cake on their birthdays.

A few years after his wedding, I asked Eliot to lend me enough money so I could take a two-month trip to Bolivia. He said no. "I have enough money for the trip," I explained helpfully. "I just need money to pay rent when I get back." He still said no. I felt judged, I told him. He said that I shouldn't ask for a favor unless I was okay with hearing *no*. I started crying—*I'm sad at you*, I used to say to my brothers when I was young—because some part of me knew he was right. It wasn't needing the money that made me cry so much as the thought that I had disappointed him. I'd spent so much of my life straining toward his praise like a houseplant leaning into sunlight, begging for something from that voice on the other end of the line—not just love, but the assurance that I deserved it.

*　　*　　*

When Marshall was dying, nearly two decades after my parents had divorced, my mother wrote him a card that she asked me to read over his body. "Thank you thank you thank you thank you," she wrote—one thanks for my father, and one for each of the children they'd had together. Her words created a solid surface around the hollowness in me where grief should have been. "I've always admired your willingness to dream big dreams," she wrote. His body on the bed seemed so unbelievably small. I touched his arm and held his hand, but could not bring myself to touch his face.

Beneath my feet, his basement was full of the detritus of his ongoing projects, their uneasy marriage of mania and brilliance: a library of sandpaper so he could make his own nail files, index cards scribbled with to-do lists, *Send Israel-Palestine Resolution to Senator Warner; Finish Afghanistan Exit Plan.* He could make you see the wonder in anything, my aunts told me, even a little bug or a weed. The poem they read to him as he was dying—with its gull's way, its whale's way—didn't end with the whetted knife of wind or the vagrant gypsy life. It ended with rest: *And all I ask is a merry yarn from a laughing, fellow-rover, / And quiet sleep and a sweet dream when the long trick's over.*

The day after he died, I made brunch for everyone, fried oysters, palming the glistening ovals of muscle and crusting them with bread crumbs, willing them to become something edible. I wanted to be useful. I wanted to feed the bereaved. I'd bought these oysters from a gas station near Rappahannock, where the man behind the counter sold me a glass jar full of their slippery bodies and then announced to me, for no apparent reason, that he wanted a root beer and a moon pie. The world seemed full of desires that couldn't always be explained, but could sometimes—in surprising ways—be met.

Over oily breaded oysters, Kelda told us Marshall had always talked easily about the early years of his life—his childhood, his service in the Air Force—but there were thirty years he rarely spoke about at all: the years of raising his first family. When my father heard that, his face showed no expression. Later that day, when I saw an empty wine bottle in his hotel room, I thought of his face at the table. What lay behind it? His empty bottle summoned all the empty wine bottles that I'd dumped in neighbors' recycling bins during the months my grandmother was dying, many decades after she and Marshall had divorced, when I was living in her home and caring for her imperfectly, as best I could. My grandfather was the only other person in my family who'd ever gotten sober, but I didn't know anything about what sobriety had been like for him. Had he also drunk seltzer water straight from the bottle? Had he also spent days in an apartment that smelled like too much toothpaste, remembering his bungled love affairs? Probably not. He'd had his own, worse journeys.

Among other things, sobriety was teaching me that I loved nothing better than telling inflated stories about my own ordinary dysfunction. And maybe I'd corralled the men in my family into another one of these tales: the story of a little girl yearning for elusive men—the pilot, the frequent flier, the silent voice at the other end of the line—whose bodies and attention were often directed somewhere else. But the story was more complicated than that. Because at some point I'd developed an attachment to the state of yearning itself. I no longer desired presence; in fact, I often had no idea what to do with men when they stuck around. It was like staying at my father's apartment for a single night after months away from him. Everything was uncomfortable. There was no food for my school lunch, only chardonnay in the fridge. I just wanted to go home. It was easier to miss him than to have him close.

It was years before I discovered the second definition of the word *saudade*. In this meaning, *saudade* doesn't describe longing for any particular object, but longing for that very state of yearning. As critic

F. D. Santos writes: "It is no more the Loved One or the 'Return' that is desired. Now, Desire desires Desire itself." This kind of desire doesn't know what to do with being met. It has trouble with the proximity of white rooms. It can't see the ways in which elusive men sometimes show up. It has trouble fitting their presence into the frame.

The truth is, the elusive men in my family also showed up plenty of times. Marshall built a second family and loved his daughters well. Sometimes he escaped to Brazil, and sometimes he escaped to his basement projects, but through it all he built a thirty-year life in an old wooden house by the Chesapeake Bay. My father was often gone, but there were plenty of times he was there—making me ramen and popcorn for dinner when my mom was out of town, or waiting in the hospital cafeteria during my heart surgery, years later. If I was attached to stories about my restless father and his restless father, then maybe once my grandfather died I could let him live as something more than myth, more than godhead; and maybe I could let my father live as something more complicated and contradictory as well, which is to say: devoted, imperfect, trying his best. Maybe I could start to see that while I had been longing for him, he'd been longing for me as well.

Two days after our grandfather died, Eliot and I woke up early to go running in the rain. "I love running in the rain," I told him, even though I didn't. I just wanted to be a person who loved running in the rain: stoic, unflappable. Eliot asked if I had a rain jacket. I didn't. He gave me his. I got soaked anyway. We both did. He got more so. Our shoes slapped sodden on the dirt road and brown grass, then on the asphalt two-lane highway, past wooden farmhouses. I resolved to run until Eliot suggested we turn around, which meant we kept going. Eliot regularly ran marathons. I'd already traded my running regimen for a smoking habit. Once we got back to the house where we were staying,

I asked Eliot how far he thought we'd gone. He guessed four miles and I guessed seven. It's always been this way: He undersells himself and stays in it for the long haul. I want credit and tire easily.

Before we got back, however, before we even turned around, we followed the highway turnoff for Omega Protein. We followed asphalt through the trees until we spied the plant itself: a collection of squat towers—huge boiling vats, probably—and a posse of forklift trucks, a few rusted boats. "What if we were spies from a rival fish-processing plant?" I asked him. "How would we take this place down?" We speculated about angles of approach, scaling chain-link fences, spoiling tanks of fish with something rotten. I have always liked laughing with Eliot because the way we laugh remains somehow untouched by the differences between the lives we've built. Eliot was one of the first people in the world I ever found hilarious.

We passed a tiny airfield at the edge of the Omega complex. It was patchy with grass and soggy with rain. It wasn't a mythic airstrip. It was more like an abandoned soccer field. It insisted on the muddy ground more than it suggested the possibility of leaving it behind. Who knew who flew there, or why? It was a field where fish were ferried to the sky in boneless lumps; where men who would someday be grandfathers did things they would someday tell their grandchildren about: carried briefcases full of Atlantic menhaden or documents they would or wouldn't send to congressmen, documents that would or wouldn't save the world. The world would keep on needing saving. We kept on running. The sky kept on raining. We knew the sky would keep pulling men into the clouds and sending them back underground. We knew that life was a long trick that ended with a dream; living was a gull and a whale and a whetted knife of wind.

Everyone had always told me about Marshall and the sky. It was the perfect metaphor: he was a restless pilot. But on that day, the sky felt too easy. It turned everything weightless. It felt more honest to stare at a closed place below it: the patchy grass surrounded by a chain-link fence, at the fish plant, in the rain.

Each time I try to write an elegy for my grandfather, it ends up becoming a thank-you letter to my brother instead. I want to tell him: Thank you for having sons in fleece pajamas. Thank you for being a good father, and for refusing me that loan—or at least thank you for telling me I needed to be okay with it. Thank you for staying married and not needing your marriage to be a white room in which you're always entertained. Thank you for showing me that settling was just a story I told myself about other people's lives. Thank you for crying when I cried, when you were young and I was younger, and for understanding why I didn't cry at our grandfather's deathbed. Thank you for giving me your rain jacket and your prom photo and your apple pies, and for sleeping in a bed below my bed, years ago, when I didn't know how to get through the night.

The Real Smoke

Two years into sobriety, I found myself ordering a mocktail at the heart of the Vegas Strip. This was in a three-story cocktail lounge enclosed by a giant chandelier made from two million crystal beads, their sparkling curtains wrapped around a secret place called Level 1.5, where you could order real drinks with names like the Forbidden Fruit and the Infinite Playlist. I got something that tasted like raspberry sherbet. It came in a cosmopolitan glass with coarse sugar crystals around the rim.

I'd been flown out to give a reading at a writing program in town. It was one of the first times I'd ever been flown anywhere; even the syntax felt glamorous, thrillingly passive. It seemed like proof of being wanted, though it had brought me to a city that was all about degrading yourself by wanting too much, too rashly, without any hope of getting even a fraction of what you'd fantasized. Back in New Haven, I'd been reeling from the end of a four-year relationship that I still felt constituted by. My life with Dave had cut right to the core of me and burrowed there. It wouldn't give up residence for a long time. I could say I didn't know that then, but I did. I knew. Every time I said something to anyone, I was still trying to say it to him.

After my reading, my hosts said they wanted to take me to the Strip. We were all young, none of us tired, all of us buzzed on the prospect of having an ironic experience of the city's relentless pageantry. My hosts were grad students who said they never went to the Strip unless they were taking someone from out of town, except for one woman who worked there as a cocktail waitress to supplement her financial aid.

On nights like that one, sobriety still felt like deprivation. With strangers, drinking had always been the way I'd let the night unravel into something we couldn't see the edges of. Without it, I was stuck inside a container with visible boundaries. Now I was stuck inside a three-story chandelier. When someone suggested getting a mocktail, I recoiled. I had no interest in the simulated version of the actual experience of getting drunk. But then I thought, Why not? The most authentic Vegas experience was simulated experience anyway.

As it turned out, my mocktail tasted great. I was drinking juice in the land of two million crystal beads. The night was just getting started. We went to a secret pizza joint hidden behind the slot machines, deep in the interior of the interior, far from any windows or clocks. We went to a humid greenhouse where golden trees sprouted golden coins from their branches. Red lanterns flickered in the shadows. The snails were made of roses. We passed an electronic billboard that said WE RESPECT YOUR OPINION OF ASPARAGUS BUT DISAGREE WITH IT and then HAVE A SAFE TRIP HOME! But we weren't going home. We were going to the Bellagio fountains. We watched the water dance to an instrumental version of the *Titanic* theme song. Those illuminated surging plumes stirred the part of me—deep inside—that wanted to find beauty in what other people found absurd.

One of my hosts, a man named Joe—handsome in his hipster jeans, with curly blond hair and a perpetually wry, bemused expression on his face—asked if there was anything else I wanted to see. There *was* something, I told him. I wanted to buy a onesie. It was for one of my best friends, who was about to have a baby. She was possibly the classiest woman I knew. She had an elegant West Village apartment, an elegant dog, and an elegant chef husband who made elegant farm-to-table food. I wanted to buy her the tackiest onesie I could find.

"I know a place," Joe said, and took me to the biggest souvenir shop in the world. It was closed. Nothing was supposed to be closed. He said, "I know another place." It didn't have what we were looking for. He said, "This isn't done."

It turned out the only thing better than finding the onesie was not finding the onesie, because then we got to keep looking. It felt good to cruise the mild winter night in Joe's Jeep, to see the neon blurring and dazzling around us, dispensing enchantment like an IV drip. You got it in your bloodstream and things started to hum. This night felt more like the first night I'd done cocaine than anything had since.

We cruised the clutch of all-night wedding chapels that connected the Strip to downtown. We passed the Chapel of the Flowers, the Chapel of the Bells, Graceland Wedding Chapel, and A Wee Kirk o' the Heather, as well as the grande dame, with its humble name: A Little White Chapel, where Frank Sinatra and Michael Jordan and Rita Hayworth had each gotten hitched, all their ghosts sheltered under a towering Elvis in a gold lamé suit who promised, in cursive, *with love*. It was where Britney Spears had married her best friend at three in the morning, in a rented lime-green limo. "They were laughing, but crying, too," said the chapel's owner. "I thought it was a marriage that would last forever." They signed annulment papers the following afternoon. Reality was like that here: You ordered what you wanted, and then if you didn't want it anymore, you returned it. You could switch from Paris to Venice, from Luxor to New York, from the circus to the castle. These were the fruits of restlessness, the capitalist gospel of choice. You could get married. Then you could take it back.

Joe took me to the swimming pool at the Golden Nugget, where an enclosed glass waterslide curved through a massive aquarium full of ancient-bodied sharks circling their kingdom, cool as you please. We flirted beside the sharks, in the hotel corridors, in the parking lot. If the sensation of flirting were an interior landscape, it would be a cavern lit up like Vegas at night—flickering with possibility, sizzling like moths against neon.

We ended up finding our onesie on Fremont Street, in the shadow of forty-foot Vegas Vic, who smoked a neon cigarette between his neon lips. Once upon a time, that giant glowing cigarette had sent up actual puffs of smoke. Now Fremont Street had become the Fremont Street Experience: a pedestrian walkway covered by the massive canopy of a curving LED screen. This felt like a natural extension of the logic of the casinos, which kept you far away from windows—away from the rhythms of day and night, the vast otherness of sky. Now the sky had been banished completely. Strangers screamed above us on zip lines.

For the first time since the end of Dave, I was feeling the glimmering suggestion of what it might be like to fall in love with someone else. This feeling of anticipation was quite different from actually falling in love. It was arguably even better. Nothing was really at stake. It was more like opening a window without having to go outside and face the sky. I spent the ride home wondering if Joe would kiss me when we pulled up to my hotel in his Jeep. It was like being sixteen again. He didn't kiss me, but I knew—from the particular way he hadn't, from his pause—that someday he would.

In 1968 the Yale School of Architecture offered a seminar called the "Learning from Las Vegas Research Studio." The professors who designed it, Denise Scott Brown and Robert Venturi, believed that architecture had become too "socially coercive," imposing taste rather than responding to it, and they believed the Las Vegas Strip pushed back against this coercion as the "purest and most intense" manifestation of consumer desires. Their course centered on a ten-day trip to Vegas devoted to "open-minded and nonjudgmental investigation," seeking those truths that might dwell in the urban forms that other architects regarded with disdain.

It was an unusual venture: a couple of Yale professors and their students showing up on the Strip, freshly sprung from the Brutalist concrete palace of their architecture school back in New Haven. They stayed in free rooms at the Stardust. They got an invitation to the gala opening of the Circus Circus casino, where they showed up in Day-Glo castoffs from a local Salvation Army. After they asked for local funding, one headline read: "Yale Professor Will Praise Strip for $8,925." The implication was clear: these diplomats from the land of the highbrow would not deign to praise the lowbrow for free. But Venturi and Scott Brown didn't believe the highbrow and the lowbrow were separate. They wanted to put "A&P parking lot" and "Versailles" in the same sentence. They wanted them to share a lineage. Midway through the semester, the students started calling their course "The Great Proletarian Cultural Locomotive."

Decades later, I shared their impulse to frame Vegas as an underdog in the great games of taste. It's easy to call Vegas cheesy, but what is *cheesy*, anyway? Its current meaning is an ironic reversal of what it meant in the days of the British Empire, which was *fine* or *grand*, as in *the real chīz* (*chīz* being the Urdu word for *thing*). Now it means something inauthentic and unsubtle, something that tries too hard. All of Vegas tries too hard. But is it inauthentic? I've never thought so. If inauthenticity depends on pretending you are something you're not, then Vegas has always been adamantly honest. It is all fake, all the time.

Vegas gets it. There's no escape from artifice. You can pretend you aren't performing, or you can admit you're performing, but either way you are always performing.

"Let me confess my preference for the real fakery of Las Vegas over the fake reality of Santa Fe," writes art critic Dave Hickey. "For the genuine rhinestone over the imitation pearl." That night at the Chandelier Bar, Vegas was a genuine rhinestone. It followed its fakery so far that it ended up being radically honest. Even if it was trying too hard, it wasn't trying to be something it wasn't. Sure, it was lowbrow and absurd. Sure, it was tasteless. But fuck the snobs of taste. Why disdain Vegas for openly admitting what was already true everywhere? The whole world was making promises it couldn't keep. The whole world was out to scam you. Vegas was just upfront about it. It put marquee lights around it. To me, Vegas felt like the urban-planning equivalent of the homeless man we passed whose sign said: WHY LIE? I WANT BEER.

Maybe I was just drawn to the city because I liked finding beauty in what others found ugly. My awe at the Bellagio fountains wanted to believe it was compensating for someone else's disgust. Vegas understood that any time you were somewhere, there were a thousand elsewheres you might be longing for. So it jammed them together: New York–New York, Paris, the Tropicana, the Mirage. Its glaring neon landscapes were an articulation of collective longing. It acknowledged how much of our lives we spend looking toward illusory, impossible horizons. It suggested that this longing was not delusion, but one of our central truths. It constituted us.

When I got back to my New Haven winter, Joe and I started writing to each other. We turned our lives into stories and lobbed them back and forth. He told me about breaking into the Circus Circus midway after hours and playing free Skee-Ball in its empty aisles. He told me about shattering a bunch of empty bottles by throwing them off his balcony one night. I imagined his glowing city from the middle of my Connecticut blizzards. When I told my friends about him, I started calling him Vegas Joe. This wasn't dismissal, exactly. It was more like an acknowledgment of the ways that I had already cast him as a character in the story I was trying to write about this next chapter of my life. He was the mascot of Possibility in Aftermath.

We agreed to meet in Boston, at the massive annual writers' conference that I annually dreaded attending. That year I was desperate to get there. I dug my car out of three feet of snow and fishtailed down icy highways. The swell of potential worked on me like a drug, blocking out everything else: the pelting sleet, the black ice, the road slipping under my tires. I cranked up my radio: "I'm living on such sweet nothing." Joe kept texting, "Don't die!" He texted: "When will you get here?"

We booked a room that night. Because the conference had filled the hotel, the only room left was the Presidential Suite. We got it cheap because it was already 10:00 p.m. and it wasn't occupied. It was huge, with three rooms and panoramic views of downtown Boston's glassy skyscrapers. It didn't even have a bed, because it was used exclusively for large corporate cocktail parties. It had a wet bar and sectional leather couches. We ordered a trundle bed and a bucket of seafood: crab legs, oysters, lobster tail. We didn't sleep much.

After that night we found ourselves in a state I knew well: the giddy rush of offering ourselves to each other. To start, we offered each other rough transcriptions of the ragged emotional arcs of our last long-term relationships. He wrote about driving out to a ghost town on the shores of the Salton Sea: the gutted homes full of plates, a flock of white pelicans. He wrote: "Here's to unbland wellness," a phrase I'd used in an essay about an author who'd been afraid that sobriety would make him bland for good. I wondered if I was falling in love. I wondered if I was built exclusively to fall in love. I worried, sometimes, that I was built more to *fall* in love than to *be* in love. But didn't everyone worry about that? You couldn't think your way past it. You just had to keep falling in love, over and over again, and hope that it stuck once, to prove it could.

A few weeks after getting back from Boston, I visited the Yale architecture library, looking for a book called *Every Building on the Sunset Strip*. Published in 1966 by the artist Ed Ruscha, it is an accordion style art book that unfolds to a length of twenty-five feet. As its title promises, it documents every building on the Sunset Strip between Doheny and Crescent Heights: motor inns, faux Tudor cottages, a big shed called Body Shop Burlesque, a smaller shed called Sea Witch, a café called the Plush Pup. The book had helped inspire the Yale Vegas seminar. When Venturi and Scott Brown took their students to Vegas in 1968, they drove the length of the Strip with a camera mounted on the hood of their car, just as Ruscha had done on Sunset two years earlier.

I was drawn to the premise of Ruscha's book for the same reason I'd been drawn to the premise of the Vegas seminar: both wanted to find beauty in the same bric-a-brac sprawl that others called the epitome of ugliness. This was part of my heritage. All my life I'd been told I didn't seem like a person from Los Angeles. But all my life I'd been a person from Los Angeles. The more frequently I was told I didn't seem to be from L.A., the more strongly I wanted to defend it. It was a place other people loved to call shallow or fake, but I found its strip malls and their parking lots oddly gorgeous: sunlight glimmering off gritty streets, palm trees silhouetted against smoggy sunsets.

Ruscha's book made me want to walk the Vegas Strip from north to south, four miles total, and take notes on all of it. I would find the blueprints of collective fantasy. The project started gathering the force of an ethical repo job. I'd salvage meaning from what others had called blight. But who was I kidding? I also wanted a reason to go see Vegas Joe.

I hatched a plan. A friend of mine was getting married at Zion

National Park in early July, just a three-hour drive from Vegas, and I would go out a few days early to stay with Joe and walk the Strip. Then he and I would go to her wedding together.

A few weeks before the visit, Vegas Joe told me he had bedbugs. He was trying to get rid of them by cranking his heater in 110-degree weather and opening all his windows. I knew it wouldn't work. You needed professional temperatures. But the longer his bedbug saga dragged on, the more I started to suspect he enjoyed something about the battle. Once it became clear that his bedbugs were ongoing, I booked a room for forty-nine dollars at the Flamingo. A few days before my flight, Vegas Joe sent me a photograph of his thigh with three dots of dried blood neatly aligned across his pale flesh. It was the signature trio of bedbug bites that the internet called "breakfast, lunch, and dinner." I recoiled from the image—not so much the image itself as the threshold crossing that it seemed to signify. We were no longer awestruck strangers watching a dancing fountain, or new lovers perched fifteen stories above Boston. Now we were talking about our bug infestations. His notes made me itch. It was as if his little bugs were powerful enough to reach my brick row house across the country. I was no longer sure I wanted him that close.

From the moment I stepped into Joe's Jeep, outside the baggage carousels at McCarran, I felt the whole endeavor suffocating under the weight of our expectations: four months of notes and daydreams, all built from one night by a shark tank and another spent in a skyscraper surrounded by the crystalline lights of office buildings. All that fervor had been the intimacy of two curated selves culled from the mess of two actual selves. But this was something else: the sweltering desert evening, the smell of him, the awkwardness of trying to speak to each other in his front seat after months of speaking to each other without our bodies hanging around. I tried to remember that first night in his Jeep but could access only a memory that gleamed like a sparkling awning, a night I'd already conscripted into personal mythology: *the night I knew I would survive my breakup.* As soon as I got into his car, I started wondering if it might be best for me to go to my friend's wedding alone.

We drove down Paradise Road, the street running behind the huge hotels like a desolate backyard. It had shops selling uniforms for casino dealers and costumes for strippers. It was full of the detritus that had fallen off the edges of the dream. One billboard asked: INJURED IN A HOTEL? and suggested www.injuredinahotel.com. A vasectomy ad bragged NO SCALPEL NO NEEDLE at www.ez-snip.com. At the airport, I had overheard a man telling a stranger about his battle with cancer. "They took out my bladder and made me a new one from a fifteen-inch piece of my small intestine," he'd said. "Everything works great now."

I kept imagining bedbugs in the back of the Jeep, folding their tiny bodies into the crevices of my suitcase zippers and pockets. I vaguely understood that Joe's bedbugs had become a kind of psychic stand-in for his actual and flawed humanity: all the parts of him that could not be sculpted and viewed from a comfortable distance, all the parts that were imperfect or vulnerable or struggling, trying to get his depression medications right.

He spent the night with me at the Flamingo. We lay together in a king bed that suggested certain stories—an illicit tryst between lovers, a drunken night between strangers, a wedding anniversary—but we lived another kind of story. Our bodies didn't touch at all.

* * *

What I saw when I finally walked the Strip: the Palazzo, the Venetian, the Mirage. Treasure Island, the Wynn, the Encore. Circus Circus. New York–New York. Mandalay Bay. Hooters in the distance. An animatronic Atlantis, drowning and rising every hour. A recovery meeting in a Riviera conference room that smelled like stale popcorn, where a man said it was tough for him to stay sober as an electronica DJ. What else? Jeff Koons's tulips with their own security guard. Signs advertising yoga with dolphins. A prize booth called the Redemption Center that I turned into my Twitter backdrop.

I saw a homeless man sitting in the triangular shade of a Catholic church who asked me what kind of God I believed in, then said he wanted to show me his scar but didn't want to give me nightmares. I saw a dad on crutches beside an aisle of carnival games, his wheelchair piled with the stuffed animals he'd won for his kids: a robot, a banana. I saw a T-shirt bearing the silhouette of a stripper that said I SUPPORT SINGLE MOMS, then overheard a mom telling her son, "We have to go to another branch of this fucking stupid-ass bank." A man exiting the Luxor, suspicious of the daylight, asked his friend: "Why are we going outside?" Beyond the casino doors, it was 110 degrees in the shade. A dry fountain eager to defend itself said DUE TO DROUGHT. Even illusion had its limits.

Vegas no longer seemed like a rhinestone unfairly victimized by highbrow snobbery. It was a machine designed to make money. Its cheesiness was the ultimate capitalist enterprise. Its profit margins came layered in curtains of crystals, millions of untenable promises: every bulb, every steak, every shark in every shark tank. Even if I admired the honesty of the homeless man whose sign told the truth—WHY LIE? I WANT BEER—I had no desire to defend the economic system that had made him homeless in the first place. But who was I to cry false consciousness on the strangers in two hundred thousand hotel rooms all around me, to say they didn't understand their own plight? What did it mean that everyone kept losing their money but believed they were having a good time?

After one of Siegfried & Roy's white tigers attacked Roy onstage at the Mirage in 2003, Roy kept telling everyone that Montecore hadn't meant him any harm. Montecore had just been trying to protect him. At first the live audience didn't know the attack had not been a planned part of the show. A ten-year-old British boy buried his face in his mother's sleeve. "I tried to tell him it would be okay and that it wasn't real, because this was supposed to be magic," she told one reporter. During the days afterward, her son kept saying: "You said it wasn't real, Mummy." In a land where everything was supposed to be fake, the arrival of reality functioned as the betrayal of a promise, an upending of the deal, a reversal of the plan.

During my days at the Flamingo, I woke up early each morning to work on copyedits for a book deadline. The dirty room-service dishes of strangers stayed in my hotel hallway for days, untouched: the fudge sauce–smeared remains of a brownie sundae, desolate lumps in a filmy puddle of melted ice cream. Had the people who'd ordered that sundae gotten what they wanted? I assumed everyone had been wounded by the same boom-bust cycle I'd let myself be disappointed by.

Lining up for coffee in the lobby casino at 6:30 in the morning, I stood exclusively with people who'd been up all night. The whole place smelled like coconut sunscreen and smoke. One man in line—strung out, dead tired—looked at me with pity. "Good luck," he said softly, gently touching my elbow. I took my coffee to the thick heat of the flamingo garden, where the air stank of birds and their shit. I felt so sad at the sight of a woman smoking—in such heat, so early in the morning, among flamingos—that it took me a moment to remember I was smoking, too.

While I was working on my copyedits by the hotel pool, in the blazing sun, a leathery man spotted a leathery woman across the field of plastic chaise longues. "You are a *beast!*" he yelled. "Get me a club soda." A thirteen-year-old boy wore a T-shirt down to his knees printed with two boxes marked TAKEN and SINGLE. The latter was checked. People measured the price of things in terms of blackjack hands: "I could lose that in six." At closing time, people at the pool got upset. A man threw his inflatable beach ball at a lifeguard. In a city that advertised twenty-four-hour-a-day pleasure, the next best thing to immortality, every closing time was a little death.

After he got off work, Joe took me to a fondue restaurant tucked inside the Forum Shops at Caesars Palace. Everything was simultaneously too much—chocolate-chip cookies, dipped in chocolate fondue—and not enough. I was irritated by the way Joe kept cutting me off in the middle of my sentences. His medication meant he had no appetite, and that irritated me, too. I was easily irritated. He was saying something about nihilism, how all meaning was subjective and constructed and there was no core from which…but I wasn't following, totally. I was watching the flames curl from pink crystals below the fondue pot, leaning so close my hair almost caught on fire. The waiter smiled at me knowingly. He said it happened every day. I told Joe that maybe he shouldn't come to the wedding with me after all. It was too much, too soon. What I couldn't say to him: *You were an idea. Now you're here.* He told me he was working on a novel about an alternate universe where all the Vegas hotels had been converted into prisons. I'd converted Joe into Vegas Joe, but it turned out he was an actual person. He was funny and handsome and kind but he was also struggling, he was also *real*—he needed things, he was unsure about others—and when I was around him there was a lump in my throat that I couldn't stop swallowing, a longing not for the man in front of me, but for the man who wasn't.

In the book that emerged from their Vegas seminar, Venturi and Scott

Brown argue that the signs on a commercial strip are more important than the buildings they advertise: "The sign at the front is a vulgar extravaganza; the building at the back, a modest necessity." This kind of persuasion is also the logic of long-distance daydreams. There can be truth in these dreams, in that signage—and even beauty. But the architecture of persuasion is also the opposite of proximity and inhabitance. Which is all to say: After pulling off the highway, I didn't know how to dwell in the building I'd chosen. Joe was the real smoke at the end of a fake cigarette, but I wasn't ready for another person's full humanity. We had been something far apart that we were not able to be together.

At my friend's bachelorette party the next night—in a suite at the Venetian, fifteen floors above a chlorinated Grand Canal—other women took turns describing the annoying habits of their Sig Os and passed around glasses of cheap champagne. I no longer drank champagne, or had a Sig O to be annoyed by. After dark, we strolled out of the cloud-painted Venetian sky and into the Vegas night, wearing our sparkly tiaras, walking past what appeared to be a pile of bloody rags bunched against the curb, above a drain pipe.

At the "Thunder from Down Under" male revue, under glittering disco lights at the Excalibur, a firefighter, a construction worker, a doctor, a soldier, and a milkman peeled away their uniforms to show their glinting six-packs. Baby-oiled bodies in the strobe-lit darkness collapsed the distinction between being there ironically and just being there. The emcee had a huge sobriety tattoo inked across one of his biceps—GOD GRANT ME THE SERENITY—and made an old woman cup his balls through his shiny leather pants.

As we walked home along the Strip, an SUV full of women pulled up beside us. One leaned her head out the window and asked: "Which one's the bride?" We pointed her out—with the largest tiara, and the veil—and all the women started shouting: "Don't do it!" Before they sped away, they said: "We're all divorced!"

The next time I went to Vegas, I got married there. It was just fifteen months later. I'd moved to New York and fallen in love with a man who had grown up in Vegas, the son of two pawnbrokers. Everyone he met was surprised to learn that he'd actually grown up in Vegas—that anyone had. But he did. He spent his childhood rolling quarters in the back of his parents' shops, hearing them get called dirty Jews by angry customers, watching them work seven days a week for their entire lives to give their four kids more opportunities than they'd had themselves.

For Charles, Vegas wasn't an outsized metaphor for impossible dreams or their deflation. It was Saturday-morning cartoons, and Slurpees from the 7-Eleven melting in the ruthless desert sunlight. It was playing high-school basketball at the same courts where the Runnin' Rebels played pickup games, back in the days of Tark the Shark, the legendary UNLV coach who gnawed on a wet towel when he got nervous. Vegas was where Charles and his father had cruised up I-15 with the radio tuned to the prizefights at Caesars Palace. It was where he'd made his own backyard boxing ring out of paper strips—a child inspired by the particular materials of his world, because it was the world he knew.

Charles and I met at the workspace in downtown Manhattan where we both wrote. He introduced himself by asking me to translate my tattoo. He had eleven tattoos of his own, the most recent of which was his five-year-old daughter's name, scrawled in blue across his forearm. He'd promised her that after she wrote her name for the first time, he would get it printed permanently on his skin. I would come to understand that he was always good to his word.

When we first met, I already knew his work. I'd read his first book years earlier, a big sprawling novel about Vegas that I loved for its tender evocation of outsiders: teen runaways sleeping on the streets, awkward adolescent boys who lived for their comic books, pawnbrokers mocked by their customers. And his own personal story was well known in our shared literary world. His wife had been diagnosed with leukemia when their daughter, Lily, was just six months old. She'd died just before Lily's third birthday.

The first time Charles and I talked, we talked for hours. It felt, as they say, like we could have talked forever. Except we couldn't talk forever, because Charles had to pick up Lily from after-school at five. During that first conversation, I told him about a ritual I'd taken part in a few months earlier, at a residency in Wyoming: on the night of a full moon, we'd all brought empty purses and wallets into an open meadow and asked the universe for something specific we wanted. I'd asked to care less about worldly success. At the time, this had seemed like a very enlightened thing to ask for. The guy who went after me asked for a motorcycle. Charles laughed at that, as I'd hoped—nervous—he would. When I asked Charles what he thought Lily would request during a full-moon ritual, he said she'd probably ask for a plastic ice castle. Then he paused and said, "Honestly, she would ask for a mom."

This was vintage Charles: willing to state the truth bluntly, jocular about pain because he'd lived it so fully, deeply aware of life as something simultaneously full of trauma and plastic ice castles. He asked if we could meet up again soon and do our own full-moon ritual in the communal kitchen of our workspace. I told him I would bring the empty purses if he supplied the full moon. The next time we met, at a little table by the coffee machine, he tacked up an illustration he and Lily had made together: three jagged mountains cut from brown construction paper, and a round yellow moon hanging above them.

On our first date, Charles took me out for a seven-course Italian meal, but we had to skip the last two courses so he could get back by the time he'd promised the sitter. Our second date was a midday tryst while Lily was at school. We made out in my apartment all morning and then got turkey sandwiches from the bodega at the end of my block, ate them on the grassy strip of Eastern Parkway with plastic bottles of lemonade and a box of the chicken-and-waffle crackers he loved as a child. Our third date was a road trip to the Catskills while Lily was staying with her grandmother. I booked a last-minute room at a tiny bed-and-breakfast where our room was full of animal prints and photographs of Siegfried & Roy, unmauled and beaming. Those days in the Catskills were full of morning walks down a muddy road, messy with spring thaw, to a tiny highway diner where we got eggs and bacon so salty it stung the tiny cut in my mouth. On that trip, we found bliss in all the smallest things. We bought the best snacks at gas stations: licorice and sour cherry balls. We wondered at the albino tigers on our walls. We could riff back and forth on a joke for ten minutes straight, then return to it a day later, riff a little more. Charles was candid about difficulty, and he was funnier than anyone I'd ever met.

In certain ways, the pattern of our early months—our passionate descent into love—looked like other relationships I'd had. But I trusted it more. From the start, our love was embedded in the business of daily living, in all its scattered rag dolls and bake sales and meltdowns and rubber toys under your feet before you flicked on the bathroom light in the middle of the night. Our romance wasn't charged by the possibility of total abandon; it was electrified by borders and edges. It was less about engaging with curated versions of each other and more about inhabiting ordinary days that summoned our whole selves: scattered, overwhelmed, trying. Our story wasn't about getting the skyscraper suite just because we felt like it. It was about finding pockets of effervescence in the midst of daily life—waking up on a red futon in his tiny rent-controlled apartment, kissing first thing in the morning in the shadow of a four-foot-high plastic dollhouse.

In the abstract, our love looked tethered by obligation and trauma; by the demands of raising a child, and the long shadow of loss. But there was another truth lurking under all that difficulty: a felt experience of love that didn't follow any of the scripts I'd spent my life craving. This love lived in fits of midnight laughter on a futon with a too-small blanket. It lived in an hourly motel near the Hudson, with a sitter at home and a mirror on the ceiling of our room. It lived in the shared language of days contoured by after-school pickup and ballet-class leotards, by Saturday-morning chocolate-chip pancakes and tuna melts at their favorite diner.

I'd somehow rocketed straight from single life—smoking alone on my stoop, lost to daydreams and self-pity—into this life of accountability and intimate beholdenness. It was as if I'd taken a shortcut on the banana-yellow path of the Game of Life, which we often played on the living-room carpet that Lily called "Snow Rug, Throw Rug"; as if I'd jumped straight to the family portion of the game board rather than stopping in my little plastic car and spinning the plastic wheel for my own plastic babies. Instead I'd jumped into someone else's plastic car. Now I was living out of a suitcase wedged into the corner of his crowded living room.

After barely six months together, Charles and I decided to elope to Vegas. Almost every way you looked at it, this was reckless. I had no idea what it meant to be a mother, much less what it meant to mother a child who'd lost her mother. But Charles trusted that I was capable of showing up for this life, and I wanted to show up for it—for him, and for Lily, and for myself. I trusted him because when I looked at him I saw a man who had been showing up for the people he loved, even through unimaginable pain, for years. It was our extraordinary ordinary life—this life made of actual days, striated by obligation—that we were committing to with our improbable wedding, our clandestine joy.

We got married at A Little White Chapel, under the glowing heart, beyond the Astroturf. Lily was having a sleepover at her cousin's house. We showed up at the cashier's desk—past the pink Cadillac, past the Tunnel of Love and the drive-through window—and said: "Marry us!" The woman at the register said we needed to go to City Hall for a license. What had I been expecting? One-stop shopping, I suppose, especially at a place that advertised its twenty-four-hour drive-through window. I asked the woman at the register how many people never came back once they found out they needed to go to the courthouse. She thought for a moment, then said, "Maybe fifty percent?"

When we returned with our license in hand, just before eleven, we did not purchase the flower package or the Elvis impersonator. We did not rent the pink Cadillac. We did not have our ceremony in the Chapel L'Amour, or the Crystal Chapel, or the gazebo. We did not drive our rental car under the cherubs painted across the ceiling of the Tunnel of Love. We did it old-school style, in the original chapel, while "Fools Rush In" played from speakers we could not see. The back wall looked like a quilted comforter, upholstered with white silk. Statues of cherubs held tumbling bouquets of fake white flowers. There were stained-glass windows showing roses, hearts, and doves. None of this felt wrong. It felt—weirdly, improbably—right. If I was hurling myself into something entirely unknown, with no idea what the terrain would look like, then it seemed appropriate to do it someplace so utterly strange. It was almost freeing, like an acknowledgment of all the ways I couldn't have predicted how my life would turn out.

By the end of the ceremony, we had tears in our eyes. The photographer was the witness. Father Someone quoted Nietzsche: "It is not a lack of love, but a lack of friendship, that makes unhappy marriages." He did not quote Nietzsche saying, "We ought not to be permitted to come to a decision affecting our whole life while we are in the condition of being in love."

We were in the condition. I wore a long blue-and-white dress that Charles had given me for my birthday that summer. It looked like clouds. My red nail polish was chipped. I tried to capture both our faces in a selfie with two painted turtles whose wrinkled necks stretched out from their shells so their small heads could touch.

Back at the Golden Nugget, where we were staying, we got cupcakes in the lobby. We ordered room-service steak. I told Charles that the sharks in the aquarium had once struck me as a symbol of wonder and possibility. He said their tank had been built on the land where his grandfather's first pawnshop once stood. When we tried to go swimming at the third-story infinity pool, we were told it was closing at midnight, in five minutes. A boy who looked sixteen told us so. "But we just got married!" we said. He looked unfazed. He probably heard that every night.

The next year we would have a ceremony in the woods, with a treasure hunt for a feral pack of blissful children. It would be like a postcard that day: all our people and their toddlers, wading into the glittering water. But that night we had only the absurdity of our little white chapel, our fever dream turned actual, with Father Someone consecrating our love. That night it was just us. It was just ours.

One definition of living might be the perpetual swapping of story lines. We trade in the scripts we've written for ourselves and get our real lives in return. This is what Vegas did to me—what it did *for* me. It swallowed up the story I'd written about falling in love one night by the Bellagio fountain, and gave me another story to live instead: the story of marrying a widower and helping him raise his daughter, a story in which heading back to Vegas meant visiting the in-laws and waking up to ordinary life. It meant spending more time downtown and less time on the Strip.

In that Vegas, we took Lily and her cousin Diamond to the arcade games at Circus Circus, where the Redemption Center was no longer an ironic Twitter backdrop but a physical place where I begged the woman behind the counter to replace the whoopee cushion Lily had lost beneath the twirling bodies of four Brazilian acrobats. In that Vegas, we ate soft serve in the parking lot of Luv-it Frozen Custard, while the girls pretended to hold mistletoe over our heads until we kissed. We got lost on the drive to Lake Mead, and never made it to the water: the girls grew bored in the back seat while the desert darkened around our wrong highway.

In that Vegas, Lily and I watched strangers ride on zip lines over the commotion of Fremont Street — full of panhandlers and buskers, men painted in silver and moving their limbs like robots, casinos blasting air-conditioning into sweltering summer heat — and I said, "Someday we'll do it ourselves," and Lily's small body pressed against mine, trembling with fear and desire. We spent hours waiting for a tow-truck driver after a German tourist named Wolfgang Hamburger sideswiped us near the base of the Stratosphere, in a rental car with tinted windows covered in love graffiti: *W. Hamburger* scribbled inside a big pink heart. He was in town to celebrate his twenty-fourth wedding anniversary. Vegas never made this shit up. It simply invited me to bring doughnuts to my mother-in-law at her pawnshop — its glass cases full of turquoise jewelry, dice clocks, and old war medals — where the walls were decorated with racing silks from a horse jockey her dad used to bet on, and the patchy carpet existed under the benevolent rule of a huge cat wandering among the furs hanging in back. In that Vegas, after five years of watching strangers on the zip lines, Lily and I finally did it ourselves: White Castle to the right and straight on till morning.

So much of the pleasure of Vegas — for me, at first — was about possibility, about wanting and longing, about imagining what *could be*. The pleasure of Vegas Joe was all about anticipation. It was the pleasure of fishtailing down wintry roads, trying to reach him in Boston, spending a night in a room at the top of the world and then imagining fruit-bowl shades of neon from my studio apartment during blizzards. That first night was better without the kiss, because that way I still got to imagine what the kiss would be like.

For years I'd been an expert at longing, an expert at loving from the state of not-quite-having, an expert at daydreaming and sinking back into the plush furniture of cinematic imagining. But from those early years with Charles I learned that marriage was something else. It was composed of the pleasures of dwelling, which were harder and thicker than the pleasures of conjuring. Marriage wasn't the bliss of possibility. It was the more complicated satisfaction of actually living and actually having. It was a view not from the top of the world but from the base of the Stratosphere, while we tried to understand what Wolfgang Hamburger was saying about his rental insurance. It was about realizing that when his spray-painted heart proclaimed decades of devotion, those years weren't full of the absence of longing so much as its constant renewal, its acrobatics, its shapeshifting.

Marriage isn't telling your best stories to a new lover; it's asking your husband about his day and not glazing over at his reply. Marriage isn't walking past the shark tank at one in the morning, stomach full of butterflies at the prospect of kissing someone new: an unknown taste, an unknown body. It's walking past the shark tank at nine in the morning, scouring the potted plants for the wooden nutcracker your six-year-old stepdaughter lost the night before. Marriage isn't months of fantasy. It's years of cleaning out the fridge. For a long time, I had admired the art of showing up—in my friends, my mother, my brother, the other folks in recovery meetings—but it's one thing to admire how other people live, and another thing to try to live that way yourself: not waiting for love to stick, as if love itself could do the work, but waking up to support it each day—knowing it can't promise to be anything forever, except something that is always changing.

Marriage is what happens when you take the ride despite the SUV full of women who told you, *Don't;* despite the fact that you may someday be one of them. Marriage is what happens when the mirage shimmers away to reveal plain asphalt straight ahead. It's everything you keep trying to summon faith in, and it delivers you to what you couldn't have imagined: past that first flush of falling in love, to all the other kinds of love that lie ahead. You may never reach Lake Mead, but you'll always have the drive itself—that particular glow of evening sun baking the highway, setting the cars on fire, light brighter than you can stand to look at, and already holding the night.

Daughter of a Ghost

W hen she was six, my stepdaughter told me that her favorite character in *Cinderella* was the evil stepmother. This wasn't entirely surprising. During playdates, Lily often liked to play orphan, writing down long lists of chores: *dichs* (dishes); *moping* (mopping); *feeding* (the fish). She and a friend liked to drink something they called "pepper water," which was ordinary tap water they pretended their cruel orphan-handlers had made undrinkable. Maybe it was thrilling to stage her own mistreatment, to take power over the situation of powerlessness she had imagined. Maybe she just liked a virtuous reason to dump water on the floor. When I asked Lily why Cinderella's stepmother was her favorite character, she leaned close to me and whispered, like a secret, "I think she looks *good*."

For all her cruelty, the evil stepmother is often the fairy-tale character most defined by imagination and determination, rebelling against the patriarchy with whatever meager tools have been left to her: her magic mirror, her vanity, her pride. She is an artist of cunning and malice, but still—an artist. She isn't simply acted upon; she acts. She just doesn't act the way a mother is supposed to. That's her fuel, and her festering heart.

In many ways, fairy tales—dark and ruthless, usually structured by loss—were the stories that most resembled Lily's life. Her mother died just before her third birthday, after a two-and-a-half-year struggle with leukemia. Two years later, Lily got a stepmother of her own—not a wicked one, perhaps, but one terrified of being wicked.

I wondered if it was comforting for Lily to hear stories about fairy-tale children who had lost what she had lost—unlike most of the kids at her school, or in her ballet classes, whose mothers were still alive. Or perhaps it brought the stories dangerously close, the fact that she shared so much with their heroines. Maybe it peeled away their protective skins of fantasy, made their pepper water too literal, brought their perils too near. When I read her the old fairy tales about daughters without mothers, I worried that I was pressing on the bruises of her loss. When I read her the old fairy tales about stepmothers, I worried I was reading her an evil version of myself.

When I first became a stepmother, I was hungry for company. I didn't know many stepmothers, and I especially didn't know many stepmothers who had inherited the role as I had inherited it: fully, over-whelmingly, with no other mother in the picture. Our family lived in the aftermath of loss, not rupture—death, not divorce. This used to be the normal way of being a stepmother, and the word itself holds grief in its roots. The Old English *steop* means "loss," and the etymology paints a bleak portrait: "For stepmoder is selde guod," reads one account from 1290. Another text, from 1598, says, "With one consent all stepmothers hate their daughters."

The fairy tales are obviously damning. The evil queen from "Snow White" demands the secret murder of her stepdaughter after a magic mirror proclaims the girl's superior beauty. The stepmother from "Hansel and Gretel" sends her stepchildren into the woods because there isn't enough to eat. Cinderella sits amid her fireplace cinders, sorting peas from lentils, her ash-speckled body appeasing a wicked stepmother who wants to dull her luminosity with soot because she feels threatened by it. It's as if the stepmother relationship inevitably corrupts—it is not just an evil woman in the role but a role that turns any woman evil. A "stepmother's blessing" is another name for a hangnail, as if to suggest something that hurts because it isn't properly attached, something that presents itself as a substitutive love but ends up bringing pain instead.

The evil stepmother casts a long, primal shadow, and five years ago I moved in with that shadow, to a one-bedroom rent-controlled apartment near Gramercy Park. I sought the old stories in order to find company—out of sympathy for the stepmothers they vilified—and to resist their narratives, to inoculate myself against the darkness they held.

The early days of my relationship with Charles, Lily's father, held the kind of love that fairy tales ask us to believe in: encompassing and surprising, charged by a sense of wonder at the sheer fact of his existence in the world. I uprooted my life for our love, without regret. Our bliss lived in a thousand ordinary moments: a first kiss in the rain, over-easy eggs at a roadside diner, crying with laughter at midnight about some stupid joke he would make during an *American Ninja Warrior* rerun. But our love also held the art and work of parenting, and much of our bliss happened on stolen time: that first kiss while the sitter stayed half an hour late; those diner eggs on a spontaneous road trip possible only because Lily was staying with her grandmother in Memphis; our hands clamped over our mouths during those fits of midnight laughter so we wouldn't wake Lily in the next room. This felt less like compromise and more like off-roading, veering onto terrain I'd never imagined.

I approached the first evening I spent with Lily as a kind of test, though Charles tried to stack the deck in my favor: he decided we would get takeout from the pasta place Lily liked, then spend the evening watching her favorite movie—an animated film about two princess sisters, one with a touch that turned everything to ice. That afternoon, I went to find a gift at the Disney Store in Times Square—not only a place I had never been but a place I had never imagined going. I hated the idea of bribing Lily, trading plastic for affection, but I was desperately nervous. Plastic felt like an insurance policy.

The clerk looked at me with pity when I asked for the *Frozen* section. I suddenly doubted myself: Was it not a Disney movie? The clerk laughed when I asked, then explained: "We just don't have any merchandise left. There's a worldwide shortage."

She was serious. They had nothing. Not even a tiara. Or they had plenty of tiaras, but they weren't the right tiaras. I scanned the shelves around me: Belle stuff, Sleeping Beauty stuff, Princess Jasmine stuff. Lily had to like other movies, right? Other princesses? There was a moment when I considered buying something related to *every* princess, just to cover my bases. I had some vague realization that the low-level panic in the back of my throat was the fuel capitalism ran on. On my cell phone, I was on hold with a Toys"R"Us in the Bronx. On my way out, I spotted something shoved into the corner of a shelf. It looked wintry. It had ice-blue cardboard packaging: a sled.

I cannot even tell you my relief. My sense of victory was complete. The sled came with a princess, and also maybe a prince. (A Sami ice harvester, I would learn.) The set came with a reindeer! (Named Sven.) It even came with a plastic carrot for him to eat. I tucked the box under my arm protectively as I walked to the register. I eyed the other parents around me. Who knew how many of them wanted this box?

I called Charles, triumphant. I told him the whole saga: the clerk's laughter, the *worldwide shortage,* the frantic phone calls, the sudden grace of glimpsing that pale-blue cardboard.

"You won!" he said, then paused. I could hear him deciding whether to say something. "The princess," he asked, "what color is her hair?"

I had to check the box. "Brown?" I said. "Sort of reddish?"

"You did great," he said after a beat. "You're the best."

But in that beat, I could hear that I'd gotten the wrong princess. Charles wasn't criticizing; he just knew how much a princess could mean. He had spent the last two years knee-deep in princesses, playing mother and father at once. The truth of the wrong princess was also the truth of unstable cause and effect. With parenting, you could do everything you were supposed to and it still might backfire, because you lived with a tiny, volatile human who did not come with any kind of instruction manual. The possibility of failure hung like a low sky, pending weather, over every horizon.

In his book *The Uses of Enchantment*, the psychoanalyst Bruno Bettelheim makes a beautiful argument for the kinds of reckoning that fairy tales permit: they allow children to face primal fears (like parental abandonment) and imagine acts of rebellion (like defying authority) in a world reassuringly removed from the one they live in. Enchanted woods and castles are so conspicuously fantastical, their situations so extreme, that children don't need to feel destabilized by their upheavals. I wondered if that was still true for Lily, whose loss showed up more frequently in fairy tales than in the world around her. It can be a fine line between stories that give our fears a necessary stage and stories that deepen them—that make us more afraid.

In an 1897 letter to the editor in *Outlook*, a high-circulation American lifestyle magazine, one correspondent lamented the effects of reading "Cinderella" to young children: "The effect or impression was to put stepmothers on the list of evil things of life." But in our home, it was less that "Cinderella" put stepmothers on an evil list and more that the story raised the question—with a kind of openness that might otherwise have been impossible—of whether stepmothers belonged there. Often, Lily used the figure of a fairy-tale wicked stepmother to distinguish our relationship from the one we had just read. "You're not like her," she would say. Or when it came to the stepmother she admired from "Cinderella," she was generous: "You look better than her anyway."

Perhaps claiming the stepmother as her favorite character was a way for Lily to grasp the source of her fears and take some control over them. Perhaps it was another version of playing orphans. Did she worry I would turn cruel? Did she love me fiercely so I wouldn't? I wondered if it helped her to see us reflected and distorted by a dark mirror, if these more sinister versions of our bond made her feel better about our relationship—or gave her permission to accept what might feel hard about it. I found a strange comfort in the nightmare visions of mean stepparents I found in popular media—at least I wasn't cruel like them. It was a kind of ethical schadenfreude.

In many ways, the stories my family inherited mapped imperfectly onto ours. In fairy tales, the father-king was often duped and blind. He had faith in a woman who didn't deserve it. His trust, or his lust, permitted his daughter's mistreatment. Charles was like these fairy-tale fathers in only one way: he trusted me from the beginning. He believed I could be a mother before I believed it. He talked openly about what was hard about parenting, which made it feel more possible to live in love and difficulty—love *as* difficulty. He knew what it meant to wake up day after day, choose three possible dresses, pour the cereal, repour the cereal after it spilled, wrestle hair into pigtails, get to school on time, get to pickup on time, steam the broccoli for dinner. He knew how much it meant to learn the difference between the animated ponies with wings and the animated ponies with horns and the animated ponies with *both*—the alicorns. He knew what it meant to do all that, then wake up the next day and do it all over again.

My relationship with Lily, too, was not like the story we inherited from fairy tales—a tale of cruelty and rebellion—or even like the story of divorce-era popular media: the child spurning her stepmother, rejecting her in favor of the true mother, the mother of the bloodline and womb. Our story wasn't about rejection; it was about pure, primal, overwhelming need. I was never going to replace her mom, but I was here. I was something. We were forging a story of our own—a story built from a hundred tiny conversations on the 6 train, built from painting Lily's nails and trying not to smudge her tiny pinkie, built from telling her to take deep breaths during tantrums, because I needed to take deep breaths myself. Our story began that first night when I felt her small, hot hand reach for mine during the scene when the abominable snowman swirled into view on an icy mountain and almost overwhelmed the humble reindeer.

That night, when we sang songs at bedtime, she scooted over and patted the comforter, in the same bed where her mother had spent afternoons resting during the years of her illness, directly below the hole Charles had made—angrily swinging a toy train into the wall—after a telephone call with an insurance company, a hole now hidden behind an alphabet poster. "You lie here," Lily told me. "You lie in Mommy's spot."

If the wicked stepmother feels like a ready-made archetype, then its purest, darkest incarnation is the evil queen from "Snow White." In an 1857 version of the Brothers Grimm tale, she goes wild with jealousy and asks a hunter to bring back her stepdaughter's heart. After this attack fails (the hunter has a bleeding heart of his own), the stepmother's aggression takes the form of false generosity. She goes to her stepdaughter disguised as a beggar crone and offers Snow White items that seem helpful or nourishing: a corset, a comb, an apple. These are objects a mother might give her daughter—as forms of sustenance, or as ways of passing on a female legacy of self-care—but they are actually meant to kill her. They reach Snow White in the folds of her new surrogate family, where the seven dwarves have given her the opportunity to be precisely the kind of "good mother" her stepmother never was. Snow White cooks and cleans and cares for them. Her virtue is manifest in precisely the maternal impulse her stepmother lacks.

The evil stepmother is so integral to our familiar telling of "Snow White" that I was surprised to discover that an earlier version of the story doesn't feature a stepmother at all. In this version, Snow White has no dead mother, only a living mother who wants her dead. This was a pattern of revision for the Brothers Grimm; they transformed several mothers into stepmothers between the first version of their collected stories, published in 1812, and the final version, published in 1857. The figure of the stepmother effectively became a vessel for the emotional aspects of motherhood that were too ugly to attribute to mothers directly (ambivalence, jealousy, resentment) and those parts of a child's experience of her mother (as cruel, aggressive, withholding) that were too difficult to situate directly in the biological parent-child dynamic. The figure of the stepmother—lean, angular, harsh—was like snake venom drawn from an unacknowledged wound, siphoned out in order to preserve the healthy body of a maternal ideal.

"It is not only a means of preserving an internal all-good mother when the real mother is not all-good," Bettelheim argues, "but it also permits anger at this bad 'stepmother' without endangering the goodwill of the true mother, who is viewed as a different person." The psychologist D. W. Winnicott puts it more simply: "If there are two mothers, a real one who has died, and a stepmother, do you see how easily a child gets relief from tension by having one perfect and the other horrid?" In other words, the shadow figure of the fairy-tale stepmother is a predatory archetype reflecting something true of every mother: the complexity of her feelings toward her child, and her child's feelings toward her.

Even if Lily didn't split her ideas of motherhood into perfect absence and wicked presence, I did—assigning precisely that psychic division of labor. I imagined that her biological mother would have offered everything I couldn't always manage: patience, pleasure, compassion. She would have been *with* Lily in her tantrums, as we'd once been advised—a bit opaquely—by a therapist. Her real mother wouldn't have bribed her with ridiculous amounts of plastic. She wouldn't have gotten so frustrated when bedtime lasted an hour and a half, or else her frustration would have had the counterweight of an unconditional love I was still seeking. I knew these self-flagellations were ridiculous—even "real" parents weren't perfect—but they offered a certain easy groove of self-deprecation. A woman mothering another woman's child, Winnicott observes, "may easily find herself forced by her own imagination into the position of witch rather than of fairy godmother."

In a study called "The Poisoned Apple," the psychologist (and stepmother) Elizabeth Church analyzed her interviews with 104 stepmothers through the lens of one particular question: How do these women reckon with the evil archetype they stepped into? "Although their experience was the opposite of the fairy-tale stepmothers," she reported, insofar as "they felt powerless in the very situation where the fairy-tale stepmothers exerted enormous power," they still "tended to identify with the image of the wicked stepmother." She called it their poisoned apple. They felt "wicked" for experiencing feelings of resentment or jealousy, and this fear of their own "wickedness" prompted them to keep these feelings to themselves, which only made them feel more shame for having these feelings in the first place.

*　　*　　*

Folktales often deploy the stepmother as a token mascot of the dark maternal—a woman rebelling against traditional cultural scripts—but the particular history of the American stepmother is more complicated. As the historian Leslie Lindenauer argues in *I Could Not Call Her Mother: The Stepmother in American Popular Culture, 1750–1960*, the figure of the American stepmother found her origins in the American witch. Lindenauer posits that the eighteenth-century popular imagination took the same terrible attributes that the Puritans had ascribed to witches—malice, selfishness, coldness, absence of maternal impulse—and started assigning them to stepmothers instead. "Both were examples of women who, against God and nature, perverted the most essential qualities of the virtuous mother," Lindenauer observes. "Moreover, witches and stepmothers alike were most often accused of harming *other* women's children."

The stepmother became a kind of scapegoat, a new repository for aspects of femininity that had been threatening for a long time: female agency, female creativity, female restlessness, maternal ambivalence. By the late eighteenth century the stepmother was a stock villain, familiar enough to appear in grammar books. One boy was even injured by his dead stepmother *from beyond the grave* when a column above her tombstone fell on his head. The particular villainy of the stepmother—the duplicity of tyranny disguised as care—enabled colonial rhetoric that compared England's rule to "a stepmother's severity," as one 1774 tract put it. In an article that ran in *Ladies' Magazine* in 1773, on the eve of the American Revolution, a stepdaughter laments her fate at the hands of her stepmother: "Instead of the tender maternal affection...what do I now see but discontent, ill-nature, and mal-a-pert authority?" The stepmother offers bondage cunningly packaged as devotion.

But the American popular imagination hasn't always understood the stepmother as a wicked woman. If it was true that she was an eighteenth-century gold digger—a latter-day witch—then it was also true that she was a mid-nineteenth-century saint, happily prostrate to the surge of her own innate maternal impulse. In the Progressive Era, she was proof that being a good mother was less about saintly instincts and more about reason, observation, and rational self-improvement. You didn't have to have a biological connection—or even an innate caregiving impulse—you just had to *apply* yourself.

When I interviewed Lindenauer about her research, she told me that she had been surprised to discover these vacillations—particularly surprised to find the figure of the virtuous stepmother showing up in the very same women's magazines that had vilified her a few decades earlier. She eventually started to detect a pattern. It seemed as if the stepmother found redemption whenever the nuclear family was under siege: in the immediate aftermath of the Civil War, or when divorce emerged as a social phenomenon in the early twentieth century. The stepmother became a kind of "port in the storm," Lindenauer told me. "It's better to have a stepmother than no mother at all."

The golden era of the American stepmother archetype—the summit of her virtue—was the second half of the nineteenth century, during and after the Civil War, when sentimental novels and women's magazines were full of saintly stepmothers eager to care for the motherless children who stumbled into their laps. In Charlotte Yonge's 1862 novel, *The Young Step-Mother; or, A Chronicle of Mistakes,* the protagonist, Albinia, is portrayed as a woman with a surplus of goodwill, just waiting for people with needs (read: grief) deep enough to demand the deployment of her excess goodness. Her siblings worry about Albinia marrying a widower with children, afraid she will become a kind of indentured servant, but the novel reassures us that "her energetic spirit and love of children animated her to embrace joyfully the cares which such a choice must impose on her." When her new husband brings her home, he apologizes for what he is asking from her. "As I look at you, and the home to which I have brought you, I feel that I have acted selfishly," he says. But she won't let him apologize. "Work was always what I wished," she replies, "if only I could do anything to lighten your grief and care." With the children, Albinia doesn't simply say but truly *feels* all the right things: she is sorry they have her in place of their mother; they can call her Mother, but they don't have to. Although the novel is subtitled "A Chronicle of Mistakes," Albinia doesn't seem to make many.

When I read in the novel's epigraph, "Fail—yet rejoice," it felt like a lie and an impossible imperative at once. In fact, the entire voice of the saintly stepmother felt like an elaborate humblebrag. She knew she would always be second—or third! or fifth! or tenth!—but she didn't care. Not one bit. She just wanted to be useful. I thought I would be glad to discover the existence of these virtuous stepmothers, but instead I found them nearly impossible to accept—much harder to stomach than the wicked stepmothers in fairy tales. My poisoned apple wasn't the wicked stepmother but her archetypal opposite, the saint, whose innate virtue felt like the harshest possible mirror. It would always show me someone more selfless than I was. These stories forgot everything that was structurally difficult about this kind of bond, or else they insisted that virtue would overcome all. This is why fairy tales are more forgiving than sentimental novels. They let darkness into the frame. Finding darkness in another story is so much less lonely than fearing the darkness is yours alone.

I punished myself when I lost patience, when I bribed, when I wanted to flee. I punished myself for resenting Lily when she came into our bed, night after night, which wasn't actually a bed but a futon we pulled out in the living room. Every feeling I had, I wondered: *Would a real mother feel this?* It wasn't the certainty that she *wouldn't* that was painful, but the uncertainty itself: How could I know?

Initially I imagined that I might feel most like an "actual" mother among strangers, who had no reason to believe I wasn't one. But it was usually among strangers that I felt most like a fraud. One day early in our relationship, Lily and I went to a Mister Softee, one of the ice-cream trucks parked like land mines all over New York City. I asked Lily what she wanted and she pointed to the double cone of soft serve, the biggest one, covered in rainbow sprinkles. I said, "Great!" I was still at the Disney Store, still thrilled to find the sled set, still ready to pass as mother by whatever means necessary, whatever reindeer necessary, whatever soft serve necessary.

The double cone was so huge that Lily could barely hold it. *Two hands*, I would have known to say a few months later, but I didn't know to say it then. I overheard the woman behind me in line ask her friend, "What kind of parent gets her child that much ice cream?" My face went hot with shame. *This* parent. Which is to say: not a parent at all. I was afraid to turn around and at the same time I desperately wanted to turn around, to make the stranger feel ashamed, to speak back to the maternal superego she represented by saying: "What kind of mother? A mother trying to replace a dead one." Instead I grabbed a wad of napkins and offered to carry Lily's cone back to our table so she wouldn't drop it on the way.

As a stepparent, I often felt like an impostor—or else I felt the particular loneliness of dwelling outside the bounds of the most familiar story line. I hadn't been pregnant, given birth, felt my body surge with the hormones of attachment. I woke up every morning to a daughter who called me Mommy but also missed her mother. One of Lily's favorite dolls—a goth character called Spectra Vondergeist, with purple-streaked hair and a skeleton-key belt—was advertised on her cardboard packaging as the "Daughter of a Ghost."

I often called our situation "singular." But as with so many kinds of singularity, it was not only a double-edged blade—a source of loneliness and pride at once—but also a delusion. "Lots of people are stepparents," my mother told me once, and of course she was right. A recent Pew Research Center survey found that four in ten Americans say they have at least one step-relationship. Twelve percent of women are stepmothers. I can guarantee you that almost all these women sometimes feel like frauds or failures.

In an essay about stepparents, Winnicott argues for the value of "unsuccess stories." He even imagines the benefits of gathering a group of "unsuccessful stepparents" in a room together. "I think such a meeting might be fruitful," he writes. "It would be composed of ordinary men and women." When I read that passage, it stopped me dead with longing. I wanted to be in that meeting, sitting with those ordinary men and women—hearing about their ice-cream bribes, their everyday impatience, their frustration and fraudulence, their desperate sleds.

In the methodology portion of her "Poisoned Apple" study, Elizabeth Church admits that she disclosed to her subjects that she was also a stepmother before interviewing them. After an interview was finished, she sometimes described her own experiences. Many of her subjects confessed that they had told her things during their interviews that they had never told anyone else. I could understand that—that they somehow would feel, by virtue of being in the presence of another stepmother, as if they had been granted permission to speak. It was something like the imagined gathering of unsuccessful stepparents, as if they were at an AA meeting in a church basement, taking earned solace in the minor triumphs and frequent failures of their kind: not blood, but a kind of kin.

The decision to call the stepmother Mother, or the decision *not* to call her Mother, is often a dramatic hinge in stories about stepmothers. It usually functions as a climactic moment of acceptance or refusal. In a story called "My Step-Mother," published in the *Decatur Republican* in 1870, a young girl regards her new stepmother with skepticism. When her stepmother asks her to play a song on the piano, trying to earn her trust and affection, the girl decides to play "I Sit and Weep by My Mother's Grave." But lo! The stepmother is undeterred. She not only compliments the girl on her moving performance, she shares that she *also* lost her mother when she was young and *also* used to love that song. The story ends on a triumphant note, with the daughter finally calling her Mother, an inverted christening—child naming the parent—that inaugurates the "most perfect confidence" that grows between them.

For Lily, calling me Mother wasn't the end of anything. The day after Charles and I married in a Las Vegas wedding chapel, Lily asked almost immediately if she could call me Mommy. It was clear she had been waiting to ask, and I was moved by her desire—as if we had landed in the closing credits of a movie, the soundtrack reaching a crescendo all around us.

But we weren't in the credits. We were just getting started. I was terrified. What would happen next? What happened next: pulling into a 7-Eleven for snacks as Lily tugged on my sleeve to tell me she'd had an "adult drink" at the laser-tag birthday party she'd just attended and now she felt funny. She didn't want me to tell her dad. It was like the universe had sent its first maternal test. Was she drunk? What should I do? If I was going to let myself be called Mommy, I had to be prepared to deal with the fallout from the laser-tag birthday party. Charles eventually deduced that she had had a few sips of iced tea.

It felt less as if I had "earned" the title of *mother*—the way it has figured in so many sentimental stories, as a reward for behaving the right way and defying the old archetypes—and more as if I'd stepped into a cutout doll already sculpted for me by a little girl's yearning. It was as if I'd landed in the 1900 story called "Making Mamma," in which six-year-old Samantha layers a dressmaker's dummy with old fabric in order to make a surrogate mother for herself. It was as if Lily had bestowed a deep and immediate trust in me—unearned, born of need—and now I had to figure out how to live inside that trust without betraying it.

Once I stepped into the costume of a well-worn cultural archetype, I got used to hearing other people's theories about my life. Everyone had ideas about our family without knowing anything about our family. One woman said our situation was easier than it would have been if I'd had a terrible ex to compete with; another woman said I would be competing with the memory of Lily's perfect biological mother forever. When I wrote an article about a family trip for a travel magazine, the editor wanted a bit more pathos from my account: "Has it been bumpy?" she wrote in the margins of my draft. "What are you hoping for from this trip? A tighter family bond? A chance to let go of the sadness? Or...?? Tug at our heartstrings a bit." When this editor imagined our family, she envisioned us saturated by sadness, or else contoured by resistance. More than anything, I liked her "Or...??" It rang true. It wasn't that every theory about our family offered by other people felt wrong; it was more that most of them felt right, or at least held a grain of truth that resonated. Which felt even more alarming, somehow, to be so knowable to strangers.

But every theory also felt incomplete. There was so much more truth around it, or else something close to its opposite felt true as well. I rarely felt like saying, "No, it's nothing like that." I usually wanted to say: "Yes, it *is* like that. And also like this, and like this, and like this." Sometimes the sheer fact of those assumptions—the way they churned inside everyone we encountered—made stepmotherhood feel like loving someone in front of an operating theater full of strangers.

I was convinced that I was constantly being dissected for how fully or compassionately I had assumed my maternal role.

Ultimately I found only two fairy tales with good stepmothers, and they were both from Iceland. In one, a woman named Himinbjorg guides her stepson through his mourning by helping him fulfill a prophecy delivered to him by his dead mother in a dream: that he will free a princess from the spell that turned her into an ogre. By the time the prince returns from his mission, victorious, the royal court is ready to burn Himinbjorg at the stake, because everyone is convinced that she is responsible for his disappearance. Her selflessness moved me. She is willing to look terrible in order to help her stepson pursue a necessary freedom, while I worried that I cared too much about proving I was a good stepmother—worried that wanting to *seem* like a good stepmother might get in the way of *being* a good stepmother. Perhaps I wanted credit for mothering more than I wanted to mother. Himinbjorg, on the other hand, is willing to look like a witch just to help her stepson break the spell he needs to break.

Then there was Hildur. Her husband had vowed never to marry after the death of his first queen, because he feared his daughter would be mistreated. "All stepmothers are evil," he tells his brother, "and I don't wish to harm Ingibjorg." He is a fairy-tale king who has already absorbed the wisdom of fairy tales. He knows the deal with stepmoms. But he falls in love with Hildur anyway. She says she won't marry him, though—not unless he lets her live alone with his daughter for three years before the wedding. Their marriage is made possible by her willingness to invest in a relationship with his daughter that exists apart from him, as its own fierce flame.

The closest thing Lily and I ever had to an Icelandic castle was a series of bathrooms across downtown Manhattan. Bathrooms were the spaces where it was just the two of us: the one with wallpaper made from old newspapers, the one where she insisted that people used to have braids instead of hands, the one at a Subway with a concrete mop sink she loved because it was "cool and simple."

Bathrooms were our space, just as Wednesdays were our day, when I picked her up from school and took her to the Dunkin' Donuts full of cops at Third Avenue and Twentieth before I rushed her to ballet, got her squeezed into her rhinestone-studded leotard, and knelt before her tights like a supplicant, fitting bobby pins into her bun. At first I expected an Olympic medal for getting her there only two minutes late. Eventually I realized that I was surrounded by mothers who had done exactly what I'd just done, only they had done it two minutes faster, and their buns were neater. Everything that felt like rocket science to me was just the stuff regular parents did every day of the week.

But those afternoons mattered, because they belonged to me and Lily. One day, in a cupcake-shop bathroom in SoHo—a few months before Lily, Charles, and I moved into a new apartment, the first one we would rent together—Lily pointed at the walls: pink and brown, decorated with a lacy pattern. She told me she wanted our new room to look like this. Ours. She had it all planned out. In the new place, Daddy would live in one room, and Lily and I would live in the other. Our room would be so dainty, she said. She wasn't sure boys would be allowed. This was what Hildur knew: we needed something that was for the two of us alone.

A few months later, reading Dr. Seuss's *Horton Hatches the Egg* to Lily in that new apartment, I felt my throat constricting. Horton agrees to sit on an egg while Mayzie the bird, a flighty mother, takes a vacation to Palm Beach. Mayzie doesn't come back, but Horton doesn't give up. He sits on a stranger's egg for days, then weeks, then months. "I meant what I said, and I said what I meant," he repeats. "An elephant's faithful, one hundred percent!"

When the egg finally hatches, the creature that emerges is an elephant-bird: a bright-eyed baby with a small, curled trunk and red-tipped wings. Her tiny trunk made me think of Lily's hand gestures—how big and senseless they got, like mine—and how she was starting to make to-do lists, as I did, just so she could cross things off them. But she also had a poster of the planets in her bedroom, because her mom had loved outer space, and she was proud to say she always had her "nose in a book," just as her grandmother told her that her mother always had.

For me, the stakes of thinking about what it means to be a step-mother live not in statistical relevance—*slightly more than 10 percent of American women might relate!*—but in the way stepparenting asks us to question our assumptions about the nature of love and the boundaries of family. Family is so much more than biology, and love is so much more than instinct. Love is effort and desire—not a sentimental story line about easy or immediate attachment, but the complicated bliss of joined lives: ham-and-guacamole sandwiches packed in a My Little Pony lunchbox, or growing pains at midnight and car seats covered in vomit. It's the days of showing up. The trunks we inherit and the stories we step into, they make their way into us—by womb or shell or presence, by sheer force of will. But what hatches from the egg is hardly ever what we expect: the child that emerges, or the parent that is born. That mother is not a saint. She's not a witch. She's just an ordinary woman. She found a sled one day, after she was told there weren't any left. That was how it began.

Museum of Broken Hearts

The Museum of Broken Relationships is a collection of ordinary objects hung on walls, tucked under glass, backlit on pedestals: a toaster, a child's pedal car, a handmade modem. A toilet-paper dispenser. A positive pregnancy stick. A positive drug test. A weathered ax. They come from Taipei, from Slovenia, from Colorado, from Manila. All donated, each accompanied by a story: *In the 14 days of her holiday, every day I axed one piece of her furniture.*

One of the most popular items in the museum gift shop is the "Bad Memories Eraser," an actual eraser sold in several shades. But in truth the museum is something closer to the psychic opposite of an eraser. Every object insists that something *was*, rather than trying to make it disappear. Donating an object to the museum permits surrender and permanence at once: you get it out of your home, and you make it immortal. *She was a regional buyer for a grocer and that meant I got to try some great samples*, reads the caption next to a box of maple-and-sea-salt popcorn. *I miss her, her dog, and the samples, and can't stand to have this fancy microwave popcorn in my house.* The donor couldn't stand to have it, but he also couldn't bear to throw it away. He wanted to put it on a pedestal instead, honor it as the artifact of an ended era.

When it comes to breakups, we are attached to certain dominant narratives of purgation, liberation, and exorcism: the idea that we're supposed to want to get the memories out of us, free ourselves from their grip. But this museum recognizes that our relationship to the past—even its ruptures and betrayals—is often more vexed, that it holds gravity and repulsion at once.

Exhibit 1: Clamshell Necklace
Florence, Italy
It's a simple necklace: a tiny, brown-striped clamshell tied to a black leather cord. The shell was gathered from a beach in Italy and attached to the cord by means of two holes drilled into the shell with a dental drill. The person who made the necklace for me was a dental student in Florence at the time. He did it secretly, in one of his classes, while he was supposed to be learning how to make crowns. I wore that necklace every single day, until I didn't anymore.

When I visited the museum in Zagreb, Croatia—where it occupies a baroque aristocratic home perched at the edge of Upper Town—I was on my own, though almost everyone else had come as part of a couple. The lobby was full of men waiting for wives and girlfriends who were spending longer with the exhibits. I imagined all these couples steeped in schadenfreude and fear: *This isn't us. This could be us.* In the guest book, I saw one entry that said simply: "I should end my relationship, but I probably won't," and fingered my own wedding ring—as proof, for comfort—but couldn't help imagining the ring as another exhibit, too.

Before flying to Zagreb, I'd put out a call to my friends—*What object would you donate to this museum?*—and got descriptions I couldn't have imagined: a clamshell drilled by a dental student, a steel-guitar slide, a shopping list, four black dresses, a single human hair, a mango candle, a penis-shaped gourd, the sheet music from Rachmaninoff's Concerto no. 3 for Piano. One friend described an illustration from a children's book that her ex had loved when he was young, showing a line of gray mice with thought bubbles full of the same colors above their heads, as if they were all dreaming the same dream. The objects my friends described all reached toward obsolete past tenses: *that time we dreamed the same dream*. The objects were relics from those dreams, as the museum exhibits were relics from the dreams of strangers—attempts to insist that these dreams had left some residue behind.

Walking through the museum felt less like voyeurism and more like collaboration. Strangers wanted their lives witnessed, and other strangers wanted to witness them. The curatorial notes quoted Roland Barthes: "Every passion, ultimately, has its spectator…[there is] no amorous oblation without a final theatre." I felt weirdly necessary, as if my attention offered proof—to the strangers who had donated these objects—that their thwarted love was worth paying attention to. There was a democratic vibe to the place. Its premise implied that anyone's story was worth telling, and worth listening to. The people who had donated items weren't distinct, in any meaningful sense, from the ones who were observing them. By contributing an item, any observer—anyone with a broken heart and a toilet-paper dispenser—could become an author.

The caption beside a small travel bottle of conditioner described a man named Dave, who had been "welcomed" into the open marriage of Mr. and Mrs. W. She had left the conditioner behind after a weekend visit to Dave's cabin, but after she and Mr. W. were killed in a car crash, Dave had "no public forum to grieve." The caption seemed to be addressing me directly when it said: "You are giving Dave his public forum."

Exhibit 2: Shopping List

Princeton, New Jersey

I spent the first seven years of my twenties in serious long-term romantic relationships, and then I got my heart broken when I was 27 and never dated again. Ten years into my singleness, having moved four times since my last breakup, gotten a PhD and a job, gained 40 pounds, I was going through a box of old too-small summer clothes and slipped my hand into the back pocket of some abbreviated jean shorts and felt a scrap of paper which turned out to be a shopping list in my heartbreaking ex's handwriting: "batteries, lg. black trash bags, Tide (small) bleach alt., g. onion." I suddenly remembered his gratuitous use of periods—oddly, always after he signed his name, every email and every letter ending with a punctuation mark of finality.

The Museum of Broken Relationships began with a breakup. Back in 2003, after Olinka Vištica and Dražen Grubišić ended their relationship, they found themselves in the midst of a series of difficult conversations about how to divide their possessions. As Olinka put it: "The feeling of loss…represented the only thing left for us to share." Over the kitchen table one night, they imagined an exhibit composed of all the detritus from breakups like their own, and when they finally created this exhibition—three years later—its first object was one salvaged from their own home: the mechanical windup rabbit they'd called Honey Bunny.

Just over a decade later, the story of their breakup has become the museum's myth of origins. "It was the strangest thing," Olinka told me over coffee one morning. "The other day I was getting out of my car, right outside the museum, and I heard a tour guide telling a group of tourists about the bunny. He said: 'It all started with a joke!'" Olinka wanted to tell the tour guide it hadn't been a joke at all, that those early conversations had been deeply painful, but she realized that the story of her own breakup had become a public possession, subject to the retellings and interpretations of others. People took whatever they needed from it.

Two years after they'd moved out of their shared apartment, Dražen called Olinka with the idea of submitting their breakup installation to a local Zagreb art festival. They were rejected the first year but accepted the next—given only two weeks to plan the installation, and told they wouldn't be granted space inside the gallery itself. So they got a shipping container delivered from Rijeka, a port city on the Adriatic Sea, and spent the next two weeks collecting objects to fill it. At first they were worried they wouldn't find enough, but everyone who heard about the idea said: "I might have something for you."

Olinka met a woman under the clock tower in Ban Jelačić Square who arrived with her husband but brought an old diary filled with the name of her former lover. She met an elderly man in a bar, a wounded vet, who pulled a prosthetic leg out of a shopping bag and told the story of the social worker who'd helped him get it during the early '90s, when sanctions during the Balkan Wars made prosthetics nearly impossible to obtain. The prosthetic had lasted longer than their relationship, he said, because it was "made of sturdier material."

When Olinka and Dražen finally found a home for their permanent exhibition, four years after that first exhibit, the space was in terrible shape: the first floor of an eighteenth-century palace in utter disrepair, perched near the top of a funicular railway. "We were a little bit crazy," Olinka told me. "We had tunnel vision. Like when you fall in love." Dražen finished the floors and painted the walls, restored the brick arches. He did such a great job that people kept asking Olinka: "Are you sure you wanted to break up with this guy?"

That's the pleasing irony of the museum's premise: that in creating a museum from their breakup, Olinka and Dražen ended up forming an enduring partnership. From the museum coffee shop, the mechanical bunny was visible in its glass case—a presiding mascot and a patron saint. "People think that the bunny is our object," Olinka told me. "But really the museum is our object. Everything that it's become."

Exhibit 3: A copy of *Walden*, by Henry David Thoreau
Bucharest, Romania
R. and I both started reading Walden *in the beginning of our relationship. It takes a certain amount of solitude to grow fond of* Walden, *and our relationship was a vessel where we could put both our isolations while keeping them separate, like water and oil. We were living together, but decided to sleep in different rooms, both reading* Walden *before falling asleep. It was our proxy: our bodies were separated by the wall in between our rooms, but our minds were converging towards the same ideas. By the time we broke up, neither of us had finished. Nevertheless, we continued reading it.*

Every caption at the museum was an education in the limits of my vision. What looked like an UNO game wasn't just an UNO game. It was the UNO game that an American soldier had planned to give his long-distance girlfriend—an Australian army widow, in the service herself, raising two small kids—but when they were finally done with their tours, and he came to Australia to meet her flight from Afghanistan, she told him she wasn't ready for a commitment. Years later, when he stumbled across this museum full of the residue of lost loves, he decided to donate the UNO game they'd never played. He'd been carrying it with him all that time.

Some of the exhibits conjured grand historical dramas, like the love letter written by a thirteen-year-old boy escaping Sarajevo under fire in 1992: a note he'd written to Elma—a girl stuck in the same convoy, in the car next to his—but hadn't had the courage to give her. He'd just given her his favorite Nirvana tape instead, since she'd forgotten to bring her own music.

But the objects that moved me most were the ordinary ones, because their ordinariness suggested that every love story—even the most familiar, the most predictable, the least dramatic—was worth putting in a museum. The museum's former manager, Ivana Družetić, understood their endeavor as a descendant of the curiosity cabinet: "Since the discovery of that which is the smallest and the reaching of that which is the furthest, the criteria no longer seem to be craving the extreme, but rather attempting to capture all that which falls in between."

These ordinary objects understood that a breakup is powerful because it saturates the banality of daily life, just as the relationship itself did: every errand, every annoying alarm-clock chirp, every late-night Netflix binge. Once love is gone, it's gone everywhere. It's a ghost suffusing daily life just as powerfully in its absence. A man leaves his shopping lists scattered across your days, cluttered with personality tics and gratuitous periods, poignant in their specificity: *lg. black trash bags* summoning that time the trash bags were too small, or *g. onion,* the type necessary for a particular fish stew prepared on a particular humid summer evening. The exhibits were all vocabulary words drawn from private shared languages that I would never entirely understand—the beaten-up pot, the plastic bin—or relics from two-person civilizations that no longer existed.

Some objects felt less like relics from the past and more like artifacts from unlived futures. A crumbling gingerbread cookie endured as stale eulogy for a one-day flirtation with an engaged man, a giddy afternoon spent at an Oktoberfest in Chicago, before a text from him arrived the next day: "It is hard for me to say this to you as you are a great girl but…please don't phone or text as I fear it would only cause trouble." It was so seemingly inconsequential—the chance encounter and the dismissive text—something you'd never expect to find immortalized.

And yet, there it was. A single Oktoberfest mattered enough to make a woman save a gingerbread cookie for years, until its frosting had gathered into pale broken scabs, and these scabs held the essence of the museum itself—its commitment to the oblique sadness of the "one-day thing," to attachments that might not seem worthy of commemoration, to the act of mourning what never happened. Which is part of any breakup: grieving the enduring relationship that never came to pass, the hypothetical relationship that could have worked. One soldier's wool sock came with a caption from his lover of twenty years: *I had two children with him and we never shared a real conversation. I always thought that, one day, it would begin.*

One journal at the museum, kept by a woman during one of her lover's bipolar episodes, was full of phrases repeated like mantras: *I am keeping my heart open* and *I am living in the now,* written over and over again. It was the triteness of those phrases that moved me. They weren't brilliant. They'd just been necessary.

Exhibit 4: Envelope with Single Human Hair
Karviná, Czech Republic
In 1993 I graduated college and taught English for a year in a coal mining village on the Polish/Czech border, a depressed, polluted, communist city in which I experienced loneliness like I'd never known before or since. The summer before I left, I met a Scottish boy named Colin at the amusement park in Salisbury Beach where he was running the Ferris wheel. After the summer, we wrote letters to each other, and sometimes a letter from him was the only thing that got me through my day. He had auburn curls I adored and once when the familiar airmail-blue envelope arrived in my box I saw he had taped the flap and a single piece of his curly hair got trapped under the tape: a part of his body, his DNA, that would one day be shared with our children. After he dumped me in a pretty cowardly way—just stopped writing—I still checked my box every day and wept,

then returned to my sad communist flat and wept, then looked at the
envelope that held his single curly hair and wept some more.

"The museum has always been two steps ahead of us," Olinka told me, explaining that it's had a will of its own from the start, an impulse to exist beyond her and Dražen. It was as if all these stories had already been waiting all around them—like humidity in the air, a sky ready to rain. Immediately after their shipping-crate exhibition, Olinka and Dražen got a call from a Japanese quiz show that wanted to film an episode in their museum. But there was no museum. It was like that from the beginning: people believing in the thing, *wanting* the thing, before it even existed.

In the decade since that first shipping crate, the museum has taken many shapes: permanent installations in Zagreb and Los Angeles, a virtual museum comprising thousands of photographs and stories, and forty-six pop-up installations all over the world—from Buenos Aires to Boise, Singapore to Istanbul, Cape Town to South Korea, from the Oude Kerk in Amsterdam's red-light district to the European Parliament in Brussels, all locally sourced, like an artisanal grocer, stocked with regional heartbreak.

Olinka told me anecdotes about particular exhibits: The Mexico City exhibit was flooded with more than two hundred donations in the first twenty-four hours. The South Korean exhibit was full of objects that had belonged to high-school students who'd died in a recent ferry accident. While French donors often narrated their own captions in the third person, American narratives usually featured a prominent first person—that all-American "I." American curators were also much more likely to use the first person when they talked about their exhibitions: *My collection. The donations I've gathered.* She and Dražen tried not to speak that way. It took a few years before they even introduced the backstory of their own breakup into the public narrative of their museum. They always believed the project belonged to something much larger than their private pain.

Objects make private histories public, but they also grant the past a certain integrity. Whenever memory conjures the past, it ends up papering over it: replacing the lost partner with memories and re-constructions, myths and justifications. But an object can't be distorted in these ways. It's still just a box of popcorn or a toaster, a hoodie that got drenched with sudden rain one night in 1997.

At another Zagreb exhibit I saw that week, this one devoted to the 1991 Serbian-Montenegrin attacks on Dubrovnik, it was the objects that felt most powerful: not the massive photographs showing pale stone forts exploded into plumes of smoke, but the small grenade shaped like a miniature black pineapple, and the crude cross a family had fashioned from pieces of an exploded artillery shell that hit their home. A soldier's pink flashlight sat beside a piece of shrapnel, a square of gauze stained with his blood, and a photo of him lying in a hospital bed with a bandage over one eye, rosary against his bare chest. His name was Ante Puljiz. Those words meant nothing to me. But that piece of shrapnel—it had been lodged inside his body.

Exhibit 5: Four Black Dresses
Brooklyn, New York
I would donate to the museum the four black dresses hanging in my closet: a shirtwaist, a sundress, a ribbed turtleneck, and an A-line of raw silk. Two of these dresses were given to me by my ex, and two I bought myself, but they all date from a time in my life when I imagined I could become the person I wanted to be by adopting a uniform. I thought—we both thought—that the problem of my un-femininity, my lack of interest in clothes, my general un-hipness, could be solved by my becoming one of those literary party regulars who dresses in black, makes cutting comments, and writes bestsellers. Two months before we broke up, this

man said to me, "I'm just waiting to see if you become famous, because
then I think I might fall in love with you." A horrible thing to say,
clumsy in its attempt at honesty—yet I did see how this was what, on
some level, I'd been promising him, the fantasy of a public self we'd been
co-constructing. I would donate these dresses to the museum—except that
I still wear them. All the time. It's just that I wear other dresses—purple,
floral, geometric, pink—as well.

When I was young, before my parents separated, I believed that
divorce was a ceremony just like marriage, only inverted: the couple
walked down the aisle of a church, holding hands, and then, once they
reached the altar, they unclasped their hands and walked away from
each other. After a family friend's marriage ended, I asked her: "Did
you have a nice divorce?" It seemed like a polite question. An ending
seemed like something important enough to justify a ritual.

When performance artists Marina Abramovic and her partner Ulay
decided to end their twelve-year relationship, they marked its conclusion
by walking the length of the Great Wall of China. "People put so much
effort into starting a relationship and so little effort into ending one,"
Abramovic explained. On March 30, 1988, she started walking from the
eastern end of the Great Wall, the Bo Hai gulf on the Yellow Sea, and
Ulay began walking from the western edge, in the Gobi Desert. They
each walked for ninety days, covering roughly 1,500 miles, until they
met in the middle, where they embraced to say goodbye. At a retro-
spective of Abramovic's work in Stockholm nearly thirty years later,
two video screens showed scenes from their respective journeys: one
screen showed Abramovic walking past camels on hard dirt covered
with snow, while the other showed Ulay hiking with a walking stick
over green hills. The tapes were running on a continuous loop, and
it seemed beautiful to me that on those screens, decades after their
breakup, these two lovers still walked constantly toward each other.

If every relationship is a collaboration—two people jointly creating the selves they will be with each other—this collaboration can sometimes feel like tyranny, forcing the self into a certain shape, and it can sometimes feel like birth, making a new self possible. Sometimes the comet tail left behind—the dresses you wore, the lipstick you tried, the books you bought but never read, the bands you pretended to like—can feel like broken shackles, but sometimes it's beautiful anyway: a dress reclaimed from costume, turned into silk skin for a Saturday night.

In truth, I've been obsessed with breakups since before I was ever in a relationship. I grew up in a family thick with divorces and overpopulated by remarriages: both sets of grandparents divorced, my mother's twice; both my parents married three times; my oldest brother divorced by forty. Divorce seemed less like an aberration than an inevitable stage in the life cycle of any love.

But in my family the ghosts of prior partners were rarely vengeful or embittered. My mother's first husband was a lanky hippie with the kindest eyes who once brought me a dream catcher. My beloved aunt's first husband was an artist who made masks from the dried palm fronds he gathered on beaches. These men enchanted me because they carried with them not only the residue of who my mom and aunt had been before I knew them, but also the spectral possibilities of who they might have become. Seventeen years after their divorce, my own parents had become so close that my mother, an Episcopal deacon, officiated my father's third wedding.

Which is all to say: I grew up believing that relationships would probably end, but I also grew up with the firm belief that even after a relationship was over, it was still a part of you, and that this wasn't necessarily a bad thing. When I asked my mother what object she would contribute to the museum, she chose a shirt she had bought in San Francisco, years before I was born, with the woman she had loved before she met my father.

I grew up with the sense that a broken relationship always amounted to more than its breakage. Everything that happened before it ended was not invalidated by the fact of its ending. Those memories of the relationship—the particular joys and frictions it held, the particular incarnation of self it permitted—didn't disappear, though the world didn't always make room for them. To speak of an ex too much was seen as a sign of some kind of pathology. The gospel of serial monogamy could have you believe that every relationship was an imperfect trial run, useful only as preparation for the relationship that finally stuck. In this model, a family full of divorces was a family full of failure. But I grew up seeing them as something else, grew up seeing every self as an accumulation of its loves, like a Russian nesting doll that held all of those relationships inside.

Exhibit 6: Paisley Shirt
San Francisco, California

It was sometime in 1967. We bought our paisley shirts from an outdoor rack in Haight-Ashbury. This was in the early heady days of our relationship; for me all the more intoxicating as it was my first lesbian love affair. Our shirts almost matched, but not quite; mine was psychedelic pink and hers purple. They were definitely first worn at a Jefferson Airplane concert, though the shirt carries memories of places it never went: a year backpacking and picking crops in Europe, leading an olive picker strike in Provence, a camping trip in Death Valley where we watched the sun set on one horizon while the moon rose on the other. It was all so good and right and full of hope, until it wasn't. I never understood why we ended, although my wanting children probably had something to do with it. The last time I saw her was at Gay Pride Day in Washington, D.C., in 1975. That's a long time ago but the paisley shirt has stayed with me. It reminds me of who I once was.

When I was a kid, I loved a book called *Grover and the Everything in the Whole Wide World Museum.* In the Whole Wide World Museum, Grover visits "The Things You See in the Sky Room" and the room full of "Long Thin Things You Can Write With," where a carrot has mistakenly wound up, so he returns it to an elegant marble pedestal in the middle of the otherwise empty "Carrot Room." As Grover reaches the end of the exhibits, he wonders: "Where did they put everything else?" That's when he reaches the wooden door marked: "Everything Else." When he opens it, of course, it's just the exit.

When I left the Museum of Broken Relationships, everything on the streets of Zagreb seemed like a possible exhibit, an object that had been part of a love affair or that might be, someday: a garden gnome grinning in front of lace curtains; purple modeling clay formed into uneven balls on a windowsill; orange plastic ashtrays near the top of the funicular railway; every toothpick sticking out of the sausages roasting on an outdoor griddle in Strossmartre; every cigarette butt in the clogged metal street grate on Hebrangova ulica; the scab as large as an apple on an old man's exposed shin as he rode a motorbike with an old woman gripping his waist. Perhaps someday she would wish she'd saved that scab as something to remember him by. The cloudless Zagreb day held potential heartbreak like a distant ticking bomb.

When I saw a man and woman sharing a bag of popcorn in Zrinjevac Park, I wondered if someday, once everything was broken, they would remember the accessories of this particular day like soil samples: her sunglasses, his sneakers. I imagined their popcorn on a pedestal, with a spotlight shining on it—*Bag of Popcorn; Zagreb, Croatia*—captioned by the story of another woman, or another man, or simply another year, how it dimmed exuberance into routine.

I could summon my own lost loves as an infinite catalog of ghostly objects: a pint of chocolate ice cream eaten on a futon above a falafel shop; a soggy tray of chili fries from the Tommy's at Lincoln and Pico;

a plastic vial of pink-eye medicine; twenty different T-shirt smells; beard hairs scattered like tea leaves across dingy sinks; a three-wheeled dishwasher tucked into the pantry I shared with the man I thought I would marry. But perhaps the deeper question is not about the objects themselves—what belongs in the catalog—but about why I enjoy cataloging them so much. What is it about the ache that I enjoy, that etched groove of remembering an old love, that vein of nostalgia?

After breaking up with my first boyfriend, when we were both freshmen in college on opposite sides of the country, I developed a curious attachment to the sadness of our breakup. Rather than sitting through our stilted phone conversations, I could smoke my cigarettes in the bitter cold of Boston nights and miss what it had been like to fall in love back in Los Angeles: warm evenings by the ocean, kissing on lifeguard stands. That sadness felt like a purified version of our bond, as if I was more connected to that man in missing him than I'd ever been while we were together. But it was more than that, too: the sadness itself became a kind of anchor, something I needed more than I'd ever needed him.

Exhibit 7: Steel-Guitar Slide
Fayetteville, West Virginia

The most potent relationship object in my possession is an old steel-guitar slide from the 1920s. It's a bar slide—or tone bar—meaning a simple chunk of chromed steel or brass, its original manufacture stamp worn away by constant fretting. My ex, a person of both exceptional musical ability and unusually destructive behavior, gave it to me (probably in a fit of the latter). I think it might have been his most prized possession, and he didn't tend to have many possessions. We were together for six years when I was very young, and the whole thing ended with me in a battered-women's shelter. I can't quite manage to get rid of the tone bar, though, and of course I think about all the blues that have poured through it over time: his, mine by way of his. It still seems more his than mine, though—my fingers don't even fit its edges—and I'd gladly return it to him if he wanted it back.

Olinka believes that "melancholy has been unjustly banished from the public space," and told me she mourns the fact that it has been driven into ghettos, replaced by the eerie optimism of Facebook status updates. A guitar slide can hold the blues—"his, mine by way of his"—or a museum can hold the blues, insisting we need to make room for them. Olinka has always imagined her museum as a "civic temple where melancholy has the right to exist," where sadness can be understood as something other than a feeling meant to be replaced. She doesn't like when people praise her museum's "therapeutic value." It insists that sadness needs curing.

For fifteen years of my life, between my first breakup and my last one, I was committed to a nearly opposite belief in sadness as a rarefied state: an affective distillery that could summon the strongest and purest version of me. But walking through Zagreb that week, two and a half years married and two months pregnant, I was not looking for places to smoke and feel lonely, scraping out my insides with unfiltered European cigarettes. I was looking for fresh fruit that might satisfy my sudden and overwhelming cravings: a paper bag of cherries from the outdoor market, or doughnut peaches so ripe their juice spilled onto my dress the moment my teeth punctured their skin.

I'd always struggled with relationships once they lost their earliest states of unfettered love and unbridled passion. I found the aftermath of that early glow muddy and compromised. But getting married had meant committing to another kind of beauty: the striated beauty of continuity, letting love accrete its layers over the years, showing up to intimacy in all its difficulty as well as its giddiness, staying inside something long enough to hold its previous rough patches like talismans, to tell yourself: *This has another side.*

Back in my Zagreb hotel room, my phone buzzed with a message from a friend who was waiting at an airport in Colorado to meet the flight of a man she was falling in love with, and then a text from another friend: "We just broke up. Are you around? Just don't want to be alone all weekend."

The world is always beginning and ending at once. Icarus falls from the sky while someone swipes right on Tinder.

At the Broken Relationships pop-up installation in Boise, Idaho, one man donated an answering machine that played a message from his ex, calling him an asshole, immediately followed by a message from his dad, talking about something as ordinary as the weather. This is heartbreak: rupture is huge in your heart, while the rest of the world is checking on scattered showers. Your ex can't stand the fact of your existence in the world, and your brother wants to know if you saw the Knicks game last night. The appeal of the museum is also about this: wanting company, wanting to turn the experience of becoming solitary into something social instead. *We just broke up. Are you around? Just don't want to be alone all weekend.*

French conceptual artist Sophie Calle explained the premise of her 2007 installation *Take Care of Yourself* like this: "I received an email telling me it was over. I didn't know how to respond…It ended with the words, 'Take care of yourself.' And so I did." For Calle, taking care of herself meant asking 107 women to interpret his note: "To analyze it, comment on it, dance it, sing it. Dissect it. Exhaust it. Understand it for me." Her exhibition was composed of the chorus of their reactions. A "researcher in lexicometry" noted a lack of agency in the breakup note's grammar. A proofreader highlighted its repetitions. A lawyer deemed her ex guilty of deceit. A criminologist diagnosed him as "proud, narcissistic, and egotistical."

Witnessing breakups and asking mine to be witnessed have been part of every deep friendship of my life. It's the art of collaborating as close readers, soothsayers, tea-leaf translators, alternate-narrative makers: "darlin, can i beg you for a read on this?" a friend wrote once, forwarding an email from a man she'd just broken up with. "I'm struggling to be sure I'm not being a hysterical woman...could just use someone else's eyes on this exchange, for total sense of closure. crazy grateful for you." The breakup as social experience isn't kiss-and-tell so much as a desire not to be alone in facing the end of the story. Kicked out as character, you become a reader, parsing the wreckage. It feels so much better not to read alone.

Exhibit 8: Plastic Bag of Pistachio Nuts
Iowa City

Dave and I spent four years together. We moved across the country and back. We drove a U-Haul across Pennsylvania in the middle of a rainstorm, and then we did it again, two years later, headed the opposite direction. Pennsylvania surprised us with its size; somehow it did this twice. I loved Dave with all of myself, like a wet cloth wrung out. In the first apartment we shared—once things had deteriorated and we were fighting frequently—we started to notice these gray moths flitting clumsily around our kitchen. When we smashed them against the walls, their innards left silvery trails against the pale paint. We kept killing them, kept fighting, kept hoping that if we killed enough moths, if we had enough fights, then eventually we'd get rid of them for good. After several months, we discovered where the moths were coming from: a plastic bag in the pantry full of old pistachios, thick with the white webbing of their tiny eggs. We threw it out. I kept hoping we'd discover our equivalent of that bag—the core of all our fights, their primal source—so we could banish it.

My breakup with Dave, at the end of my twenties, mattered more than any other breakup ever had, and lasted longer—the loss itself, and its aftermath. Dave and I had spent much of our relationship trying to figure out if our relationship could work, and I thought that breaking up would liberate us from that pull-and-tug. It didn't. We broke up, got back together, broke up again, then talked about getting married. Our split became my partner the way Dave had been my partner. There was an absence that held his shape, and it followed me everywhere.

We often describe our ghosts as voices whispering to us, but I felt Dave as spectral ear, someone to whom I kept wanting to whisper. For years after we broke up, every thought I had was constructed partially for him. I kept a physical list of things I wanted to tell him but couldn't—mainly silly, daily things: the snow piled between my inner and outer windows during blizzards; how I'd dug out my own car after the storm, and two lawyers had yelled at me for parking in their lot; the broiled grapefruit with a burnt-sugar crust I'd eaten at our local diner, without him, who loved grapefruits; all the men I'd seen or thought about seeing in his absence. "I want a man here to touch me," I wrote, "just so I'll put down this list and stop writing to you."

Memories came at me like the state of Pennsylvania in a rainstorm. Every time I thought he was over, that I'd traveled through him, it turned out he wasn't over yet. I could go as many miles as I wanted and there would still be more of how it felt to lose him. I seemed okay, because I said so all the time to friends, and often it felt true, as if my feelings were locked away somewhere else, and the key had been taken from me for my own protection. But sometimes in the night, alone, I woke up desperate for that key—to open the door, to get to the locked space. Maybe he would be there, waiting.

After a bad sunburn, when my skin peeled away in curling strips that wadded up like bits of dried masking tape between my fingers, I thought: *This is the skin he touched*. My ridiculous mourning. No reasoning with it. My skin kept coming off me like shredded paper, drifting in flakes all over my clothes, my little Toyota. He was everywhere, the dust of him.

Standing in an airport line, I watched a blue-eyed couple who teased each other amicably. Who would have to replace his/her passport first? He would! No, she would! He swatted her with his plush neck pillow. They had matching silver-plated luggage tags attached to their matching leather-trimmed roller duffels. In those days, I treated every couple like a crime scene to scour for clues, or a recipe to steal. How did they choose their matching luggage, and how did they stand in line without bickering, and how did it feel to be grooved into a shared last name etched in silver? I wanted to feel superior to the shallow life I projected onto them, but even that meager consolation gave way to wondering: *What did they have that we didn't? What could they manage that we couldn't?*

"Perhaps the hardest thing about losing a lover is / to watch the year repeat its days," Anne Carson wrote. "It is as if I could dip my hand down / / into time and scoop up / blue and green lozenges of April heat / a year ago in another country." When I dipped my cupped palms into the past I'd shared with Dave, every remembered moment hardened into something cleaner and more purely happy than it had really been. Nostalgia rearranges the rooms of memory: it makes the beds, puts a vase of flowers on the dresser, opens the curtains to let in the sun. It gets harder and harder to say, *It was painful to live there.* The voice of insistence goes faint: *It was.* Because we miss it. We miss what was hard about it. We miss it all.

On the first night we ever kissed, I told Dave: "I didn't feel alive. Now I do."

Exhibit 9: Bottle of Crystal Pepsi
Queens, New York
After the end of my relationship with the man I thought I would marry, I met an unexpectedly wonderful lawyer who lived in Queens. He took me to trivia night at his local bar in Astoria. He took me to

a Christmas party at his law office near Times Square. He took me to the Blazer Pub, near his childhood home upstate, where we ate burgers and played shuffle bowling. I knew he wasn't "the one" but also suspected I no longer believed in "the one"—not because I'd never met him, but because I had and now we were done. The lawyer made me laugh. He made me feel comfortable. We ate comfort food. We made pancakes with raspberries and white chocolate chips and watched movies on weekend mornings. He found old reruns of Legends of the Hidden Temple, *the stupid game show we'd both loved as kids, and gave me a ten-year-old bottle of Crystal Pepsi he'd found online—my favorite soda when I was young, discontinued for years. He was remarkable, but I couldn't ever quite see him—or see that—because I never really believed in us. Nothing about us made me feel challenged. His devotion started to feel like a kind of claustrophobia. It was like he taught me how much I struggled to live inside love—to understand something as love—without difficulty.*

Nine months after Dave and I broke up, I started to see a man who felt like his opposite. Or at least that was the story I told myself. He wasn't a poet but a lawyer, with an office job in Midtown. We didn't have explosive fights, perhaps because I hadn't placed my heart in his hands—in his in-box, in his U-Haul, in his pantry—for safekeeping. But our relationship gave me sustaining laughter and genuine joy, fluttery sensations in my stomach, after years spent fighting for and with a relationship that wasn't working. It suggested that the things I'd always thought I wanted from a partner—charisma, elusiveness—weren't necessarily the things I needed most.

In many ways, our relationship was another chapter in the unfolding story of my relationship with Dave, part of its epilogue. When the lawyer and I broke up, it felt less like a fresh sadness and more like a return to the sadness that was already there, missing the one

I'd been missing all along. A few months later, I met the man I would marry.

Before I left for Croatia, I thought of bringing the bottle of Crystal Pepsi the lawyer had given me, to donate to the museum as a memento of my last breakup before marriage. But I never put it in my luggage. Why did I want to keep it at home, on my bookshelf? It had something to do with wanting to acknowledge the man who'd given it to me, because I hadn't given him enough credit while we were together. Keeping his last gift was a way of granting him credit in the aftermath.

The whole time I wandered the Museum of Broken Relationships, I kept imagining all the objects that *hadn't* been donated, all the objects that people couldn't stand to part with, lurking like a ghost collection behind the thousands of objects (more than three thousand) that had. I thought of all the objects my friends had described—the clamshell necklace, the shopping list, the single human hair stuck on the envelope, the four black dresses, and the steel-guitar slide—some lost, some tucked away, some repurposed as part of a new life.

If I'm honest with myself, keeping that bottle of Crystal Pepsi isn't just about honoring the man who gave it to me, or what we shared. It also has to do with enjoying that glimpse of sadness and dissolution, with holding on to some reminder of the pure, riveting feeling of being broken. These days my life is less about the sublime state of solitary sadness or fractured heartbreak and more about waking up each day and making sure I show up to my commitments. My days in Zagreb were about Skyping with my husband and emailing a good-morning video to my stepdaughter. They were about feeding the fetus inside me: Istrian *fuži* with truffles, noodles in thick cream; sea bream with artichokes; something called a domestic pie; something called a vitamins salad.

Life now is less about the electricity of thresholds and more about continuance, coming back and muddling through; less about the grand drama of ending and more about the daily work of salvage and sustenance. I keep the Crystal Pepsi because it's a souvenir from those fifteen years I spent in a cycle of beginnings and endings, each one an opportunity for self-discovery and reinvention and transformative emotion; a way to feel infinite in the variety of possible selves that could come into being. I keep the Crystal Pepsi because I want some reminder of a self that felt volcanic and volatile—bursting into bliss, or into tears—and because I want to keep some proof of all the unlived lives, the ones that could have been.

The Quickening

When you were the size of a poppy seed, I sat in the bathroom of a Boston hotel room and peed on a stick I'd bought from an elderly man at a drugstore near Fenway Park. I laid the plastic on the cold tiles and waited for it to tell me if you existed. I wanted you to exist so badly. It had been a year of chipper emails from my fertility app, asking if I'd had sex on the right nights, and a year of sunken hearts whenever I spotted blood: at work, at home, in a sandy bathroom on a chilly beach just north of Morro Bay. Each rusty stain took away the narrative I'd spent the past few weeks imagining—that *this* would be the month I found out I was having a baby. My body kept reminding me that it controlled the story. But then, there you were.

A week later, I sat in a movie theater and watched aliens hatch from their human hosts in a spaceship mess hall. Their dark, glistening bodies broke open rib cages and burst through the torn skin. An evil robot was obsessed with helping them survive. When the captain asked him, "What do you believe in?" the robot said, simply: "Creation." This was just before the captain's chest ripped apart to show its own parasite baby: horrific, beetle-black, newly born.

When a nurse asked me to step on a scale at my first prenatal appointment, it was the first time I had weighed myself in years. Refusing to weigh myself had been one way to leave behind the days I'd spent weighing myself compulsively. Standing on a scale and actually *wanting* to see that I'd gained weight—this was a new version of me. One of the oldest scripts I'd ever heard about motherhood was that it could turn you into a new version of yourself, but that promise had always seemed too easy to be believed. I'd always believed more fully in another guarantee—that wherever you go, there you are.

W hen I was a freshman in college, I walked into my dorm-room closet every morning to step on the scale I kept hidden there. It was embarrassing to starve myself, and so for the ritual of weighing I retracted into the dark, out of sight, tucked into the folds of my musty winter coats. Since my growth spurt at thirteen, it seemed like I'd been looming over everyone. Being tall was supposed to make you confident, but it just made me feel excessive. There was too much of me, always, and I was always so awkward and quiet, failing to earn all the space I took up.

In the years since those days of restriction, I have found that usually when I try to articulate this to people—"I felt like I wasn't supposed to take up so much space"—they understand it absolutely or not at all. And if a person understands it absolutely, she is probably a woman.

Those hungry days were full of Diet Cokes and cigarettes and torch songs on Napster; a single apple and a small allotment of crackers each day; long walks through frigid winter nights to the gym and back again; trouble seeing straight, as dark flecks crowded the edges of my vision. My hands and feet were always cold. My skin was always pale. It was as if I didn't have enough blood to go around.

During my pregnancy, fifteen years later, my gums bled constantly. A doctor told me it was because my body was circulating more blood—four pounds more of it—to satisfy the tiny second set of organs. This extra blood swelled me. It heated me. My veins were feverish highways, thick with that hot red syrup, flooded with necessary volume.

When you were the size of a lentil, I flew to Zagreb for a magazine assignment. As our plane banked over Greenland, I ate a huge bag of Cheez-Its and wondered if this was the week your brain was being forged, or your heart. I pictured a heart made of Cheez-Its beating inside me, inside you. Much of that first trimester was spent in awe and terror: astonished that a tiny creature was being gathered in my inner reaches, petrified that I would somehow knock you loose. What if you died and I didn't know it? I obsessively googled "miscarriage without bleeding." I kept my hand over my abdomen to make sure you stayed. You were my bouquet of cells, my soft pit of becoming. I cried when I found out you would be a girl. It was as if you had suddenly sharpened into focus. The pronoun was a body forming around you. I was a body forming around you.

When I told my mom I was flying to Croatia, she asked me to consider staying home. "Take it easy," she said. But she also told me that when she was five months pregnant with my oldest brother, she'd swum the length of a bay in Bari while an elderly Italian man, worried, followed her the whole way in his rowboat.

On our plane to Zagreb, a toddler cried in front of us, and then another toddler cried behind. I wanted to tell you, *I know these wailers are your people.* I wanted to tell you, *The world is full of stories:* the men in hand-knit yarmulkes who had delayed our takeoff for an hour because they wouldn't sit next to any women; the man across the aisle who'd stabbed himself with a blood-sugar needle right after eating his foil-wrapped square of goulash, who watched the little icon of our plane creep over the dull blue screen of the Atlantic. Who could know what he was dreaming? What beloved he was flying toward? I wanted to tell you, *Baby, I've seen such incredible things in this life.* You weren't a baby yet. You were a possibility. But I wanted to tell you that every person you'd ever meet would hold an infinite world inside. It was one of the only promises I could make to you in good conscience.

When I was starving myself, I kept two journals. One tallied the number of calories I consumed each day. The other described all the food I imagined eating. One notebook was full of what I did; the other was full of what I dreamed of doing. My hypothetical feasts were collages made from restaurant menus and saturated with the minute attention of desperation: not just mac-'n'-cheese but *four-cheese* mac-'n'-cheese; not just burgers but burgers with melted cheddar and fried eggs; molten chocolate–lava cake with ice cream pooling around its gooey heart. Restricting made me fantasize about the possibility of a life where I did nothing *but* eat. I didn't want to eat normally; I wanted to eat constantly. There was something terrifying about finishing, as if I had to confront that I hadn't actually been satisfied.

In those days, I filled my mouth with heat and smoke and empty sweetness: black coffee, cigarettes, mint gum. I was ashamed of how desperately I wanted to consume. Desire was a way of taking up space, but it was embarrassing to have too much of it—in the same way it had been embarrassing for there to be too much of me, or to want a man who didn't want me. Yearning for things was slightly less embarrassing if I denied myself access to them, so I grew comfortable in states of longing without satisfaction. I came to prefer hunger to eating, epic yearning to daily loving.

But during pregnancy, years later, the ghost of that old skeletal girl sloughed off like a snakeskin. I moved toward chocolate-chip muffins of unprecedented size. At the coffee shop near my apartment, I licked the grease from an almond croissant off my fingers and listened to one barista ask another, "You know that girl Bruno was dating?" She squinted at her cell phone. "I know she's pregnant, but... what the fuck is she eating? Horses?"

It took me five or six months to show. Before that, people would say: "You don't look pregnant *at all*!" They meant it as a compliment. The female body is always praised for staying within its boundaries, for making even its sanctioned expansion impossible to detect.

W hen you were the size of a blueberry, I ate my way through Zagreb, palming handfuls of tiny strawberries at the outdoor market, then ordering a massive slice of chocolate cake from room service back at my hotel, then inhaling a Snickers bar because I was too hungry to wait for the cake to arrive. My hands were always sticky. I felt feral. My hunger was a different land from where I'd lived before.

As you grew from lime to avocado, I ate endless pickles, loving their salty snap between my teeth. I drank melted ice cream straight from the bowl. It was a kind of longing that did not imply absence. It was longing that belonged. The word *longing* itself traces its origins back to pregnancy. An 1899 dictionary defines it as "one of the peculiar and often whimsical desires experienced by pregnant women."

When you were the size of a mango, I flew to Louisville to give a talk and got so hungry after my daily vat of morning oatmeal that I decided to walk to brunch, and got so hungry on the walk to brunch that I stopped on the way for a snack: a flaky slice of spanakopita that stained its paper bag with islands of oil. By the time I got to brunch, I was so hungry that I couldn't decide between scrambled eggs with biscuits, or sausage links blistered with grease, or a sugar-dusted stack of lemon pancakes, so I got them all.

This endless permission felt like the fulfillment of a prophecy: all those imaginary menus I had obsessively transcribed at seventeen. Eating was fully permitted now that I was doing it for someone else. I had never eaten like this, as I ate for you.

When I was living on crackers and apple slices, I didn't get my period for years. It made me proud. The absence lived inside me like a secret trophy. Blood leaking out of me seemed like another kind of excess. Not bleeding was an appealing form of containment. It was also, quite literally, the opposite of fertility. By thinning my body, it was as if I'd vanquished my physical self. Starving myself testified to the intensity of my loneliness, my self-loathing, my simultaneous distance from the world and my hopeless proximity; a sense of being—at once—too much and not enough.

When I got pregnant at the age of twenty-four, a few years after I started getting my period again, I saw the telltale cross on the stick and felt flooded not by fear or wariness—as I'd imagined—but by wonder. I was carrying this tiny potential life. Even as I knew intellectually that I would get an abortion, I still felt that sharp rising lift of awe in my gut. That awe planted something deep inside me, a tether. It said: *Someday you'll be back.*

It was only after I'd gotten the abortion that I started to notice babies on the street. Their little faces watched me from their strollers. They had my number. It wasn't regret. It was anticipation. I'd been magnetized. I didn't want to hold other people's babies, I just knew that I would eventually want to hold my own—want to watch her bloom into consciousness right in front of me, apart from me, beyond me; want to be surprised and mystified by a creature who had come from me but was *not* me.

During the year I spent trying to get pregnant, a decade after my abortion, my friend Rachel told me about watching her infant son have a febrile seizure. Her description of her own terror was humbling. It wasn't something I could fully understand. I'd always resisted the idea that parenting involves a love deeper than any love you've ever felt before, and some part of me wanted to give birth just so I could argue against that belief, just so I could say: *This love isn't deeper, just different.* But another part of me knew it was possible I'd simply become another voice saying: *There is no love as deep as this.*

Once I finally got pregnant, my gratitude was sharpened by the wait. My body had decided to bestow this little purse of organs when it could have just as easily withheld it. This second heartbeat was nothing I could take for granted. After my first ultrasound, I got on the subway and looked at every single passenger, thinking, *You were once curled up inside another person.*

As you grew to the size of a turnip, then a grapefruit, then a cauliflower, I wanted to build you from joy: summer rainstorms and fits of laughter; the voices of women in endless conversation. With my friend Kyle, I swam naked in a pool at night, under eucalyptus trees shushing in the hot breeze, while your kicks swelled under my skin like waves. With Colleen, I drove to a rickety old house perched on a hill above a post office, where rattling trees tapped our windows. By lamplight, we ate eggs with bright yellow yolks. She left the sink full of their broken shells, just as she had when we lived together, after both our hearts had been broken.

Back in Los Angeles, your grandmother had a Cameroonian refugee staying with her. What can I say? This was hardly surprising. It made me clench my fists with longing, how much I wanted you and your grandmother to have a thousand years together in this world, nothing less. My hunger for my mother during pregnancy was like my hunger for fruit, for a second Snickers bar, for the scrambled eggs and the sausage links and the lemon pancakes. There was no bottom to it. She told me she could still remember looking at the snow piled on the branches outside the window of her doctor's office when he told her I would be a girl, as if all her longing had gathered on those branches—impossibly beautiful, utterly ordinary.

I wanted to give you the best parts of my love for your father—how we rented a house in a tiny town in northern Connecticut, that summer I was pregnant with you, and lay on a big white bed listening to the wail of the trains and the patter of rain on the creek and imagined it falling on the blue tarp covering the hot-dog stand across the road. We ate hamburgers at a roadside shack and swam at Cream Hill Lake, where the teenage lifeguards almost kicked us out because we weren't members. We barely deserved that deep blue water, those shores thick with trees, those wooden buoys dappled with sunshine. We'd had our whispered resentments, our nights of fighting. But I want you to picture us there: our voices bantering, our laughter entwined. I want you to know you were built from medium-rare meat and late-afternoon light.

When I finally got treatment, it gave me a sudden, liquid thrill to glimpse the diagnosis written on one of my medical forms: *eating disorder.* It was as if there was finally an official name for how I felt—the sense of inadequacy and dislocation—as if the words had constructed a tangible container around those intangible smoke signals of hurt. It made me feel consolidated.

The psychiatrist who diagnosed me wasn't interested in that consolidation. When I told her about being lonely—probably not the first college student to do so—she said, "Yes, but how is starving yourself going to *solve* that?" She had a point. Though I hadn't been trying to solve the problem, only express it, maybe even amplify it.

But how to translate these self-defeating impulses into the language of rational actors? I'd failed to justify the disorder with a Legitimate Reason, like failing to supply a parent's note excusing my absence from school.

For fifteen years after that appointment, I kept looking for that note. I kept trying to explain myself to that doctor, kept trying to purge my shame about the disorder by listing its causes: my loneliness, my depression, my desire for control. All of these reasons were true. None of them was sufficient. This was what I'd say about my drinking years later, and what I came to believe about human motivations more broadly: we never do anything for just one reason.

The first time I wrote about the disorder, six years after getting help, I thought if I framed it as something selfish and vain and self-indulgent, then I could redeem myself with self-awareness, like saying enough Hail Marys to be forgiven for my sins. I still thought of the disorder as something I needed to be forgiven for.

When I submitted that early jumbled attempt to a writing workshop, another graduate student raised his hand during the discussion to ask if there was such a thing as too much honesty. "I find it incredibly difficult to like the narrator of this essay," he said. I found his phrasing amusing, *the narrator of this essay,* as if she were a stranger we could gossip about. It was my first nonfiction class, and I wasn't used to the rules of displacement—all of us pretending we weren't also critiquing one another's lives. After class, the same man who'd found it difficult to like my narrator asked me if I wanted to get a drink. In my head I said, *Fuck you,* but out loud I said, "Sounds great." The less you liked me, the more I wanted you to.

By getting pregnant, it seemed as if I had finally managed to replace "the narrator of this essay"—a sick girl obsessed with her own pain, difficult to like—with a nobler version of myself: a woman who wasn't destroying her own body, but using her body to make another body she would care for. A stubborn internal voice was still convinced that the eating disorder had been all about the "I," all about whittling myself to the shape of that tall rail. Now pregnancy promised a new source of gravity: the "you." Strangers smiled at me constantly on the street.

At my ob-gyn, once a patient was pregnant, she got to ascend to the second floor. I no longer visited the regular gynecological suites on the lower level. I got to glide up an atrium staircase instead, destined for ultrasounds and prenatal vitamins, leaving behind those gonorrhea tests and birth-control prescriptions—as if I were advancing to the next level of a video game, or had earned a ticket to the afterlife.

By the time you were the size of a coconut, I was audibly huffing my way up the subway stairs. My belly was a twenty-pound piece of luggage I carried everywhere. My ligaments stretched and snapped, painful enough to make me gasp. Each evening, my legs were overcome by a maddening fidgeting sensation, something my doctor would call "restless legs syndrome." At a movie one night, I kept compulsively crossing and recrossing them, unable to hold still, so I left the theater to sit in a bathroom stall for ten minutes. My legs jerked and stretched as if they were being commanded by someone else, as if the tiny being inside had already taken control.

When I was in the middle of a three-month-long cold, my mother chided me for refusing to alter the pace of my life. "I know you don't want to disrupt your plans," she told me, "but there will be a point when you won't have a choice. You will go into labor, and your plans will be disrupted." It was what I was most afraid of—being disrupted. It was also what I craved more than anything.

In a way, I was grateful for the physical difficulty of my third trimester. It made me feel like I was doing my job. During the first few months, when morning sickness hadn't shown up, it had been like failing to cry at a funeral. Wasn't I supposed to feel my boundaries flooded by pregnancy? Wasn't I supposed to hurt? Wasn't that Eve's original punishment? *I will greatly multiply thy sorrow and thy conception; in sorrow thou shalt bring forth children.*

Some part of me craved pain as proof that I was already a good mother, long-suffering, while another part of me wanted to reject hardship as the only possible proof of devotion. I'd been so eager to fall in love with pregnancy as a conversion narrative, promising to destroy the version of myself who equated significance with suffering and replace her with a different woman altogether—someone who happily watched the numbers on the scale grow bigger, who treated herself well, and focused on her baby, and devoted herself wholly to un-conflicted calories and virtuous gratitude.

But as it turned out, pregnancy wasn't a liberation from prior selves so much as a container holding every prior version of myself at once. I didn't get to shed my ghosts so fully. It was easy to roll my eyes at people saying, "You don't look pregnant *at all*," and harder to admit the pride I felt when I heard it. It was easy to call my doctor absurd when she chided me for gaining five pounds in a month (rather than four!), and harder to admit that I'd honestly felt shamed by her in that moment. It was harder to admit the part of me that felt a secret thrill every time a doctor registered concern that I was "measuring small." This pride was something I'd wanted desperately to leave behind. I worried that it was impeding your growth, which was really just the distillation of a deeper fear—that I would infect you with my own broken relationship to my body, that you would catch it like a dark inheritance.

When you were the size of a pineapple, I wrote a birth plan. This was part of my birth class, but it was also a species of prophecy: telling the story of a birth before it happened.

The birth-class teacher pointed triumphantly at a model pelvis made of plastic. She said, "People think there's not that much room for the baby's head to pass through. But there's actually *a lot* of room." I squinted at the pelvis. Not *that* much room.

In a way, we all lived toward that pain. It wasn't just about suffering; it was about knowledge. It was impossible to understand the pain until you'd undergone it. That opacity compelled me. *In sorrow thou shalt bring forth children*. The pain had been punishment for eating the apple, for wanting to know. Now the pain itself had become the knowledge. Soon I would become someone who had a birth story. I just didn't know what that story would be. It was understood, of course, that there were no guarantees. Anyone could have a C-section. It cast its shadow across everything. It was what you tried to avoid. The pushing—the *labor*—was what made the delivery real. That's the implicit equation I'd absorbed.

In writing my birth plan, I saved my strongest language for the golden hour. That was what they called the first hour after birth, when your new body would rest against mine. The phrase itself sounded like a chiming bell. If I wanted this golden hour, I was told, I needed to insist on it: *I would like immediate uninterrupted skin-to-skin contact with her until the first feeding is accomplished*, I wrote in my plan. It was like casting a spell. I would bring you into the world. You would live against my skin. You would eat.

When you were larger than a honeydew but smaller than a watermelon, the new year brought a blizzard. It was three weeks before my due date. My doctor was worried you were too small, so she had scheduled another growth scan. I trudged through piles of snow to get to her office in Manhattan, wrapping my arms around the swaddled globe of my belly, around a coat that would not zip, saying, "Mine,

mine, mine." My sense of ownership was sharpened by the icy flurry all around me. It was primal.

At her office, my doctor said it was a funny thing about storms—some people believed they made a woman's water more likely to break. It had to do with the drop in barometric pressure. This seemed like something one midwife might whisper to another in the barn, while the sky filled with clouds, and like a fairy tale it came true that night. I woke at three in the morning, stepped out of bed, and the hot warmth gushed out. My mother's first birth, with my oldest brother, had also begun this way. It was almost biblical, I told myself: *As it was for the mother, so it shall be for the daughter.* There was a pleasing symmetry.

My birth-class teacher had recommended going back to sleep if my water broke in the middle of the night, because I would need the rest. I did not go back to sleep. I could not even imagine the version of myself that might go back to sleep. Plus, I still seemed to be leaking. I sat on the toilet with my laptop on my legs and felt the amniotic fluid leave my body while I edited an essay about female rage. When I sent it to my editor, I added at the bottom: "PS: I am in labor." By the time we took a cab to the hospital the following afternoon, my body was knotting with pain every few minutes as we headed up that glorious stretch of the highway beside the East River, lined by docks and basketball courts and gleaming skyscrapers looming across the water.

The pain meant my body knew what it needed to do to bring you here. And I was grateful that my body knew, because my mind did not. It was now the body's humble servant, begging with its crudest, truest words: *Please do this. I want this more than I've ever wanted anything.*

After we got to the hospital, I labored through the early evening and into the night. A monitor above my bed showed two lines: my contractions, and your heartbeat. My doctor started to get worried, because when the first line spiked, the second plummeted. That wasn't supposed to be happening. Your heartbeat always came back up, my doctor said.

But we needed to stop it from dropping. It was supposed to stay between 160 and 110. *Don't drop,* I willed the graph. *Don't drop.* I watched the monitor vigilantly. It was as if I were trying to keep your heart rate above the danger line through sheer force of will. Belief in willpower was another familiar ghost, one of the gospels of my hungry days.

When your heart rate stabilized, it felt like we were working together—you and I—as if you'd heard me calling out, as if you'd felt my stubborn insistence that you be okay settle like a sturdy floor beneath you. The contractions were an exploded version of the hot, twisting cramps I'd felt during the nights following my abortion. But really the pain was exactly like everyone had described it: impossible to describe. Someone had told me to picture myself lying on a sandy beach, that each contraction would be a wave washing over me with pain, and in between those waves my job was to soak up as much warmth as I could from the sun. But very little in that delivery room felt like waves, or sand, or sun. I asked for an epidural: a helicopter that would spirit me away from the shore entirely. Approximately ten thousand minutes passed between my saying "I'd like an epidural" and actually getting one.

Early in my pregnancy, my husband told me that his first wife had been determined to have a natural birth. "With you," he said, "I imagine it being more like, *Give me all the drugs you've got.*" I was indignant, but couldn't argue. The story of the woman determined to have a natural childbirth felt nobler than the story of the woman who asked for all the drugs right away, just as the story of the pregnant woman felt nobler than the story of the woman who starved herself. There was something petty or selfish or cowardly about insisting on too much control, about denying the body its size or its discomfort.

Around two in the morning—nearly twenty-four hours after my

water broke, following several hours of sweet epidural haze—a nurse I didn't know came into the room. "Looks like you're having problems with the fetal heart rate." Her tone sounded accusatory. It was as if I'd been withholding this information.

"What's wrong with her heart rate?" I asked. I thought you and I had managed to bring it up. But when I looked at the monitor, it was just below 110—and dipping further.

Another nurse came in. "Could you use another pair of hands?" she asked, and the first nurse said: "I could definitely use another pair of hands."

Why do you need so many hands? I wanted to ask, but I didn't want to distract them from whatever their hands needed to do. More nurses arrived. They told me they needed a better measurement of your heart rate. They stuck a wand inside me. They had me roll onto one side, then the other. They stuck the wand inside me again. They asked me to get on all fours.

"We're not finding it," the first nurse said, her voice more urgent, and I wanted to ask: *It's not there, or you can't hear it?* It was the only question in the world.

Then my doctor was in the room. She told me they were seeing what they didn't want to see. She said, "Your baby's heart rate is dropping and it's not coming up."

Everything happened very quickly after that: ten people in the room, fifteen, many of them rolling me onto the gurney, my legs still paralyzed from the epidural. Your father grabbed my hand. A voice called out, "It's in the sixties!" And another, "It's in the fifties!" I knew they were talking about your heart. Then they were pushing me down the hallway on the gurney, running. A nurse fit a surgical cap onto my doctor's head as she ran.

In the operating room, a man pinched my abdomen and asked if I could feel him pinching. I said I could. He seemed annoyed. I said they should just go ahead and cut me open anyway. He put something else in my IV and the next time they pinched me I didn't feel anything. My doctor said I was going to feel pressure, not pain. Everything would happen on the other side of the blue curtain, where the rest of my body was.

My husband sat on a stool beside the operating table—worried, in a blue surgical cap—and I watched his face like a mirror, trying to read your fate. It was only when I heard the doctor's voice say, "Hey there, cutie pie," that I knew they had opened me up and found you waiting there, ready to be born.

Every birth story is the story of two births: the child is born, and the mother is born, too—constructed by the story of how she brought her child into the world, shaped by the birthing and then again by the telling. My birth plan stayed folded in my hospital duffel bag. It was the story of a thing that never happened.

Instead, a team of doctors separated my mind from my womb with a blue tarp. The hands of another woman reached in to pull you out. My body went from collaborator to enemy. It was no longer laboring; it had failed. It needed to be cut open. The process needed to be saved by other people, because I hadn't managed it myself. I'm not saying this is the truth about C-sections. I'm saying this is the truth of what I felt. I felt betrayed.

I'd always heard labor described in terms of triumphant capacity, but giving birth to you was a lesson in radical humility. My story was disrupted. My body was disrupted. You arrived and showed me that pain had never been my greatest teacher. You arrived and showed me I'd never been in control. Giving birth to you didn't matter because my body had been in pain, or because it hadn't been in enough pain. It mattered because you showed up glistening and bewildered and perfect. You were still part of me. You were beyond me.

If the work of starvation had been as small and airless as a closet, then the work of birth was as wide as the sky. It expanded with all the unknowns of a life that would happen in the body that my body had made possible.

For much of the first hour after you were born, I was still lying on the gurney, asking if I could hold you. Your father reminded me that I was still in surgery. He was right. My abdomen was still gaping open. My body was still shaking from all the drugs they'd given me to numb the things that had gone right, and then the things that had gone wrong.

I didn't know I would keep shaking for hours. I knew only that your father was pointing to one corner of the room, where they were carrying a tiny bundle to the incubator. One little leg stuck out, impossibly small. My whole body vibrated with the need to hold you. I kept saying: "Is she okay? Is she okay?" The doctors' hands were in my belly, rearranging my organs—pressure, not pain; pressure, not pain—and then your wailing filled the room. At your surging voice, I heard my own crack open. "Oh my God."

There you were: an arrival, a cry, the beginning of another world.

Acknowledgments

―――――――――

With gratitude, as ever, to my tireless and tiring and utterly brilliant editor, Ben George; my warrior and comrade, Jin Auh; and to Michael Taeckens, who brings such soul and passion to his work it lifts my spirits every time. Deep thanks to my teams at Little, Brown, and Wylie: Reagan Arthur, Liz Garriga, Pamela Marshall, Craig Young, Ira Boudah, Brandon Kelley, Marie Mundaca, Gregg Kulick, Shannon Hennessey, Cynthia Saad, Allan Fallow, Alex Christie, and Luke Ingram; as well as my foreign editors, especially Max Porter, Anne Meadows, and Karsten Kredel. I was blessed to work on these essays with a crew of exacting and inspiring magazine editors along the way: Charlie Homans, James Marcus, Denise Wills, Roger Hodge, Brad Listi, Genevieve Smith, Tom Lutz, Derk Richardson, and Allison Wright.

To my extraordinary friends—the ones who read these essays as drafts, and the ones who simply helped me survive my own life—as well as my beloved family, thank you. I am so lucky, and so grateful.

About the Author

Leslie Jamison is the author of the *New York Times* bestsellers *The Recovering* and *The Empathy Exams*, as well as the novel *The Gin Closet*. A National Magazine Award finalist, she is a contributing writer for the *New York Times Magazine*, and her work has appeared in publications including *The Atlantic*, *Harper's Magazine*, the *New York Times Book Review*, the *Oxford American*, and the *Virginia Quarterly Review*. She directs the graduate nonfiction program at Columbia University.

ALSO BY LESLIE JAMISON
THE RECOVERING
Intoxication and Its Aftermath

"An astounding triumph...A recovery memoir like no other...There's something profound at work here, a truth about how we grow into ourselves that rings achingly wise and burrows painfully deep."

—David Canfield, *Entertainment Weekly*

"Magnificent and genuinely moving...This is that rare addiction memoir that gets better after sobriety takes hold."

—Dwight Garner, *New York Times*

"Such is Jamison's command of metaphor and assonance that she could rivet a reader with a treatise on toast. We perhaps have no writer better on the subject of psychic suffering and its consolations."

—Gary Greenberg, *The New Yorker*

BACK BAY BOOKS
Available wherever books are sold